**St. Louis Community College**

Forest Park
Florissant Valley
Meramec

Instructional Resources
St. Louis, Missouri

LINCOLN BEFORE WASHINGTON

LINCOLN
—— BEFORE ——
WASHINGTON

New Perspectives
on the Illinois Years

DOUGLAS L. WILSON

UNIVERSITY OF ILLINOIS PRESS

URBANA AND CHICAGO

This book is printed on acid-free paper.

Library of Congress Cataloging-in-Publication Data
Wilson, Douglas L.
Lincoln before Washington : new perspectives on the Illinois
years / Douglas L. Wilson.
p.   cm.
Includes bibliographical references and index.
ISBN 0-252-02331-5 (alk. paper)
1. Lincoln, Abraham, 1809–1865—Political career before 1861.
2. Illinois—Politics and government—To 1865. 3. Legislators—
Illinois—Biography. 4. Herndon, William Henry, 1818–1891.
5. Lincoln, Abraham, 1809–1865—Friends and associates.
I. Titles.
E457.35.W55   1997
973.7'092—dc21
96-45798
CIP

For Sharon, Cindy, and Tim

CONTENTS

Preface   ix

Acknowledgments   xiii

PART ONE: JEFFERSON AND LINCOLN

1. The Frigate and the Frugal Chariot: Jefferson and Lincoln as Readers   3

PART TWO: HERNDON AND LINCOLN

2. Herndon's Legacy   21

3. William H. Herndon and the "Necessary Truth"   37

PART THREE: NEW PERSPECTIVES ON LINCOLN

4. Abraham Lincoln versus Peter Cartwright   55

5. Abraham Lincoln, Ann Rutledge, and the Evidence of Herndon's Informants   74

6. Abraham Lincoln and "That Fatal First of January"   99

7. Abraham Lincoln and the "Spirit of Mortal"   133

PART FOUR: LINCOLN AND JEFFERSON

8. The Lincoln-Douglas Debates: An Unfinished Text   151

9. Lincoln's Declaration   166

Index   183

PREFACE

The essays in this book are largely the result of coming to Lincoln scholarship through the back door. The writer has no doubt that had he come to the subject in the usual way, with appropriate orientation in the accepted axioms and corollaries of Lincoln studies, things would have looked very different, and many of the questions that seemed so provocative might never have occurred to him. But the ignorance of the uninitiated can sometimes be an advantage, as the fable of the emperor's new clothes suggests. No such grandiose claim is made for the essays that follow; a more appropriate analogy might be entering the emperor's palace by way of the kitchen.

Readers should also be apprised that the investigations reflected in these essays focus on what has come to be regarded as the wrong end of Lincoln's life. For reasons touched upon in the essays themselves, Lincoln's early life has largely been abandoned as a subject for serious investigation by most Lincoln scholars, with very few exceptions. Rightly or wrongly, the presidency and the Civil War have become virtually the be-all and end-all of mainstream Lincoln scholarship. An unfortunate consequence is that many Lincoln scholars are scarcely conversant with the sources for his prepresidential years and tend to accept without question the judgments of previous generations. Until only a few years ago it almost appeared that Lincoln's early life had effectively been yielded up to folklore and fiction.

The theme of these essays taken as a whole is that, far from being an exhausted field, Abraham Lincoln's prepresidential life offers bright prospects for investigation. Why this should be the case, what kinds of investigation might be profitable, and what might be learned thereby constitute the collective burden of these essays, although individually they address such disparate subjects as William H. Herndon's informants, Lincoln's favorite poem, his mysterious broken engagement, the text of his debates with Douglas, or a previously unknown assault on Peter Cartwright. Put another way, these essays represent an effort, in the light of new evidence and perspectives, to test the validity of some long-standing assumptions about certain Lincoln sources and reopen some presumably settled questions about his early life. In short, this collection of essays is offered in the hope that the whole is more than the sum of its parts.

What first prompted these unorthodox excursions into Lincoln sources was the idea of comparing Lincoln and Thomas Jefferson as readers. Having spent many years studying Jefferson's youthful commonplace books, his classical education, his library, and pondering his lifelong inveteracy as a reader, the writer set out to investigate the historical circumstances behind the sharply contrasting legend of the frontier boy reading borrowed books by firelight. Any search for information on Lincoln's formative years leads inevitably to the letters and interviews collected by his law partner, William H. Herndon, a manuscript archive that is far and away the richest source of information on Lincoln's early life. Sometimes characterized as the first oral history project in American history, Herndon's extensive collection of testimony about Lincoln by people who knew him is unlike anything available for the study of Jefferson or of virtually anyone else before the twentieth century.

The lure of so much firsthand testimony about Lincoln's early reading habits led to an extensive exploration of the material Herndon had collected and the body of correspondence that accompanies it. The writer was thus thoroughly immersed in Herndon's extraordinary archive before looking into the body of scholarly commentary it had attracted, the reading of which produced two startling reactions. The first was that even though Herndon's project had produced the kind of biographical evidence that students of Jefferson, as the saying goes, would kill for, Lincoln scholars were generally united in disparaging Herndon's efforts and holding at arm's length the resulting body of testimony. The second reaction was even more startling and more consequential, namely that the characterization of the Herndon materials that uniformly prevailed among Lincoln scholars was dramatically at odds with what the writer had found in the documents themselves. Many of the essays that follow are part of an attempt to understand and account for this discrepancy.

Readers will soon discover that the writer makes some presumptuous claims. He argues, for example, that in some important respects the great Lincoln scholars of this century have been wrong about Herndon and his informant testimony, that this judgment has prejudiced their constituency unduly against Herndon, and that Herndon's neglected materials still have new and unexpected things to tell us about Lincoln's prepresidential life. Many of these claims can only be adjudicated by an appeal to Herndon's hard-to-access and often hard-to-read documents, which are now being made available in a scholarly edition.

In addition to bearing the stamp of a preoccupation with William H. Herndon and his informant materials, the essays in this book reflect a long-term interest in the affinities between Abraham Lincoln and Thomas Jefferson. The contrasts and similarities of these two great Americans as writers and statesmen formed the basis of a course that the writer was privileged to teach for several years at Knox College in partnership with Rodney O. Davis. Yearly opportunities to reread and discuss the Lincoln-Douglas debates in this stimulating context contributed to the findings offered in the concluding two essays, and the writer is pleased to acknowledge his considerable indebtedness to Knox College, his longtime teaching partner, and his students.

ACKNOWLEDGMENTS

For information, advice, criticism, and valuable assistance in locating and working with sources, the author is indebted to Jeff Douglas and Terry Wilson of the Knox College Library; William Beard and Cullom Davis of the Lincoln Legal Papers Project; James Gilreath, Oliver Orr, and John R. Sellers of the Library of Congress; John Hoffman of the Illinois Historical Survey; Mark Johnson and Richard S. Taylor of the Historic Sites Division, Illinois Historic Preservation Agency; Thomas F. Schwartz and Janice Petterchak of the Illinois State Historical Library; Jennifer Lee of Brown University Library; Margaret Moser of Allegheny College Library; and John Rhodehamel, Martin Ridge, Virginia Renner, and Robert Skotheim of the Huntington Library. Special thanks are due Richard L. Wentworth and Mary Giles of the University of Illinois Press. Thanks are also due to Robert Bray, Roger D. Bridges, Michael Burlingame, Richard N. Current, Rodney O. Davis, Mark E. Neely, Jr., George Painter, Merrill D. Peterson, Jerry Sanders, John Y. Simon, John Strassburger, Linda Norbut Suits, Terence A. Tanner, John E. Walsh, Garry Wills, and Paul M. Zall.

Most of the essays in this book have appeared previously in periodicals. Some were published under different titles, and some first appeared in somewhat different form. Permission to reprint them has been generously extended and is hereby gratefully acknowledged.

"The Frigate and the Frugal Chariot: Jefferson and Lincoln as Readers" first appeared as "What Jefferson and Lincoln Read" in *The Atlantic Monthly* 267 (Jan. 1991): 51–62.

"Herndon's Legacy" was published as "William H. Herndon and His Lincoln Informants" in the *Journal of the Abraham Lincoln Association* 14 (Winter 1993): 15–34.

"William H. Herndon and the 'Necessary Truth'" first appeared in *Abraham Lincoln in the American Mind: Papers from the Eighth Annual Lincoln Colloquium,* edited by Linda Norbut Suits and George Painter (Springfield: Lincoln Home National Historic Site, 1994), 31–41.

"Abraham Lincoln versus Peter Cartwright" first appeared in a much abridged version as "'A Most Abandoned Hypocrite'" in *American Heritage* 45 (Feb.–March 1994): 36–49.

"Abraham Lincoln, Ann Rutledge, and the Evidence of Herndon's Informants" was first published in *Civil War History* 36 (Dec. 1990): 301–24. Reprinted with permission of Kent State University Press.

"Abraham Lincoln and 'That Fatal First of January'" first appeared in *Civil War History* 38 (June 1992): 101–30. Reprinted with permission of Kent State University Press.

"Abraham Lincoln and the 'Spirit of Mortal'" was published in the *Indiana Magazine of History* 87 (June 1991): 155–70.

"The Lincoln-Douglas Debates: An Unfinished Text" appeared as "The Unfinished Text of the Lincoln-Douglas Debates" in the *Journal of the Abraham Lincoln Association* 15 (Winter 1994): 70–84.

LINCOLN BEFORE WASHINGTON

PART ONE

Jefferson and Lincoln

1

The Frigate and the Frugal Chariot: Jefferson and Lincoln as Readers

A little-noticed account of how Abraham Lincoln rose from obscurity to political greatness calls attention to the two years he spent as a member of Congress in Washington. Hubert M. Skinner believed that it was there he laid the basis for his later political triumphs by taking advantage of the resources of the Library of Congress to study the great documents and issues of American history. "In Washington," according to Skinner, "Mr. Lincoln had been a puzzle, and a subject of amusement to his fellows. He did not drink, or use tobacco, or bet, or swear. It would seem that he must be a very rigid churchman. But no, he did not belong to any church; and he soon became reckoned an 'unbeliever.' How did he occupy his spare time? He was mousing among the books of the old Congressional Library. . . . 'Bah!' said his fellow Congressmen, 'He is a book-worm!'"[1]

Skinner's depiction of Lincoln as a congressional bookworm with a reputation for mousing around in the Library of Congress is undocumented, nor can it be confirmed from what little is known of Lincoln's activities in Washington between December 1847 and March 1849. But there is no reason to doubt that he frequented the congressional library, which was directly across the street from where he lived, and every reason to believe that he found it inviting. Housed in the Capitol in what some regarded as the most beautiful suite of rooms in the city, the Library of Congress was a popular Capitol Hill meeting place, and for a sociable young member of Congress living most of the time alone in a boardinghouse, the library's social aspect would have been appealing.[2] For the research that went into his congressional speeches, its resources were clearly indispensable.

One of the things about the congressional library that would have interested Lincoln and that might have prompted him to "mouse" in it more than usual was that a large number of the books had once belonged to one of his earliest heroes, Thomas Jefferson. When the British troops burned the Capitol in 1814 and destroyed the congressional library, Jefferson had promptly offered his own magnificent collection as a replacement. The acquisition of Jefferson's 6,700 volumes more than doubled the size of the previous congressional collection, but an even more consequential result was that it dramatically broadened its scope and started the notion that the Library of Congress ought to become the basis of a national library.[3] In Lincoln's time, and until the end of the century, the books were still arranged according to Jefferson's classification system, which was prominently displayed at the beginning of the printed catalog then in use, and the titles therein were still listed in Jefferson's format. In perusing the catalog, Lincoln could easily identify the many books that had once belonged to Jefferson, for they were plainly marked. As explained by a note on the first page, "The Works to which the letter J. is prefixed, were in the Library of the late President Jefferson, when it was purchased by Congress in 1815."[4] In his first year in Congress, Lincoln had an opportunity to vote for the purchase of Jefferson's papers. If, in researching his speeches, Lincoln carried home Library of Congress books, as he did books from the library of the Supreme Court, with a stick and a large bandana, some of the books in that bandana may have once belonged to Thomas Jefferson.[5]

Thomas Jefferson and Abraham Lincoln were as different as the centuries that fostered them, but the virtue of comparisons is that they tend to throw into relief qualities and characteristics that might otherwise be minimized or escape notice. Books and learning, which constitute the focus of this brief comparison, were important in the lives of both Jefferson and Lincoln, and they often figure as important elements in the legends of both, which, in some respects, are as noteworthy as their lives. In characterizing the transformation of the Lincoln of legend—"Honest Abe becomes Father Abraham; the rail splitter becomes the Savior of the Union; the most comic of our major figures becomes the supremely tragic figure"—the great Jefferson biographer Dumas Malone confessed that "by comparison the Jefferson legend seems rather pale, and one wonders if it can be properly called a legend in the same sense."[6] But the legends are still building. John F. Kennedy's remark in April 1962 to the assembled Nobel laureates— that never had so much talent and human knowledge been present in the White House, "with the possible exception of when Thomas Jefferson dined alone"—has gained enormous currency and is now irrevocably part of the Jefferson legend.[7]

As one would expect, the formative years of Jefferson and Lincoln represent a study in contrasts, for they began life at opposite ends of the social and economic spectrum. There are, however, some intriguing parallels. Both Jefferson and Lincoln suffered the devastating loss of a parent at an early age. Jefferson's father, an able and active man to whom his son was deeply devoted, died when Thomas was fourteen, and the boy was left to the care of his mother. His adolescent misogyny and his subsequent glacial silence on the subject of his mother strongly suggest that their relationship was strained. Conversely, Lincoln suffered the loss of his mother at the age of nine, and although he adored his father's second wife he seems to have grown increasingly unable to regard his father with affection or perhaps even respect. Both Jefferson and Lincoln had the painful misfortune to experience in their youth the death of a favorite sister. And both were marked for distinction early by being elected to their respective legislatures at the age of twenty-five.

But the differences are great. Jefferson was born into the Virginia gentry. Along with a privileged position in society, he inherited a small fortune in land and slaves. The poverty and obscurity into which Lincoln was born, on the other hand, were nearly complete. His father owned land but had great difficulty holding onto it and finally retreated with his family to southwestern Indiana, which in 1816 was little more than a wilderness, and where Abraham grew up with only the homemade clothes on his back.[8]

In the matter of education, the contrasts are equally great. Jefferson had a superb education, even by the standards of his class. It included formal schooling from the age of five, expert instruction in classical languages arranged for by his father, two years of college (then the regular course), and a legal apprenticeship. Along the way, he had the benefit of conspicuously learned men as his teachers—the Rev. James Maury, Dr. William Small, and George Wythe—in addition to a seat at the table of Francis Fauquier, the cultivated governor of Virginia. Lincoln had almost no formal education. Growing up in a family of barely literate parents and in an atmosphere with, as he tells us, "nothing to excite ambition for education," Lincoln was essentially self-taught. The backwoods schools he attended sporadically were conducted by teachers who had meager qualifications. "If a straggler supposed to understand latin happened to sojourn in the neighborhood," Lincoln wrote, "he was looked upon as a wizzard."[9] Where Jefferson, after studying classical languages and French, was able to teach himself Italian, Lincoln at about the same age was teaching himself the principles of grammar in order to be able to speak and write standard English.

However different in their educational opportunities, both Jefferson and Lincoln as young men became known to their contemporaries as "hard students." As a schoolboy, Jefferson was remembered as always preparing his lessons before joining in the games of his schoolmates and as carrying his Greek grammar with him wherever he went. He is reputed to have studied fifteen hours a day at college, and his classmate, John Page, said that Jefferson could "tear himself away from his dearest friends, to fly to his studies."[10] Upon deciding to practice law, he studied for nearly three years before taking his bar examination (where others spent only a few months) and then put in an additional year of study, making extensive extracts from law reporters and legal treatises before opening his practice.

Lincoln was remembered by those with whom he grew up as an exceptionally studious boy who "read everything he could get his hands on." His family testified that in his adolescent years he was constantly reading and making notes on what he read, even when he had no paper and had to write on boards. His stepmother told how he would wrestle tenaciously with words, passages, and ideas he did not understand. When he went out on his own, his absorption in his studies was a source of astonishment to his neighbors in New Salem, where, in addition to studying history and biography, he immersed himself in technical books on grammar, surveying, and the law. His legal studies became so intensive that his friends feared for his health, and when he became temporarily deranged after the death of Ann Rutledge some thought the cause must be excessive application to his studies.[11]

A comparison of the earliest reading of Jefferson and Lincoln is instructive. The tradition in Jefferson's family is that he had read all the books in his father's library by the time he was five. The inventory of that library made nine years later, when Peter Jefferson died, shows a planter's library of about two dozen titles, consisting of a Bible, a dictionary, and books on Virginia law with an admixture of such political and literary standards as Rapin's *History of England* and *The Spectator*.[12] The earliest entries in the commonplace book that the young Jefferson kept of his literary and philosophical reading are Latin excerpts from Horace, Virgil, Cicero, and Ovid. These and excerpts from Pope, Milton, and Shakespeare date from his teens and suggest that he was being introduced systematically to the standard classical and English writers.[13]

Lincoln's first book was undoubtedly the Bible, one of the very few books in the Lincoln home. Apart from the school books to which he was introduced, such as *Dilworth's Spelling-Book*, Lincoln's earliest reading was largely confined to what he could borrow from his neighbors. Like Jefferson, he kept a notebook of his early readings, but unfortunately it has not survived.[14] His Indiana acquaintances agree that he read and reread all the books he could get hold of, which, given the primitive character of the neighborhood, was not a large number. They seem to have included Aesop's *Fables*, Bunyan's *Pilgrim's Progress*, Defoe's *Robinson Crusoe*, James Riley's *Narrative*, a life of Franklin, and lives of Washington by both Mason Weems and David Ramsey.[15] The early reading of Jefferson and Lincoln reflects the differences in their circumstances and may provide clues to the incipient genius of each. But what is perhaps most striking is that both, as boys and young men, seized all available opportunities for reading.

Despite the radical differences of their situations, Jefferson and Lincoln must be judged equal in the dedication and effort they brought to their youthful studies. They appear to have been equally disciplined and equally determined to achieve their objectives through reading and study, but those objectives were markedly different. Jefferson set out to become a learned man. From an early age, he aspired to the eighteenth-century ideal of the *philosophe*, the universally informed philosopher, whose knowledge was built on a classical base and whose efforts were committed to reason and the pursuit of objective truth. Jefferson's intellectual endeavors were a source of personal pleasure, and although he felt obligated to steer them in a useful direction they clearly yielded satisfaction as ends in themselves. He often said that he was ill-suited by nature for politics and would have followed a life of study but for the accident of the times in which he lived.

Lincoln's reasons for applying himself so assiduously to his studies appear to have been very different. In part he must have been motivated by an intelligent backwoods boy's curiosity about the great world beyond, but his consuming ambition was to rise. The poverty into which he was born entailed a life of manual labor, the unremitting regimen of the axe and plow. Lincoln's youthful commitment to study, which his neighbors and perhaps even his father saw as a species of laziness, may be regarded instead as a manifestation of self-knowledge. Even as a boy he recognized and began to indulge his differentness, and by the time he was a young man his distinctive ways had set him apart. The qualities that Skinner says were remarked by other members of Congress twenty years later—his abstinence from liquor, tobacco, and profanity—were already in evidence in his youth, and if such qualities were unusual for a politician in Washington they were almost unheard of on the midwestern frontier.

In addition to reading books, the young Lincoln became an avid reader of newspapers. These highly partisan sheets no doubt sharpened his interest in politics, for his stepmother remembers that in the period from 1827 to 1830 he was "a constant reader of them."[16] One of his boyhood friends in Indiana remembered that this was about the time he broke rank with most of his friends and neighbors and proclaimed himself an anti-Jackson man. Another remembered loaning Lincoln a newspaper with an editorial on Thomas Jefferson, which Lincoln was able to repeat word for word.[17] In this context, Louis A. Warren's suggestion that the editorial may date from the time of Jefferson's death on the Fourth of July in 1826 takes on added interest because Lincoln insisted in later life that his politics derived from the Declaration of Independence.[18]

But Lincoln's legendary feats of reading, book-borrowing, and diligent study belong only to his youth and early manhood. Once established as a successful legislator and licensed to practice law, he put his days as a hard student behind him. Thereafter, he seems to have done little more in the way of serious reading than his professional and political interests required. His law partner, William H. Herndon, an avid reader who had a good library, said emphatically that Lincoln read little. Philosophical and reflective as he undoubtedly was, the mature Lincoln contented himself with newspapers and brief forays into Herndon's scientific and philosophical books, rarely reading one all the way through. Lincoln "read less and thought more than any man in his sphere in America" was the way Herndon phrased it. "No man can put his finger on any great book written in the last or present century that Lincoln ever read."[19]

He could still set himself to a particular task that required disciplined reading, as when he undertook to master the six books of Euclid. His son Robert remembered his father's studious attention to Euclid, as did some fellow lawyers on the circuit, and Lincoln was sufficiently proud of this feat to point it out in an autobiographical statement.[20] He still relished poetry, which had early been a favorite recreation. It seemed to some of his friends that he could recite all of Burns by heart, and his marked fondness for recitation may indicate that he preferred it to solitary reading.[21] In fact, much to the annoyance of his law partner, Lincoln did his office reading aloud, claiming that both hearing and seeing the words reinforced his grasp on the material. If there was an exception to his lapse from intensive study in his maturity, it was Shakespeare. "When he was young he read the Bible," said Herndon, "and when of age he read Shakespeare. This latter book was scarcely ever out of his mind and his hands."[22] Although the observation sounds like the kind of hyperbole that Herndon sometimes employed, it is confirmed by Lincoln's son Robert, who, in describing his father's books, told a correspondent, "Shakespeare, of course, he always had by him."[23]

Jefferson, by contrast, remained a hard student all his life. What became legendary with him was the incredible range and depth of his knowledge, something that impressed not only his friends and fellow Americans but sophisticated Europeans as well. As one might expect, nearly all of Jefferson's great learning was gleaned through diligent reading and study. There was, he believed, no substitute for research, no matter how tedious. "A patient pursuit of facts, and cautious combination and comparison of them," he wrote in a footnote to *Notes on the State of Virginia*, "is the drudgery to which man is subjected by his Maker, if he wishes to attain sure knowledge."[24] Books were the indispensable tools of his work, whether as lawyer, architect, farmer, legislator, or revolutionary statesman. Merely the books referred to and discussed in his famous correspondence with John Adams would establish Jefferson's credentials as an incessant and omnivorous reader, but his general correspondence and other writings present unmistakable evidence of a habitual recurrence to books. Isaac Jefferson, who grew up as a slave at Monticello, remembered his master in the characteristic act of poring over books spread out on the floor of his library and said that whenever someone asked him a question, "He go right straight to the book and tell you all about it."[25]

Both Jefferson and Lincoln were lawyers, and both readied themselves for the law by a course of intensive reading and study. But once admitted to the bar, they diverged. When Jefferson's law books were destroyed by fire in 1770, he wrote to his friends in despair, for he believed he could not represent his clients without books. Indeed, his surviving opinions show frequent references to the printed case law and other legal authorities and suggest that his great strength as a lawyer was his legal knowledge. Lincoln was not known for his legal scholarship but was virtually unexcelled as an advocate in jury trials. In this context, legend has Lincoln saving Duff Armstrong, the son of his old friends Jack and Hannah Armstrong, from a murder conviction by the shrewd use of a book, an almanac showing that certain testimony about the moonlight was questionable. But a close look at the case indicates that it was Lincoln's highly personal and strongly emotional appeal to the jurors, which reduced everyone in the courtroom to tears, that carried the day.[26] One is reminded of Edmund Randolph's famous comparison of the legal talents of Jefferson and Patrick Henry: "Mr. Jefferson drew copiously from the depths of the law, Mr. Henry from the recesses of the human heart."[27]

⤺

Telling stories and reading the works of humorists to his cabinet are part of the Lincoln legend, and yet one of the truly remarkable things about Lincoln as president is the extent to which he resorted to literature. Perhaps no president turned to English poetry while in office with the frequency that Lincoln did. He continued to recite his old favorites, such as "O Why Should the Spirit of Mortal Be Proud?" or Holmes's "The Last Leaf," their melancholy and brooding concern for human mortality having been rendered even more apt by the somber circumstances of civil war. And he read poets such as Thomas Hood to invoke the lighter side. But he repeatedly returned to Shakespeare, whom he had probably first read as a boy in William Scott's *Lessons in Elocution* and for whom he had a lifelong fascination. "Some of Shakespeare's plays I have never read," he wrote to the Shakespearian actor James Hackett, "while others I have gone over perhaps as frequently as any unprofessional reader. Among the latter are Lear, Richard Third, Henry Eighth, Hamlet, and especially Macbeth. I think nothing equals Macbeth."[28]

Upon moving into the White House, the Lincolns purchased a number of books, a list of which survives.[29] One of the titles that we know Lincoln made considerable use of during those four years was an edition of Shakespeare. "He read Shakespere more than all other writers together," John Hay reported of Lincoln's habit of reading aloud. "He would . . . read Shakespere for hours with a single secretary for audience."[30] There is abundant evidence that Lincoln sought out Shakespeare's plays during the most trying hours of his presidency as sources of strength and consolation. Don E. Fehrenbacher relates this affinity for Shakespeare to Lincoln's keen sense of his role and ultimate responsibility in the carnage of the Civil War. "To some indeterminable extent and in some intuitive way Lincoln seems to have assimilated the substance of the plays into his own experience and deepening sense of tragedy."[31]

Jefferson had been extremely fond of poetry in his youth, as his literary commonplace book and other evidence indicates. His poetic acquaintance was wide, although his tastes were fairly conventional. Like many sophisticated readers of his day, he was smitten by the works of Ossian, the putative third-century Celtic bard whose poems were actually the work of James McPherson. One of the things that attracted Jefferson to Ossian was the supposed similarity of his bardic offerings to the writings of Homer and Virgil, whom Jefferson also greatly admired. He was decidedly partial to the classics, including Horace, the great favorite of the Enlightenment. And, like most readers of his time, Jefferson revered Shakespeare, whom he singled out as the English writer to be studied most diligently. His library contained, at one time or another, many different editions of Shakespeare, and he was quite familiar with the efforts of eighteenth-century editors who vied with each other to improve the reliability of the text.[32]

But Jefferson's taste for poetry declined as he grew older. He confessed to a correspondent about the time he assumed the presidency that his youthful relish for poetry had almost completely deserted him. Unlike Lincoln, he seems to have faced the problems of his presidency without resorting to literary works for perspective or inspiration. It would have been out of character for him to have read aloud, let alone to members of his cabinet, and he probably allowed himself comparatively little time while president for purely personal reading. A notable exception was his discovery of John Baxter's history of England, which he embraced and recommended enthusiastically as an alternative to the "subversive" history of David Hume.[33] Another exception was a purposeful excursion into the New Testament, his first effort to extract the "diamonds" of authentic Christianity from the corrupted text of the Gospels.[34] This strictly private project may serve as the appropriate counterpart to Lincoln's reading Shakespeare aloud to his visitors, for it exemplifies Jefferson's characteristic retreat to his study and his need to concentrate his own "recreational" activities on what he would have called "useful objects."

↩

Nowhere is the difference between Jefferson and Lincoln more dramatically demonstrated, or more characteristic, than in their personal libraries. Jefferson's famous library, which became the foundation of the Library of Congress, was his most cherished possession, on which he lavished vast amounts of time and money for nearly fifty years. Having started out in life as a reader and collector of books, Jefferson already owned a sizable library when, at the age of twenty-six, his mother's house burned, and he lost most of his books. So determined was he to replace his library with one grander in scale that within three years he had acquired a collection that was three to four times as large. In the face of great difficulties during the revolutionary years, although effectively cut off from the chief sources of books abroad, Jefferson managed steadily to build his library. He recorded in 1783 that he possessed the resounding total of 2,640 volumes, but even then he was assembling a large list of the books he hoped to acquire abroad. In fact, he collected so assiduously during his five years in France that he nearly doubled the size of his holdings. When he retired from the presidency many years later, his library had grown to unprecedented proportions and may well have been, as he believed it to be, "the choicest collection of books in the United States."[35]

Lincoln, again, presents a notable contrast. As a poor boy and later, as a young man heavily in debt, he owned little. But even when he could afford books he rarely bothered to acquire them. Indeed, it is difficult to find a record of his buying a book. While at New Salem, upon being advised to study English grammar by Mentor Graham, he reportedly walked several miles to acquire a copy of Kirkham's grammar. But when he had mastered it, he apparently gave it away—to Ann Rutledge.[36] To Herndon, who was a voracious reader and an eager collector of books, it seemed that Lincoln had, "aside from his law books and the few gilded volumes that ornamented the centre-table in his parlor at home, comparatively no library." This may understate the case somewhat, for Robert Lincoln remembered that his father "had some books at home. I remember well a large bookcase full of them." But Herndon is probably justified in his conclusion that Lincoln "never cared to own or collect books."[37] Upon leaving Springfield for Washington and the presidency, he apparently gave most of the books he did own to Herndon.

↬

Lincoln was martyred at the moment of his greatest achievement. Jefferson lived on for many years after his presidency. Ever active, although reclusive, he achieved much during those seventeen years, not the least of which was a lasting persona: the Sage of Monticello. He had long anticipated his return to private life and the blessings of the triad he often named: his family, his farm, and his books. In the first two, he experienced bitter trials and disappointments because he found himself powerless to reconcile the quarreling and disaffected members of his family and just as powerless to manage his lands on a paying basis and extricate himself from an increasing burden of debt. But in his books he found solace and satisfaction, and he indulged himself during these years in what he described as "a canine appetite for reading." Although he sold his library to Congress in 1815, he was never without books— "I cannot live without books," he confessed to John Adams.[38] The carefully selected library he assembled as a replacement during the last eleven years of his life eventually numbered more than 2,200 volumes.[39]

Because Lincoln was a self-taught man, his biographers have made much of his reading. But as the author of the best study of the subject, David C. Mearns, has noted, they have overdone it, for he could not possibly have "read, digested, absorbed all of the books imputed to him."[40] If it would be hard to exaggerate the range and extent of Jefferson's prodigious reading, the opposite is true of Lincoln. What is hard in his case is to come to terms with the limitations of his learning while doing justice to the critical role reading played in his character and career. Without reading books he could never have risen from a life of manual labor. Without books he could never have developed the surpassing prose style that marked his most memorable utterances. And without books—particularly, one feels, without Burns and Shakespeare—he would never have developed the humane sensibility and deep regard for the complexities of experience that tempered his ambition and elevated him to greatness. But having said this, one must acknowledge that Lincoln was neither widely read nor deeply learned. He savored what he read and liked, retained it with a nearly photographic memory, and often referred to or recited favorite passages from his reading. But it was not a large body of material; by comparison with what Jefferson had at his command, it was modest indeed.

Reading, as Robert Darnton has observed in another context, is more than the "straightforward process of lifting information from a page."[41] It has the unique power to transform. In thinking about ways of gauging the role and importance of reading in the lives of these two men, one is reminded of Emily Dickinson's poem on the subject, which begins with one distinctive metaphor and ends with another.

> There is no Frigate like a Book
> To take us Lands away
> Nor any Coursers like a Page
> Of prancing Poetry —
> This Traverse may the poorest take
> Without oppress of Toll —
> How frugal is the Chariot
> That bears the Human soul.[42]

The poem presents reading as a mode of transport, and the poet recognizes that it takes more than one form. A frigate is swift and wide-ranging; it is commodious and global in its reach. As an image, it embodies the potentiality that reading offers in its more expansive and elaborate forms. But traveling by frigate is beyond the means of most, whereas reading itself, the poem insists, is not. It is a venture in transport that the poorest may take "without oppress of Toll." This sets the stage for the poet's final reflection on reading, which is projected in the image of a simple, cartlike conveyance with overtones of grandeur—the chariot. Although sharply contrasting with the capacities of the ocean-conquering frigate, the chariot is nonetheless capable of performing the quintessential function of reading: It transports the human soul.

Jefferson's natural predilection for the studious life, his massive personal library, and his knowledge of six languages afforded him extraordinary means for extensive intellectual travel. Like Dickinson's frigate, his reading could thus take him to any port of call in the world of learning. By contrast, Lincoln's reading might be likened to Dickinson's frugal chariot. The startling adjective *frugal* is the poet's way of emphasizing the utterly basic nature of the metaphorical mode of transport, an unexpected choice of words that suggests the affinity of the parsimonious with the penurious. Although beginning his life in penury, Lincoln was able early to avail himself of the benefits of reading "without oppress of Toll." And though his career as a reader had distinct limitations and may not have made him a learned man, it accomplished something profound and essential to his greatness. In the terms of Emily Dickinson's poem, it afforded him a mode—not so grand and stately as the frigate of Thomas Jefferson, but a mode nonetheless—of imaginative transport, the means by which it is possible to engage the events of previous times and experience the tragedies and triumphs of the world's great heroes.

Unlike many of the world's great political leaders, Jefferson and Lincoln shared a greatness of mind and imagination. We continue to value them not only for what they did but also for what they thought and said. The words and ideas that continue to challenge and inspire us are undoubtedly the ripened fruit of experience, but in the case of both Jefferson and Lincoln we do well to remember that it was an experience of which reading—whether frigate or frugal chariot—was an indispensable part.

NOTES

1. Hubert M. Skinner, *The Lincoln-Douglas Debate* (Lincoln-Jefferson University, 1909), 7. Whether Skinner based his characterization on credible evidence is unknown.

2. For a description of the library, see William Dawson Johnston, *History of the Library of Congress*, vol. 1: *1800–1864* (Washington: Government Printing Office, 1904). For an account of Lincoln's life in Mrs. Spriggs's boardinghouse, see Samuel C. Busey, *Personal Reminiscences and Recollections* (Washington: Dornan, 1895).

3. For details of the sale of Jefferson's library to Congress, see Johnston, *History of the Library of Congress*. For the number of volumes and other details, see Douglas L. Wilson, "Jefferson's Library," in *Thomas Jefferson: A Reference Biography*, ed. Merrill D. Peterson (New York: Charles Scribners Sons, 1986), 157–79.

4. *Catalogue of the Library of Congress in the Capitol of the United States of America, December, 1839* (Washington: Langtree and O'Sullivan, 1840), [9]. A note in the OCLC record for this book estimates the size of the collection at "about 30,000 volumes."

5. Elihu B. Washburne tells the story of the books and the bandana in *Reminiscences of Abraham Lincoln by Distinguished Men of His Time*, ed. Allen Thorndike Rice (New York: North American Publishing, 1886), 20. Henry Rankin reported that Lincoln used the same technique to transport books from the State Library in Springfield, another library that functioned as a social center and that Lincoln was known to frequent. Henry B. Rankin, *Personal Recollections of Abraham Lincoln* (New York: G. P. Putnam's Sons, 1916), 30. Congress voted to purchase Jefferson's papers on August 12, 1848.

6. Dumas Malone, "Jefferson and Lincoln," *Abraham Lincoln Quarterly* 5 (June 1949): 328–29.

7. "Legend" is used here, as in Malone's essay, to denote the aspects of biography and reputation that are popularly emphasized, regardless of their accuracy or biographical significance.

8. "It was a wild region," Lincoln wrote of his boyhood home in Indiana, "with many bears and other wild animals, still in the woods. There I grew up." Abraham Lincoln to J. W. Fell, Dec. 20, 1859, in *The Collected Works of Abraham Lincoln*, ed. Roy P. Basler, asst. eds. Marion D. Pratt and Lloyd A. Dunlap (New Brunswick: Rutgers University Press, 1953), 3:511 (hereafter cited as *Collected Works*).

9. *Collected Works*, 3:511.

10. *Virginia Historical Register*, July 1850, 151, quoted in Dumas Malone, *Jefferson and His Times*, vol. 1: *Jefferson the Virginian* (Boston: Little, Brown, 1948), 58.

11. For Lincoln's New Salem years, the basic source is the Herndon-Weik Collection in the Manuscript Division, Library of Congress (hereafter cited as H-W). The speculation about Lincoln's excessive application to his studies is reported in Henry McHenry to William H. Herndon, Jan. 8, 1866.

12. For the inventory of Peter Jefferson's library, see *Virginia Magazine of History and Biography* 10 (1902–3): 391.

13. See Douglas L. Wilson, ed., *Jefferson's Literary Commonplace Book*, in *The Papers of Thomas Jefferson*, 2d ser., ed. Charles T. Cullen (Princeton: Princeton University Press, 1989).

14. Lincoln's stepmother, Sarah Bush Johnston Lincoln, told Herndon: "He had a copybook, a kind of scrapbook, in which he put down all things and then preserved them." William H. Herndon interview, Sept. 8, 1865, H-W.

15. This list combines the testimony of Indiana informants and what Lincoln told John Scripps for his campaign biography. For the Indiana testimony, see Herndon's letters and interviews in the Herndon-Weik Collection and the interviews of William Fortune in Bess V. Ehrmann, *The Missing Chapter in the Life of Abraham Lincoln* (Chicago: Walter M. Hill, 1938), 75. John Locke Scripps, *Life of Abraham Lincoln*, ed. Roy P. Basler and Lloyd A. Dunlap (Bloomington: Indiana University Press, 1961), 353–56.

16. Sarah Bush Johnston Lincoln to William H. Herndon, Sept. 8, 1865, H-W, in *The Hidden Lincoln: From the Letters and Papers of William H. Herndon,* ed. Emanuel Hertz (New York: Viking Press, 1938), 351.

17. John Romine loaned Lincoln the paper; see Romine to William H. Herndon, Sept. 14, 1865, H-W. Nathaniel Grigsby remembered Lincoln changing his politics. Grigsby to William H. Herndon, Sept. 12, 1865, H-W.

18. Louis A. Warren, *Lincoln's Youth: Indiana Years* (Indianapolis: Indiana Historical Society, 1959), 169.

19. Hertz, ed., *The Hidden Lincoln,* 417.

20. See *A Portrait of Abraham Lincoln in Letters by His Oldest Son,* ed. Paul M. Angle, with the assistance of Richard G. Case (Chicago: Chicago Historical Society, 1968), 47; John T. Stuart to William H. Herndon, Dec. 20, 1866, H-W; *Collected Works,* 4:62.

21. "He could very nearly quote all of Burns' Poems from memory." Milton Hay to John Hay, Feb. 8, 1887, in "Recollection of Lincoln: Three Letters of Intimate Friends," *Bulletin of the Abraham Lincoln Association* 25 (Dec. 1931): 9.

22. Hertz, ed., *The Hidden Lincoln,* 417.

23. For Lincoln's habit of reading aloud, see William H. Herndon to Jesse W. Weik, Oct. 21, 1885, in *The Hidden Lincoln,* ed. Hertz, 95; Angle, ed., *A Portrait of Abraham Lincoln,* 48.

24. Thomas Jefferson, *Notes on the State of Virginia,* ed. William H. Peden (Chapel Hill: University of North Carolina Press, 1954), 277.

25. James A. Bear, Jr., ed., *Jefferson at Monticello* (Charlottesville: University Press of Virginia, 1967), 12.

26. See Albert J. Beveridge, *Abraham Lincoln, 1809–1858* (Boston: Houghton Mifflin, 1928), 1:567–58. Students of Lincoln's legal career have recently been put on notice by the remarkable findings emanating from the Lincoln Legal Papers Project sponsored by the state of Illinois and the Abraham Lincoln Association. There is little doubt that Lincoln's ability as a skilled appeals lawyer and his legal skills generally will have to be seriously reappraised in view of the massively detailed record of his law practice now in preparation.

27. Edmund Randolph quoted in Malone, *Jefferson the Virginian,* 121.

28. Abraham Lincoln to James H. Hackett, Aug. 17, 1863, *Collected Works,* 6:392.

29. See appendix to Harry E. Pratt, *The Personal Finances of Abraham Lincoln* (Springfield: Abraham Lincoln Association, 1943).

30. John Hay, "Life in the White House in the Time of Lincoln," in *Addresses of John Hay* (New York: Century, 1906), 335, 334.

31. Don E. Fehrenbacher, "The Weight of Responsibility," in *Lincoln in Text and Context: Collected Essays* (Stanford: Stanford University Press, 1987), 158.

32. For an account of Jefferson's familiarity with Shakespeare and a listing of the editions he owned, see *Jefferson's Literary Commonplace Book,* ed. Wilson, 180–81.

33. See Douglas L. Wilson, "Jefferson vs. Hume," *William and Mary Quarterly,* 3d ser., 46 (Jan. 1989): 49–70.

34. See Dickinson W. Adams, ed., *Jefferson's Extracts from the Gospels,* in

The Papers of Thomas Jefferson, 2d ser., ed. Charles T. Cullen (Princeton: Princeton University Press, 1983).

35. Thomas Jefferson to Samuel H. Smith, May 8, 1815, quoted in Dumas Malone, *Jefferson and His Times*, vol. 6: *The Sage of Monticello* (Boston: Little, Brown, 1981), 181. For details on Jefferson's library building, see Wilson, "Jefferson's Library," 157–79.

36. This book, handed down in the Rutledge family and vouched for by members who knew Lincoln and Ann, is now in the Rare Book Division, Library of Congress.

37. William H. Herndon and Jesse W. Weik, *Herndon's Life of Lincoln*, ed. Paul M. Angle (Cleveland: World Publishing, 1949), 386; Angle, ed., *A Portrait of Abraham Lincoln in Letters by His Oldest Son*, 47.

38. Thomas Jefferson to John Adams, May 17, 1818, June 10, 1815, in *The Adams-Jefferson Letters*, ed. Lester J. Cappon (Chapel Hill: University of North Carolina Press, 1959), 524, 443.

39. There were about 1,600 volumes in Jefferson's Monticello library that was sold at auction in 1829 and about 650 volumes in his library at Poplar Forest. See Nathaniel Poor, *Catalogue. President Jefferson's Library* (Washington: Gales and Seaton, 1829) and *Catalogue of a Private Library . . . Also, the Remaining Portion of the Library of the Late Thomas Jefferson, Comprising Many Classical Works and Several Autograph Letters, Offered by His Grandson, Francis Eppes. of Poplar Forest, Va.* (n.p., 1873).

40. David C. Mearns, "'The Great Invention of the World': Mr. Lincoln and the Books He Read," in *Three Presidents and Their Books: The Reading of Jefferson, Lincoln, and Franklin D. Roosevelt* (Urbana: University of Illinois Press, 1955), 46.

41. Robert Darnton, "Toward a History of Reading," *Wilson Quarterly* 13 (Autumn 1989): 102.

42. Thomas H. Johnson, ed., *The Complete Poems of Emily Dickinson* (Boston: Little, Brown, 1960), 553.

PART TWO

Herndon and Lincoln

2

Herndon's Legacy

Why is it that the name of William H. Herndon is Mudd? How does it happen that the man who interviewed and corresponded with scores of Abraham Lincoln's friends and acquaintances, who carefully preserved the resulting documents and information for posterity, who freely shared with all comers his personal knowledge of his law partner in hundreds of letters and interviews, who fearlessly challenged the hagiographers attempting to transform a mortal politician into a martyred saint, and who, in the face of strong opposition and popular derision, championed veracity in all matters and insisted that the greatness of Abraham Lincoln could not be diminished by the truth—how does it happened that such a man should be so mistrusted by the great Lincoln scholars, so belittled by his biographer, and so disparaged by others that we should find him, as we do today, in the doghouse of Lincoln scholarship?

It is scarcely necessary to document this state of affairs. For those even superficially acquainted with the Lincoln literature of recent years, it is virtually self-evident. Every school child knows that the Ann Rutledge story, first discovered and put forward by Herndon, is a myth. The most casual reader of modern Lincoln biography soon learns how Herndon botched the story of Lincoln's courtship of Mary Todd and described, down to the bridal flowers, an aborted wedding ceremony that never happened. And the aficionados of Mary Todd Lincoln, whose numbers are steadily growing, know all too well that Mary's character and reputation have had to be rescued from an opprobrium unfairly inflicted on her by Herndon's harsh and malicious portrait. The well-informed student knows that Herndon was a drunk, that he was self-important and boastful of his intuitive powers, that he claimed credit for having introduced Lincoln to advanced views, that he coached his informants to tell him what he wanted to hear, and that he ignored testimony that he did not believe or could not accept while at the same time giving credence to doubtful evidence. His considerable contributions, which once seemed to assure him the acclaim of a grateful posterity, appear so decidedly overbalanced by the prejudices of the present that it is only fair to ask how this came about. Does Herndon deserve the unenviable reputation he presently enjoys?

There is not much doubt that Herndon's slide into disfavor was coincidental with the rise of a new breed of student in the Lincoln field in the second quarter of this century, the academically trained historians. These scholars—one thinks of people such as Paul M. Angle, Benjamin Thomas, Harry Pratt, Roy P. Basler, and James G. Randall—were less interested in the Lincoln of popular legend, the inspirational embodiment of American virtues and values that had held the stage for years, than in what they saw as the Lincoln of history, the politician and the president who made a difference. In their view, the popular Lincoln had already gotten out of hand and had ascended (or descended) to the level of folklore. Folklore might feed on rumor or conjecture, but historical inquiry must be based upon evidence, and that evidence must be genuine. This brilliant corps of Lincoln students were scholars first and brought to Lincoln studies a healthy professional skepticism that balked at much of what had passed for evidence with many of their popularizing predecessors.

The appearance of these scholars in the 1920s and 1930s brought about a new order of Lincoln scholarship, with its own emphasis and standards. What made their achievement so notable and their contribution so important and lasting is that they went back to basics and undertook much of the hard, grinding, unglamorous research that put Lincoln studies on a solid footing—studies of things like Lincoln's finances and the communities in which he lived, the invaluable series that charted his activities day-by-day, and the well-crafted edition of his writings. The movement away from the popular Lincoln and the insistence upon more rigorous standards for historical evidence constituted something of a scholarly juggernaut that took few prisoners and inflicted heavy casualties. Among the first of these casualties were the reputation and standing of William H. Herndon.

Paul M. Angle's attack on Herndon in 1927 is particularly revealing, for it sounded the keynote for what was to come. Fresh out of graduate school and recently installed as executive secretary of the Lincoln Centennial Association, the twenty-seven-year-old Angle took almost the first opportunity presented him as a Lincoln authority to strike out sharply at the authenticity of the Ann Rutledge story, calling it "one of the great myths of American history."[1] Angle's reasons are well known—principally that Herndon relied exclusively on the unconfirmed reminiscences given thirty years after the fact and that he ignored or suppressed conflicting evidence—but his attack struck, and presumably was intended to strike, much deeper than the Ann Rutledge story. It called into question the entire body of evidence associated with Herndon by charging that such reminiscences were not only subject to the hazards of memory but also that the testimony of such informants was suspect because of a natural eagerness to associate themselves with the legendary career of the martyred president.[2] This was indeed a potent charge, for these were grounds upon which virtually all of the testimony Herndon gathered could be readily impeached.

꜄

Although one could not have guessed it from his critique, Angle himself had not seen a fraction of Herndon's testimony concerning the Ann Rutledge affair, much less a sizable portion of Herndon's collection of letters and interviews on Lincoln. Angle based his indictment on the documents cited by Herndon and his collaborator, Jesse W. Weik, and possibly a look at the copies of some of the documents Herndon had sold to Ward Hill Lamon, which had ended up in the Huntington Library.[3] Not until the Library of Congress purchased the Herndon-Weik Collection in 1941 were scholars able to examine the original documents for themselves, and it is hardly surprising that one of the first to avail himself of the privilege was the leading Lincoln scholar of the day, James G. Randall.

In preparing his landmark study of Lincoln's presidency, Randall duly consulted and made use of the testimony Herndon collected in his early chapters on Lincoln's background. But such was Randall's concern for the Ann Rutledge story that he included in his manuscript an entire chapter on the Ann Rutledge evidence, which, after some indecision, he decided to relegate to an appendix. In the famous essay "Sifting the Ann Rutledge Evidence," Randall brought the full weight of his authority to bear on a subject that, as he was willing to admit, was extraneous to his study of Lincoln's presidency. He was taking up the question, he wrote, "not for any intrinsic importance at all, but because historical criticism finds here a challenge and a needful task."[4]

I have offered an exposition and critique of Randall's arguments elsewhere and will not rehearse them here.[5] Suffice it to say that Randall confirmed Angle's charges against Herndon and handed down a verdict that drew a line between personal reminiscences, such as those on which the Ann Rutledge story is based, and acceptable historical evidence. Randall's verdict amounted to a proscription of the Ann Rutledge story in serious Lincoln biography, and it is a measure of Randall's standing and influence that his interdiction prevailed virtually unquestioned until John Y. Simon challenged his conclusions at the Abraham Lincoln Symposium in 1988.[6]

It is not an accident, nor is it without significance, that Randall's attack on the Ann Rutledge story was gratuitous. As he admits, it formed no part of the story of Lincoln's presidency, and he had every right to ignore it. But the Ann Rutledge story disturbed Randall more than a little, as the files and correspondence on the subject in his personal papers at the Library of Congress show. In his view, it was a story that had "usurped the spotlight," and he aimed to discredit and crush it.[7] That he hoped to influence a broader audience than Lincoln scholars is clear from his attempt to have his Ann Rutledge chapter published separately in *The Readers Digest*.[8]

Soon after the appearance of Randall's appendix in 1945, Louis A. Warren published two concurring briefs: one on what he called "Herndon's Contributions to Lincoln Mythology" and one more openly acknowledging its debt to Randall, "Sifting the Herndon Sources."[9] In the first, he charged Herndon with the invention of at least a dozen popular myths about Lincoln, and in the second he ratified Randall's conclusions about the Ann Rutledge story and pointed to its more general application in connection with other Herndonian "myths." Warren's essays and their timing were an indication that the tide of opinion had turned decisively against Herndon, but David Donald's biography, published in 1948, was to carry him far out to sea.

↩

Donald's biography had been begun at Randall's direction, presumably as part of the mentor's program to investigate the man and methods responsible for such unfortunate red herrings in the Lincoln story as the Ann Rutledge episode. There is, indeed, much to be said in criticism of Herndon, his methods, and especially his intuitive judgments, and the young David Donald managed to say it all. Although a rewritten doctoral dissertation by another fledgling scholar, *Lincoln's Herndon* is an extremely impressive piece of work: thoroughly, one might almost say massively, researched, richly informed, and written in a lively, engaging style. Donald strove to uncover the facts of Herndon's life and ca-

reer and tell his story with due regard for his subject's virtues and vic-
es, but he could not suppress a tendency to satirize his subject nor disguise his belief that Herndon was not quite worthy of respect.

It must be allowed that Donald attempts to render Herndon his due.
He writes: "There is not, to the present writer's knowledge, a single
letter or other manuscript of Herndon's that reveals a desire or willingness to tell an untruth about Lincoln. . . . Herndon may have been in
error, but he was not a liar."[10] The difficulty lies in the fact that this
tribute to Herndon's truthfulness comes almost as a surprise announce-
ment near the end of the book. Had it appeared at the outset and been
one of the themes of the work, there is no doubt that it would have made
for a very different overall impression of Herndon and perhaps for a
different book.

Donald's actual presentation of his subject proved so irresistible that
his picture of Herndon has fixed itself with the reading public as indel-
ibly as Herndon's picture of Lincoln. But what needs to be noted is that
Donald's is an extremely limited, tightly focused picture that concen-
trates on one aspect of a man's life rather than a full-scale biography.
An indication of the kind of thing left out in Donald's book is revealed
in the following passage: "It was a busy time with him. Herndon was
attending court, collecting his Lincoln records, leading a fight against
Springfield's flourishing houses of prostitution, and heading a committee which planned removal of the county courthouse. There was a new
and ailing baby at the Herndon house, who might, it was feared, die any
moment. During all this confusion William Lloyd Garrison paid Springfield an unsolicited visit and was invited to stay with the Herndons."[11]
Few of these interesting topics is pursued further; indeed, there is very
little about Herndon's family or personal life in this biography and only
a few provocative references to his active and extensive public life. With
these critical dimensions of the man and his character almost entirely
missing, Donald's biography, to reverse one of his own figures, is something like a head without a body.

↩

But none of these considerations were part of the heady response that
made Donald's brilliant performance a popular book in 1948. Following his and Randall's lead, Lincoln scholars began in the 1950s to take
it as axiomatic that Herndon and his evidence were unreliable, and some
respected authorities, such as Ruth Painter Randall and John J. Duff,
would go further and picture him as a biographical assassin.[12] By the
1960s it was open season on Herndon. An indicative example is a remark by Paul Simon in his invaluable book on Lincoln's career in the

Illinois General Assembly. In discussing Lincoln's alleged logrolling in the Illinois legislature, Simon disputes some pertinent testimony offered by Stephen T. Logan, saying that "Herndon did not hesitate to change interviews to make them fit his preconceived theories."[13] Simon had no way of knowing that the Logan interview to which he referred was taken by John G. Nicolay, not Herndon, but the telling point here is that he offered no explanation or documentation for such a serious charge. Herndon's perfidy was presumably common knowledge among Lincoln scholars and required no justification.

In these circumstances, it comes as no surprise to find Herndon represented unsympathetically in a standard reference work. In *The Abraham Lincoln Encyclopedia*, Mark E. Neely, Jr., questions even Herndon's humanitarian sympathy for blacks.[14] The status that Herndon occupies at present is perhaps perfectly exemplified in a passage in Jean H. Baker's biography of Mary Todd Lincoln: "Later his law partner and biographer William Herndon incorrectly charged that Lincoln had contracted venereal disease in Beardstown in the 1830s."[15] The basis of this statement is that Herndon informed his collaborator, Jesse W. Weik, after their biography had appeared, that Lincoln had once told him that, as a young man, he had contracted syphilis from a girl in Beardstown, a fact Herndon was anxious not to have repeated.[16] Baker unhesitatingly transforms this into an accusation, a "charge" made by Herndon against Lincoln, and one she does not hesitate to label as "incorrect." In fact, we have no way of knowing whether Herndon's story or his information is correct or incorrect. The point she wants to make does not require this tack: "More likely Lincoln feared the intimacy and sexual union of marriage, not because he suffered from syphilis but because like many Victorian males, he thought he might have the disease."[17] The slur against Herndon is thus gratuitous. As has become all too typical, Baker accepts the information that Herndon conveys—that Lincoln feared he had venereal disease and once spoke of it to Herndon—but in so doing she needlessly and quite unfairly makes Herndon the author of a false accusation.

Far from being intentionally unfair to Herndon, it would seem that Baker inadvertently slipped into this distortion because of Herndon's abysmally low standing with contemporary historians. Baker is fully aware of the insidious nature of the situation I have been describing. In a commentary on a paper by Charles B. Strozier, she wrote: "Now Herndon, it seems to me, is every Lincoln scholar's reserve army—available to make a point when he agrees with whatever conclusion we wish to establish, but having been so often discredited, easily dismissed when we disagree."[18] Exactly. Anyone who wants to deal with

Lincoln's early life has no alternative but to resort to Herndon's evidence, for there is precious little else. Yet Herndon's standing is such that we are free to reject with impunity anything Herndon or his informants say that does not jibe with our own conceptions. But when we reflect that those conceptions are themselves largely the products of selective readings of Herndon's evidence, we may begin to fathom the depth of our dilemma.

To address this dilemma, one must begin with Herndon himself. Although we have had two good books on Herndon—Joseph Fort Newton's study published in 1910, which is still useful, and David Donald's biography—we still lack a full and balanced portrait of the man. Donald is good, wickedly good, on the foibles of Herndon, which were not inconsiderable and can not be overlooked. But by a curious inversion Herndon's shortcomings bring out the best in his biographer, for his style never appears so scintillating nor his wit so sharply engaged as when he is ridiculing or running down his subject. But he is notably restrained and circumspect when it comes to discussing his virtues. It is precisely this skewed emphasis and lack of proportion that characterize the picture most modern Lincoln students have of William H. Herndon.

One cannot hope to redress the balance here, but I propose, more than a hundred years after his death, to say something in mitigation. I offer no defense of Herndon's claims to superior intuitive insight or his many speculations about Lincoln's motivations and inner life. I merely note that although he made, in his letters and early lectures, some unguarded and rather extravagant claims along these lines that are often used against him, the finished biography is far less subject to this charge. Neither do I defend Herndon's claims to have influenced his law partner's views on important political issues, although one can see how Herndon might conclude that Lincoln's adoption of some of his own positions was evidence of that.

Nonetheless, I will address a few of the serious charges commonly made against Herndon as a biographer. Take his drinking, for example. Although a responsible and respected citizen, a dutiful and devoted father and family man, Herndon was subject at certain times in his life to drunken sprees, which sometimes had to be terminated by the intercession of his friends—or the law. "That Herndon drank excessively during this period [i.e., when he was researching his biography] is undeniable," Donald writes, but he acknowledges that during the same period Herndon "retained an upstanding leadership in Springfield affairs.

In the decade following 1865 he was in constant demand. It is hard to find a single month in that period when Herndon was not called on to head some committee, promote some reform, speak for some civic cause. In every public meeting of importance held in Springfield during the decade (except church gatherings) Herndon was asked to speak."[19]

The truth seems to be that Herndon was, in this respect, a good deal like Ulysses S. Grant. And like Grant, the evidence is not so much that drinking affected the quality of his work but rather that he could not work as long as he was drinking. Although Herndon's detractors point it out over and over, his susceptibility to drunken sprees has never been shown to have seriously compromised his abilities or performance as a biographer of Lincoln. For this reason it is greatly to Donald's credit that he confesses in the preface to a new edition of his biography that he tended, when writing the book, "to think of alcoholism as evidence of moral depravity, rather than of disease" and admits that this prejudice is probably reflected in its pages.[20]

Much fault has been found with Herndon as an investigator, but I believe that there is much more to be said in his defense. As the documents in the Herndon-Weik archive attest, Herndon spent a prodigious amount of time and effort pursuing and procuring information about Abraham Lincoln. They show that he examined and cross-examined his informants with care, that he sought information both open-endedly and on a wide variety of specific topics, that he checked up on doubtful or conflicting stories, and that he acted in accordance with his stated purpose, which was to learn and publish the truth about his great law partner. There is very little indication that Herndon led or coerced his informants to tell him what he wanted to hear in spite of the currency of this charge. Donald, for example, wrote: "From Mary Lincoln's sister, Mrs. Ninian W. Edwards, Herndon coaxed an account of that 'fatal 1st of January, 1841.'"[21] But there is no evidence that the imperious Elizabeth Edwards had been *coaxed* by Herndon to invent an aborted wedding ceremony for her sister; she told him the same story twice and repeated it independently to Weik.[22]

Herndon has also been accused of things for which there is little or no evidence but only a presumption of guilt. Consider Donald's remark: "From a knowledge of Herndon and from the extant letters in which he quizzed witnesses, it may be assumed that he harped on certain episodes in the Lincoln story—tales of the President's domestic infelicity, for example—to the neglect of other, and perhaps more important points."[23] But note that this harsh judgment is not based on any cited evidence but on an undocumented assumption. Far from corroboration for this charge, what one finds in the documents themselves is a rather scrupulous questioner who is genuinely interested in what his informants have to say, not what he expects or wants them to say.

There is also very little indication that he suppressed important testimony that undermined his own theories, another common charge. He certainly did not believe all he was told, and he admits he did not write down all the stories offered him. On the other hand, misunderstanding abounds about what is in the collection and how it was gathered. Louis A. Warren, although he wrote knowingly about Herndon's evidence, seemed to have had no idea that it was far more extensive than the modest selection printed in Emanuel Hertz's *The Hidden Lincoln*, a small fraction of the letters and interviews.[24]

The chief difficulty, and the crux of the problem, is that few students of Lincoln and Herndon have had the leisure or taken the trouble to read widely in the great mass of hard-to-read, handwritten material that is the Herndon-Weik Collection in order to be able to judge Herndon's evidence and the performance of his informants for themselves. Most are familiar with some of the more famous letters and interviews and with the badly edited sample published in *The Hidden Lincoln*. But for judgments on the collection as a whole, students of Lincoln continue to rely on the damning estimates of Angle, Randall, and Donald, estimates that I believe are far from even-handed, often quite unfair, and frequently more adversarial than judicial.[25]

᠆

As interest in Mary Todd Lincoln is revived and new estimates of her life and character are brought forward, it is inevitable that Herndon's treatment of her and her relationship with Lincoln should come under scrutiny. Because the picture of Mary Todd Lincoln in Herndon's biography is unflattering, especially because it represented Lincoln's domestic life as often difficult and unpleasant, Ruth Painter Randall believed Herndon was little short of wicked, and she attacked him repeatedly in her biography of Mary Todd Lincoln as malicious and as a distorter of the truth. She rationalized her running excoriation by saying, "In telling Mary Lincoln's life story it is necessary to take Herndon along as excess baggage."[26] This was apparently her way of admitting that, in telling the Lincoln story, it is utterly impossible to leave Herndon behind.

Nothing invokes Randall's scorn more than what she calls Herndon's "framed-up account" of the story of Lincoln as a defaulting bridegroom, which she insists Herndon made up "out of his 'intuitive' knowledge."[27] But anyone familiar with Herndon's letters and interviews knows that

Herndon did not make up this story. He got it from Mary's sister, Elizabeth Edwards, who repeated it years later to Jesse Weik. Although Randall does not advertise it, the long statement Elizabeth Edwards gave to Herndon constitutes the heart and soul of her own reconstruction of the troubled courtship, the story of the defaulting bridegroom being almost the only part that Randall rejects. One may agree that she was right to reject this highly unlikely story, but why she should charge Herndon with making it up to do mischief to the memory of Mary Todd is another question.

But did Herndon set out to malign Mary Todd? To document what she calls Herndon's "hatred" of her, Randall cites Donald's listing of a string of unflattering phrases that Herndon applied to Mary Todd in a series of letters to Weik.[28] But if one reads the letters themselves, the charge of hatred appears well off the mark. Herndon does indeed call her a "she wolf" and "a tigress," but he also credits her with an essential role in Lincoln's success. What is more, one finds Herndon explaining Mary Todd Lincoln's situation to Weik with understanding and sympathy: "In her domestic troubles I have always sympathized with her. The world does not know what she bore and the history of the bearing. I will write it out some time. This domestic *hell* of Lincoln's life is not all on one side."[29] In another of these letters, he tells Weik, "I have always sympathized with Mrs. Lincoln. Remember that Every Effect must have its Cause. Mrs. Lincoln was not a she wolf—wild Cat without a Cause."[30] Ignoring such important ingredients in Herndon's complex attitude toward Mary Todd Lincoln and passing it off as nothing but hatred indicates what is clear in many other ways: that neither Donald nor Randall is disposed to be scrupulously fair or even-handed in their treatment of the hapless Herndon.

In short, these letters do not establish anything like a hatred for Mary Todd Lincoln, nor does Herndon's portrait of her in his biography. As Donald admits, Mary Lincoln was not popular in Springfield, and Herndon's biography, drawing on the voluntary testimony of people who knew her and on his personal knowledge, tells why.[31] Although she was proud of her husband and doted on her children, townspeople (and her own sister) perceived her as aristocratic, willful, inconsiderate, quarrelsome, and possessed of a violent temper. Her subsequent behavior in Washington, where she was out of the range of Herndon and her Springfield neighbors, did nothing to improve her behavior or her reputation. Herndon had his own interpretation of why, as he believed, Mary Lincoln made Lincoln's domestic life a trial, and that interpretation is no more than speculation. But he did not invent her abundantly documented foibles or create her Springfield reputation. The picture he draws squares much more closely with what knowledgeable witnesses agreed upon than that put forth by Randall and other defenders of Mary Lincoln, who have labored to create, in the words of John Y. Simon, "an alternate legend of Lincoln's happy marriage."[32]

⤺

In some ways, the most abused characters in this drama are Herndon's informants, most of whom gave their testimony on the subject of Abraham Lincoln in good faith and to the best of their ability. Although much of what is known about Lincoln's early life comes from these informants, Herndon's critics have been very hard on them as witnesses and people. Angle and J. G. Randall are often condescending about the young Lincoln's unlettered neighbors and friends, and Donald delights in picturing them as willing collaborators with Herndon in either fabricating a romance out of rumor or as participants in a contest to stretch the truth about their old friend.[33] Informants whose information is approved are generally tolerated, but bearers of unwelcome testimony are singled out for harsher treatment. Angle, for example, in the face of Isaac Cogdal's testimony that Lincoln once admitted he had been in love with Ann Rutledge and had gone off the track at her death, disputed Cogdal's claim to be a friend of Lincoln's at all and dismissed him as "a mediocre lawyer."[34] Angle seems to have known very little about Cogdal, who turns out to have been an old friend and political associate from Lincoln's New Salem days and a fellow Whig from Democratic Menard.[35] Randall is equally distrustful of Cogdal's "effusive" testimony, and although he took the trouble to look into his background and reported that Cogdal was licensed as a lawyer, he suppressed the relevant information from the same source that it was Lincoln who had encouraged and abetted Cogdal's study of the law.[36] The point is that Angle and Randall had no more reason to doubt Cogdal's testimony than that of many other witnesses they chose not to question. Their disposition to treat Isaac Cogdal as untruthful is clearly the result of their disinclination to accept what he had to say. It does Angle and Randall's cause no credit that their approach reverses the accepted practice of first establishing the unreliability of a witness in order to cast doubt on his or her testimony.

James G. Randall's most pervasive contention is that the testimony of Herndon's informants is dubious because it is subject to the notorious fallibility of human memory. Even when presenting the recollections of a witness he seems to respect, Randall qualifies: "The testimony of James Short, a close and true friend of Lincoln and of the Rutledges, deserves consideration if one has to deal with far-off rememberings."[37]

When he encounters inconvenient testimony that seems to have every right to be believed, he reminds us that it is "dim and misty with the years."[38] And there is no doubt that this is a telling consideration. As Randall insists, all of Herndon's collected testimony is after the fact; it consists almost exclusively of the reminiscences of older people about what happened long ago.

It is sometimes maintained by an appeal to common experience that Herndon's informants could not have been expected to summon obscure events from the distant past with anything like accuracy, much less historical reliability, and that Herndon was naive to have believed them. But such objections are problematic. They make it appear that Herndon asked his informants to recall obscure events, things they had not thought about or discussed with anyone for twenty-five or thirty years. That this is very far from the case can be seen from the example of the people of Menard County, the area that has been called Herndon's "most fruitful source of information about Lincoln."[39] Lincoln was considered a remarkable man from the time of his first appearance in New Salem. As one of the neighborhood's stalwarts, Coleman Smoot, expressed it, "Not only did his wit, kindliness, and knowledge attract people, but his strange clothes and uncouth awkwardness advertised him, the shortness of his trousers causing particular remark and amusement. Soon the name 'Abe Lincoln' was a household word."[40] Although poor, in debt, and making his living by a motley assortment of work, Abraham Lincoln was nonetheless a successful politician and very much in the public eye well before he left New Salem in 1837. And after departing for Springfield, less than twenty-five miles away, he not only continued to rise as a politician but also remained active in the area as a lawyer at a time when ordinary citizens were frequently at law with each other and court sessions were important public events.

In these circumstances, Abraham Lincoln continued as a familiar presence to the people of Menard, even though many of them were Democrats and remained at odds with him politically. As he rose to prominence as a legislator, member of Congress, leading lawyer, senatorial candidate, national celebrity, and finally as president, they had frequent occasion to recall their personal contacts with him and keep alive their memories of his early days in the neighborhood of New Salem. George Spears endeared himself to James G. Randall for confessing, "At that time I had no idea of his [Lincoln's] ever being President, therefore I did not notice his course as close as I should of had."[41] But far from being typical, Spears's remark is, among informants, almost unique. The experience of most seems to have been much more like that of Aunt Louisa Clary.

Mrs. Clary had been born in 1834 at Clary's Grove and, as a young girl, had lived for two years in New Salem shortly after Lincoln left. Her ability to remember the physical details and precise locations of buildings of the long-since-deserted village greatly impressed Thomas P. Reep and his fellow members of the Old Salem Lincoln League as they attempted to piece together an accurate picture of the New Salem in Lincoln's time. Reep reported that he said to Aunt Louisa: "How in the world is it you can remember these things and locate these places so closely?" She replied, "When we went away from there I was a child eight years old, and it wasn't long after that until Lincoln began to be preeminent, and whenever they would talk about Lincoln, it would always recall Lincoln living there, and our folks knew about it. They talked about Lincoln having lived there seven or eight years, and I would think about New Salem. Every time I thought about it the picture would come back to my mind just about where all these places were, about where the road was, the buildings in regard to one another that were standing, and I would just get a picture again. In all these years my mind has kept the picture fresh by frequently having it recalled to me."[42] For many of Herndon's informants, and for much of their testimony about Lincoln as a young man, keeping the picture fresh by frequently having it recalled to them would seem a more apt characterization than Randall's "dim and misty with the years."

But was Herndon as naive about the problems of memory and the accuracy of reminiscences and long-range recollections as his critics often charge? In November of 1888, Herndon was reading proof on his biography, which was already set in type and would be published a few months later. Writing to Jesse W. Weik, he carefully specified errors and corrections that still needed to be made. Here is what he wrote his collaborator about the account of his first glimpse of Abraham Lincoln in 1832: "Be sure that Lincoln Came all the way up to Bogue's Mill. It *seems* to me that he did and that, I at that time, saw Lincoln, but be sure that I am right. The records [i.e., his letters and interviews, then in Weik's possession] will fix it — it has now been 56 years since I saw what now *Seems* to be the truth to me. Try and get me right. If L Came up to Bogues mill I saw Lincoln & if he did not then I did not see him at Bogues mill."[43]

What does this passage reveal? That Herndon, at the age of seventy, was losing his grip? That when it came right down to it, he was confused about this and probably many other matters as well? That even his firsthand recollections of Lincoln were, at bottom, shaky and uncertain? The passage could perhaps be taken to suggest any of these, and in the present climate of opinion contemporary students of Lincoln might be expected to embrace any or all with scarcely a second thought. But surely fairness to Herndon requires acknowledging other things as well: that this passage is clear and convincing evidence that Herndon cared deeply for historical accuracy, that he was keenly aware that there is a difference between what only seems to be and what is historical fact, that even his most vivid memories of Lincoln could be subject to error, and that if there were ways to test them and they proved incompatible with more solid historical evidence, they would have to be sacrificed in the interest of truth.

It is evident that the Herndon who worried about the accuracy of his first glimpse of Abraham Lincoln is a virtual stranger to contemporary students and deserves to be much better known. Moreover, the rectitude and good faith of his Lincoln informants generally have been unfairly discounted and deserve to be reconsidered. As a consequence, the extensive body of material that Herndon collected and preserved must be judged far more valuable than has been realized and deserves to be treated accordingly. It should, perhaps, come as no surprise that in great human endeavors there is frequently a hidden cost in the reckoning. Shelby Foote has said that Gettysburg was the price the Confederacy had to pay for having Robert E. Lee. The overly severe and biased treatment of Herndon and his Lincoln informants is part of the price Lincoln scholarship has had to pay for the great contributions of some of its finest historians, but it is never too late to redress the balance.

NOTES

1. Paul Angle, "Lincoln's First Love?" *Bulletin* (Lincoln Centennial Association), Dec. 1, 1927, 1.

2. Angle, "Lincoln's First Love?" 5.

3. That Angle could not have made a careful study of even the Lamon copies is evident from his misconceptions about how Herndon first heard the story and how and when he gathered his information. See "Abraham Lincoln, Ann Rutledge, and the Evidence of Herndon's Informants" in this volume.

4. J. G. Randall, "Sifting the Ann Rutledge Evidence," in *Lincoln the President: Springfield to Gettysburg* (New York: Dodd, Mead, 1945), 2:321. In his papers at the Library of Congress are copies of letters in which he discusses his indecision about where to include the Ann Rutledge chapter. I am grateful to John R. Sellers for assistance in consulting the Randall family papers at the Manuscript Division, Library of Congress, and to David H. Donald for permission to examine them.

5. See "Abraham Lincoln, Ann Rutledge, and the Evidence of Herndon's Informants" in this volume.

6. John Y. Simon, "Abraham Lincoln and Ann Rutledge," *Journal of the Abraham Lincoln Association* 11 (1990): 13–33.

7. Randall, "Sifting the Ann Rutledge Evidence," 2:321.

8. Copies of letters in the Randall Papers show that he offered his Ann Rutledge chapter to *The Reader's Digest.*

9. Louis A. Warren, "Herndon's Contribution to Lincoln Mythology," *Indiana Magazine of History* 41 (Sept. 1945): 221–44; Louis A. Warren, *Sifting the Herndon Sources* (n.p.: Lincoln Fellowship of Southern California, 1948).

10. David Donald, *Lincoln's Herndon: A Biography* (1948, repr. New York: DaCapo Press, 1989), 347.

11. Donald, *Lincoln's Herndon*, 198.

12. Ruth Painter Randall, *Mary Lincoln: Biography of a Marriage* (Boston: Little, Brown, 1953); John J. Duff, *A. Lincoln: Prairie Lawyer* (New York: Rinehart and Company, 1960). Apparently on the assumption that Lincoln scholars acknowledge Herndon to be a controversial source of information Duff accuses him of all manner of malfeasance.

13. Paul Simon, *Lincoln's Preparation for Greatness: The Illinois Legislative Years* (Urbana: University of Illinois Press, 1971), 80. The interview ascribed to Herndon and printed in the *Bulletin of the Abraham Lincoln Association,* Sept. 1, 1928, was one of several interviews John G. Nicolay conducted with Lincoln's oldest friends in June and July 1875. Michael Burlingame has discovered copies of these interviews in Nicolay's hand in the John Hay Papers at Brown University Library and the Library of Congress and has published them in *An Oral History of Abraham Lincoln: John G. Nicolay's Interviews and Essays* (Carbondale: Southern Illinois University Press, 1996). I am grateful to him for generously sharing these long-lost documents in advance of publication.

14. Mark E. Neely, Jr., *The Abraham Lincoln Encyclopedia* (New York: McGraw Hill, 1982), 145–48.

15. Jean H. Baker, *Mary Todd Lincoln: A Biography* (New York: W. W. Norton, 1987), 88.

16. William H. Herndon to Jesse W. Weik, January 1891, Herndon-Weik Collection, Manuscript Division, Library of Congress (hereafter cited as H-W), printed in *The Hidden Lincoln: From the Letters and Papers of William H. Herndon,* ed. Emanuel Hertz (New York: Viking Press, 1938), 259.

17. Baker, *Mary Todd Lincoln,* 88.

18. Jean Baker, "Commentary on 'Lincoln's Quest for Union,'" in *The Historian's Lincoln: Pseudohistory, Psychohistory, and History,* ed. Gabor S. Boritt (Urbana: University of Illinois Press, 1988), 244.

19. Donald, *Lincoln's Herndon,* 259. It is interesting, given his strictures on Herndon's reliance on reminiscence, that Donald's most telling evidence for Herndon's drunkenness is John Hill's recollections twenty-five or thirty years after the fact.

20. Donald, *Lincoln's Herndon,* viii.

21. Ibid., 355.

22. See Herndon's undated interview with Elizabeth Edwards (ca. 1865–86) and one dated July 27, 1887, H-W; the first is printed in *The Hidden Lincoln,* ed. Hertz, 373–76. For Weik's interview, see Albert J. Beveridge, *Abraham Lincoln, 1809–1858* (Boston: Houghton Mifflin, 1928), 1:313–14n.

23. Donald, *Lincoln's Herndon,* 196.

24. "Most of the items in the collection of the Library of Congress appear in Emanuel Hertz, *The Hidden Lincoln.*" Louis A. Warren, *Lincoln's Youth: Indiana Years Seven to Twenty-one 1816–1830* (Indianapolis: Indiana Historical Society, 1959), 274.

25. A basis for settling this question is now at hand. See Douglas L. Wilson and Rodney O. Davis, eds., *Herndon's Informants: Letters, Interviews, and Statements about Abraham Lincoln* (Urbana: University of Illinois Press, 1997).

26. Randall, *Mary Lincoln*, 36.

27. Ibid., 36, 40.

28. Donald, *Lincoln's Herndon*, 303–4.

29. Herndon to Weik, Jan. 9, 1886, H-W, printed in *The Hidden Lincoln*, ed. Hertz, 131.

30. Herndon to Weik, Jan. 16, 1886, H-W, printed in *The Hidden Lincoln*, ed. Hertz, 136.

31. Donald, *Lincoln's Herndon*, 172.

32. Simon, "Abraham Lincoln and Ann Rutledge," 33.

33. Donald, *Lincoln's Herndon*, 186–87, 353.

34. Angle, "Lincoln's First Love?" 6.

35. See "Abraham Lincoln, Ann Rutledge, and the Evidence of Herndon's Informants" in this volume; for information on Cogdal, see also Alice Keach Bone, *Rock Creek: A Retrospect of One Hundred Years* (n.p., n.d.), 66, and [R. D. Miller], *History of Mason and Menard Counties* (Chicago: O. L. Baskin, 1879), 749.

36. See Randall, "Sifting the Ann Rutledge Evidence," 2:333, citing Miller, *History of Mason and Menard Counties*, 749.

37. Ibid., 2:330.

38. Ibid.

39. Donald, *Lincoln's Herndon*, 184.

40. Coleman Smoot quoted in Benjamin Thomas, *Lincoln's New Salem* (1934, repr. Chicago: Americana House, 1961), 112.

41. George Spears to William H. Herndon, Nov. 3, 1866, H-W.

42. From an interview with Thomas P. Reep conducted by Joseph Booton, printed in *The New Salem Tradition*, ed. Richard S. Taylor (Springfield: Illinois Department of Conservation, 1984), 321. I am grateful to Richard S. Taylor for making this valuable compilation available.

43. William H. Herndon to Jesse W. Weik, Nov. 10, 1888, H-W. Donald cites a portion of this passage in *Lincoln's Herndon* (349), but only to illustrate the problem of evaluating a collaborative work.

3

William H. Herndon and the "Necessary Truth"

Less than two weeks after his father's assassination, Robert Todd Lincoln received a letter from his Harvard professor, Francis James Child. Child was writing in behalf of his colleague, Charles Eliot Norton, who wished to compose a biography of the fallen president and presumably sought the encouragement or cooperation of the president's son. Neither was forthcoming, for, as Robert explained, "It will be impossible . . . for the complete work which Mr. Norton contemplates to be written for a number of years, exactly how long it is impossible to say because there are no doubt many documents (I myself know several) which are necessary to the history but which would be damaging to men now living."[1]

Robert Lincoln was writing at a time of great bereavement, but neither this nor the importunities of eminent Harvard professors could submerge his immediate sense of the problems presented by a complete biography of his father—bringing to light facts and documents that were "necessary" but were at the same time "damaging" to persons still alive. What constitutes "necessary" biographical information and in what circumstances it should be withheld if considered "damaging" were then, and still are, vital questions in the biography of public figures and are central considerations of the discussion that follows.

↬

Probably the last person that Robert Todd Lincoln wanted to write a biography of his father was William H. Herndon. There was nothing in the distinctive nature of his father's verbose and unconventional law partner that would have appealed to the reticent and reserved young Robert. He had rebuffed Herndon's avuncular attempts to engage him intellectually by writing him while at Harvard what Robert described as "absurd pseudophilosophical letters." Many years later he wrote to his old school friend Clinton C. Conkling, "I confess to you that it is one of my puzzles to understand how it was my father stuck to Herndon as long as he did. Personally, I regarded him as insane."[2]

But Herndon had decided soon after the assassination that he would write something about his longtime friend and partner, although his initial conception seems to have been fairly modest. In May he wrote to the prospective biographer, Josiah G. Holland, "When you were in my office I casually informed you that it was my intention to write & publish the *subjective* Mr Lincoln — 'The inner life' of Mr L." This remark in itself would have given Robert Todd Lincoln pause, but the Herndonian sentence that followed would have given him nightmares: "What I mean by that Expression is this — I am writing Mr L's life — a short little thing — giving him in his passions — appetites — & affections — perceptions — memories — judgements — understanding — will, acting under & by motions, just as he lived, breathed — ate & laughed in this world, clothed in flesh & sinew — bone & nerve."[3]

Unfortunately for Robert, this was only the thin end of the wedge. Herndon had, as yet, scarcely begun the extensive correspondence and fieldwork that was to result in the massive archive on which his biography would eventually be based. But within a few weeks, after returning from his first round of interviewing, he wrote excitedly to Holland:

> since I wrote to you some days since, I have been searching for *the facts & truths* of Lincoln's life — not fictions — not fables — not floating rumors, but *facts — solid facts & well attested truths.* I have 'been down' to Menard County where Mr L first landed and where he first made his home in old Sangamon. . . . From such an investigation — from records — from friends — old deeds & surveys &c &c I am satisfied, in Connection with my own Knowledg of Mr L. for 30 years, that Mr Ls whole Early life *remains to be written.*[4]

Herndon's astonishment was undoubtedly genuine. He thought he had known his law partner well, so well that he was prepared to write his subjective, inner life. And because he also knew personally many of the Menard County residents he had interviewed, he was amazed to discover from their stories of Lincoln's days in New Salem that he had actually known very little about his great partner's formative years. The more he corresponded and interviewed, the more surprising things he learned; the more he learned, the more he became convinced that he had uncovered important information about Lincoln's early life that bore significantly on the formation of his character and thus on his later accomplishments.

While Herndon was busily engaged in his research into Lincoln's life, he was becoming increasingly appalled by the distorted image of Lincoln that was emerging in the public press. The man described in countless eulogies and worshipful biographies, whose name was becoming synonymous with selfless nobility and unalloyed virtue, was not the man Herndon had known but was rather an imaginary person—and something of a plaster saint. As David Donald puts it, "Lincoln had already become a myth, about whom clustered a voluminous body of apocrypha."[5] Herndon's disgust was only accentuated by the startling things he was learning about Lincoln's background and early life. If what his informants were telling him was true, the man whom a grieving nation was rapidly raising to sainthood had actually been born of questionable parentage; he had been subject to deep and even tragic disappointments in love; he had bouts of mental derangement and had been suicidal on more than one occasion; he had been a rank unbeliever in religion and had openly ridiculed the tenets of Christianity; he had proposed marriage to several women; after becoming engaged to Mary Todd he had fallen in love with someone else; and after a long period of guilt and indecision he had finally gave himself up to a loveless marriage only to satisfy his sense of honor. Nearly all of this was news to Herndon, and when he saw that even such things as his personal belief that Lincoln's marriage had been a "domestic hell" were strongly supported by the voluntary testimony of others, Herndon realized that he was in the process of documenting a story that was scandalously at odds with what other biographers had presented and with the singularly edifying and untroubled image the public had come to expect.

Discovering new and surprising things about Lincoln's life was stimulating to Herndon, as his biographer has emphasized, but what has not been so clearly recognized is that it eventually caused him great difficulty. After less than a year's research, he began to express doubts that he could do justice to the task as he had conceived it. One of Herndon's idiosyncrasies was that he could enter into correspondence with perfect strangers and confide in them with remarkable candor. Thus one Charles H. Hart, a young law student at the University of Pennsylvania in Philadelphia, became one of Herndon's most intimate correspondents in the years when he was gathering his material on Lincoln. An ardent devotee of Lincoln and an admirer of Herndon's lectures, Hart quickly became a sounding board for Herndon's ideas and hopes as well as his doubts and fears. In April of 1866 Herndon confessed to Hart, "I

sincerely wish I were a competent, a great man to write my friend's life
— but I *can* gather facts and give *truth* to mankind."[6]

That this was not mere modesty but an expression of something that
was genuinely troubling Herndon becomes clear in a letter he wrote to
Hart a few months later. "I hope to write a correct biography when it
can be done. I shall make it truthful or not at all. . . . The trouble is very,
very great, I assure you. Thousands of floating rumors — assertions and
theories, etc., etc., have to be hunted down — dug out — inspected —
criticized, etc., etc., before I can write. I can't scribble on a sentence
without knowing what I am doing."[7] The Herndon who worried about
the character of the evidence he had collected has had little exposure
in Lincoln scholarship, and it is common to assume that he was care-
less and uncritical, if not downright naive, about the conflicting and
inconsistent testimony he received. But his correspondence with Hart
makes it clear that he was highly aware of this problem and increasingly troubled by the difficulties the evidence presented.

In the same letter, written in June of 1866, Herndon confided to Hart,
"Between you and I, I am as busily engaged today in collecting materials
— times — places, etc., etc., etc., as ever — am going to Kentucky in July
— in search of new and important facts."[8] The trip to Kentucky projected for the following month had long been contemplated, but it was more
urgently needed now because Herndon felt he had to confront his informants directly and attempt to resolve some important issues. Many of
the contacts he had established in Kentucky, none of whom he knew
personally, had raised questions about the reputation of the Hanks family, of Nancy Hanks in particular, and about the paternity of her son,
Abraham Lincoln. Herndon already knew that Lincoln believed his mother illegitimate, for his partner had told him so on a memorable buggy ride
on the road to Menard County, but the other allegations were new to
him.[9] Because they were not consistent and came from people he didn't
know, the only way he could think to sort them out, not surprisingly for
a lawyer, was to cross-examine his informants in person.

But the trip to Kentucky in the summer of 1866 did not work out,
and Herndon continued to collect information and ruminate on the
necessity for resolving these issues. By the fall, he seems to have regarded his research as largely completed and engaged John G. Springer to
transcribe everything that he had acquired—informant letters and interviews, newspaper articles, speeches and letters by Lincoln, statistics,
and other miscellaneous data. He now began to confront the other side
of his problem: Once you have arrived at the truth about delicate and
sensitive matters, how do you tell it? For reasons that may have been
forced upon him, Herndon decided to try out in a public lecture his

findings and conclusions regarding one of these sensitive matters—Lincoln's tragic love affair with Ann Rutledge.[10]

~

Writing to Hart on the day of his lecture in Springfield, November 16, 1866, Herndon said: "I claim no literary power, taste, etc., but I do claim to possess *the wish* to tell the truth."[11] But as Herndon was soon to discover, neither the wish itself nor the fact that what is told is the truth mattered to the public nearly so much as the proprieties one is expected to observe. In going public with the story of Lincoln's love for Ann Rutledge and his emotional devastation upon her death, Herndon managed to offend a large segment of his public, including some who were quite friendly to him and believed in his efforts. It seemed, said one, "an invasion of a sacred chamber — a tearing away of the veil which conceals the 'holy of holies.'"[12] But in suggesting that Lincoln never got over his attachment to Ann Rutledge and had known no joy in the last twenty-three years of his life (precisely the period of his marriage), Herndon succeeded in offending nearly everybody.

A loud and hostile reaction was swift to descend. Herndon's lectures, of which this was the fourth, had already become national news, and this one quickly became notorious. As David Donald has written, "It is difficult to recapture the intensity of this feeling. It can be understood only if one remembers that Lincoln to his countrymen was more than a man with mortal failings; he had become in a real sense an American demigod."[13] Herndon had done more than merely offend Lincoln's family and a worshipful public; he had seriously undermined his standing and credibility as a reputable authority on Lincoln. John Y. Simon has shown that in deciding to deliver the Ann Rutledge lecture as he did and consequently giving widespread offense Herndon "grossly mishandled a major incident in the Lincoln story" from which "neither Herndon's reputation nor that of Ann Rutledge ever recovered."[14]

Herndon refused to reply publicly to any of the critical blasts aimed at him, but he did offer a vigorous defense of his methods and purposes to an old friend, Isaac N. Arnold, a prominent Chicago attorney and Republican member of Congress who had just published a book on Lincoln and the overthrow of slavery. Arnold wrote that he found the lecture fascinating, but he was concerned that such revelations might do injury, albeit unintentionally, to the memory of their great friend. Herndon replied in his inimitable prose: "Don't scold and suspicion even by shadowy vision indirectly your true friend, your co-laborer, till you know all — know it as I do, and as time *will have* it and make it irrespective of you and myself."[15]

Herndon's defense of this and other revelations to come has two thrusts. The first is that because the sensitive and potentially embarrassing aspects of Lincoln's life would eventually become known in any event, it would be better for Lincoln's friends to acknowledge them while they could so that such matters could be put in the best possible light. He gave as an example Lincoln's writing in New Salem a "book on *Infidelity*," which Herndon intended to acknowledge and use to show that although Lincoln's essay apparently took issue with and perhaps even ridiculed the Bible and certain doctrines of orthodox Christianity, it was a response to the loss of Ann Rutledge and "written through the spirit of his misery, through the thought and idea that God had forsaken him, and through the echoes of Lincoln's mental condition, suffering, a burden of wild despair."[16]

If this sounds suspiciously like rationalization, the second thrust of Herndon's defense is more substantive. It is that certain facts or conditions, private and inappropriate to published biography as they might ordinarily be considered, are necessary to the understanding of Lincoln's character, which in turn is the key to what he ultimately accomplished. A prime example would be Lincoln's having to live with the shame that attached to his family and his origins. Herndon put it to Arnold circumspectly: "Did you know that Mr. Lincoln was informed of *some facts* that took place in Kentucky *about the time he was born* (was told so in his youth), that eat into his nature, and as it were crushed him, and yet clung to him, like his shadow, like a fiery shirt around his noble spirit?" These "facts" and Lincoln's brooding awareness of them had consequences. "What made him so tender, so good, so honest, so just, so noble, so pure, so exalted, so liberal, so tolerant, so divine, as it were?" Herndon asked. "It was the fiery furnace through which God rolled him, and yet the world must not know it, eh!" Knowing about this shaping experience and failing to tell it, according to Herndon, would be unthinkable. It would be, he says with characteristic hyperbole, to "shut out all light, freeze up all human sympathy from *this sacred man!*"[17]

This line of reasoning leads Herndon to what might be described as the doctrine of necessary truth. After noting that Lincoln stood for truthfulness and that it ill-behooved his biographers to settle for less, he announced to Arnold: "The man that dares *now* tell the truth, all and every necessary truth in reference to Lincoln, mankind will bless, and curse him that lies. Mark my words, friend. All truths are necessary that show, explain, or throw light on Mr. Lincoln's mind, nature, quality, characteristics, thoughts, acts and deeds, because he [suppressed] the Rebellion . . . and guided the grandest of Revolutions through its grand consumation."[18]

The "grandest of Revolutions" refers, of course, to the abolition of slavery, and Herndon's reference to it seems to imply that so historic and momentous an event justifies extraordinary measures. Herndon's doctrine of necessary truth thus insists that, at least in the case of Abraham Lincoln, even the most private and painful secrets must come out when they are necessary to explain the extraordinary character and accomplishments of the man. If his unique and enabling qualities were molded in a fiery furnace, and the biographer knows what that furnace was, he has an obligation to reveal it, for such a revelation explains and exalts his subject rather than degrades him.

Herndon thought so well of the rationale of necessary truth that he saved a copy of his long letter to Arnold for his files and sent one a few days later to Charles H. Hart. In it he followed up on the question of the biographer's responsibility, telling Hart: "Mr. Arnold is *afraid*[,] that is the word — that I shall drop some *necessary* truth that Lincoln's enemies will use to unholy purposes. I am not responsible for the misapplication — misappropriation, or other wrong use of a *great necessary truth in Mr. Lincoln's life.*" The greater danger is for the friendly biographer not to act: "My Judgment is — poor as it may be, that if these facts are concealed from mankind by his — L's — biographers now, that they will grow and develope into a huge ever discussed lie, bothering and fretting mankind forever. I know human nature; hide a mouse in a crack, and shade it, it will in the minds of men grow and expand into an elephant."[19]

Herndon knew perfectly well that he was proposing something that would be strongly resisted and resented, not only by Lincoln partisans but also by society at large. "I know I shall have to appeal to Time," he wrote to Francis B. Carpenter a few days later. "I cannot argue with a sacred feeling; it is deaf, dumb, blind, and holy. It must argue with itself. Hence, I want time." But he also thought that the times, like time itself, were on his side and that there was in the air a movement away from what he called "blind bat-eyed hero worship" and toward a greater regard for "absolute Truth." "Philosophy is marching that way; history will soon follow — so will biography."[20]

↩

No one saw the implications of Herndon's Ann Rutledge lecture more quickly or more clearly than Robert Todd Lincoln. Within a few days he knew all about it and wrote immediately to his father's executor, Supreme Court Justice David Davis, "Mr. William H. Herndon is making an ass of himself."[21] Robert had been leery of Herndon's lectures from the beginning. He had described them to Davis several months earlier as "rather odd literary efforts" and added, "I hope he will stop it."[22] But Herndon had not, and now Robert recognized with something akin to clairvoyance that the fat was in the fire. His letter to Davis continued, "If you have seen his lecture on 'Abraham Lincoln & Ann Rutledge,' I have no doubt you will feel the impropriety of such a publication even if it were, which I much doubt, all true. His reflections, which make up a large portion, would be very ludicrous if I did not feel strongly that he speaks with a certain amount of authority from having known my father so long."

Not surprisingly, truth was not, for Robert, an acceptable defense for such an "impropriety" as he believed this to be. "Do you think it would be advisable to write to him? He is such a singular character that I am afraid of making matters worse, but I think something ought to be done to stop his present course."[23] It is a measure of the young Robert's alarm and concern that although he disliked contention and confrontation, he traveled to Springfield within a few days of writing those words to speak to Herndon about the matter personally. Herndon's recollection of the meeting makes it sound as though Robert was in a fighting mood, but the cautionary note in his letter to Davis and the diplomatic tone of the letter he wrote to Herndon after their meeting suggest otherwise.[24] Indeed, Robert's letter, written on December 14, is a model of diplomacy and restraint:

> My dear Sir:
>   Your letter of Dec 10 is received and it contains just what I understood to be the result of our conversation at Springfield.
>   As I said then, I have never had any doubt of your good intentions but inasmuch as the construction put upon your language by everyone who has mentioned the subject to me was so entirely different from your own, I felt justified in asking you to change your expression. Beyond this, I do not wish, nor have I any right to go. Your opinion may not agree with mine but that is not my affair. All I ask is, that nothing may be published by you, which after *careful consideration* will seem apt to cause pain to my father's family, which I am sure you do not wish to do.[25]

Robert here shrewdly conciliates Herndon and works the discussion around to what almost everyone of that day would have considered a reasonable criterion of contemporary biography—to write nothing that would "cause pain" to Lincoln's bereaved family.

But Herndon was no ordinary biographer and had already made up his mind that he had to address necessary truths in his book. Whatever he wrote to Robert in reply must have made reference to his proposed treatment of Robert's mother, for Robert responded in considerable alarm:

I *infer* from your letter, but I hope it is not so, that it is your purpose to make some considerable mention of my mother in your work — I say I hope it is not so, because in the first place it would not be pleasant for her or for any woman, to be made public property of in that way — With a man it is very different, for he lives out in the world and is used to being talked of — One of the unpleasant consequences of political success is that however little it may have to do with that success, his whole private life is exposed to the public gaze — that is part of the price he pays. But I see no reason why his wife and children should be included — especially while they are alive — I think no sensible man would live in a glass house and I think he ought not to be compelled to do so against his will. I feel very keenly on this subject, for the annoyance I am subjected to sometimes is nearly intolerable I hope you will consider this matter carefully, My dear Mr Herndon, for once done there is no undoing —[26]

Three days later Robert wrote to Herndon again, and although he acknowledged Herndon's reassurance on the point in question, there is a note of resignation in his reply that suggests that Robert knew very well where all this was leading: "Your letter of yesterday is at hand and I am very glad to find that I misunderstood your language and that you do understand my feelings on that subject. There is no need of saying anything more about it."[27]

❧

But if Robert had resigned himself to the notion that Herndon could not be inhibited or deterred by family sensitivities, biographical proprieties, and the expectations of the public at large, he was mistaken. Although Herndon had experimented with the Ann Rutledge lecture and boldly justified making controversial revelations to Isaac Arnold, his letters to Charles Hart reveal that he was deeply conflicted on the issue. In spite of the doctrine of necessary truth so boldly laid out, he had, in fact, admitted in his letter to Arnold, "All these facts are not to go into my biography now, and yet the world will know all in spite of your wish or my desire, or any man's will."[28] In other words, Herndon seemed to admit that he could not print such sensational truths, however necessary, at the present time, which was less than two years after Lincoln's assassination. His letters to Hart show that he felt the pressure from critics "who do not & cannot Know what I am at." Herndon knew only too well the traditional fate of the messenger bringing unwelcome news. "Would to God the world knew what I do, and save me the necessity of being the man to open and explain all clear as the noonday sun."[29] A short time later he complained to Hart, "Mr. Lincoln is hard to get at

— i.e., it will take so much talk, explanation, etc., to get him properly before the world, that I almost despair."[30]

Herndon's frustration comes into focus when he tries to explain to Hart the secret at which he had only hinted previously and that he believed was partly responsible for Lincoln's melancholy. It had to do, according to Herndon, with Lincoln's knowledge that not only was his mother illegitimate but also that she was a fallen woman. Herndon wrote to Hart, "Lincoln's mother, *fell — fell* in Kentucky about 1805 — *fell* when unmarried — *fell* afterward. Thomas Lincoln left Kentucky on that account; and on no other as I understand the story."[31] What Herndon is describing for Hart is perhaps the most harrowing as well as the most telling aspect of the "fiery furnace" through which Herndon believed Lincoln was rolled. Needless to say, it was also the most sensitive and controversial.

Herndon's belief that this set of embarrassing revelations constituted a necessary truth about Lincoln's makeup and character rested on what seemed to him reasonably solid ground, for Lincoln had told Herndon about his mother's illegitimacy and drawn the conclusion that his distinctive talents came to him in this way. The two partners had been on their way to try a case in Menard County "which required a discussion on hereditary qualities of mind, natures, etc.," Herndon recalled for Ward Hill Lamon. Twenty years later he reconstructed what Lincoln had said to him out of the blue as they rode along: "Billy, I'll tell you something, but keep it a secret while I live. My mother was a bastard, was the daughter of a nobleman so called of Virginia. My mother's mother was poor and credulous, etc., and she was shamefully taken advantage of by the man. My mother inherited his qualities and I hers. All that I am or hope ever to be I get from my mother, God bless her. Did you never notice that bastards are generally smarter, shrewder, and more intellectual than others?"[32] Remembering this colloquy years later, after he had gathered considerable testimony from Kentucky to the effect that Lincoln had been fathered by someone other than Thomas Lincoln, Herndon added that "in these last expressions I have sometimes thought that Lincoln intended to include himself."[33]

But in telling Hart in December 1866 about the allegations of Lincoln's disputed paternity, Herndon admitted to having serious misgivings. "There can be not much doubt of this as I now think, and *yet there is room for mistake.* I am going to Kentucky to search this whole matter to the bottom, and if false I shall scare some wicked men, I assure you. I must get *absolutely* right myself before I dare open."[34] By January of 1867 Herndon had determined that he could not write his biography until he had gone to Kentucky so that he could "look into the eyes of men and women, watch their features, investigate their motives, inquire into their characters, opportunities, veracity, etc., etc., thoroughly, well, to the bottom and below the bottom, if I can go below." He was fearful that the things he had been told by his unfamiliar informants did not quite add up. "There is some mistake as to identity, or something," he told Hart, "and I'll find it out and expose those engaged in it. I am decided on this, cost what it may — even life. I feel there is a wrong somewhere, but can't tell you now."[35]

Not only had Herndon decided that he could not go ahead with his biography until he had resolved what were clearly for him critical questions about Lincoln's family and paternity, but he had also reconsidered the degree of explicitness requisite in rendering necessary truths. He told Hart, "When I spoke of making these revelations to the world I did not intend to tell what I write you, only a part of it in very indirect language, by hints, saying that some of the near and dear relatives of L. so acted as to crush the soul of Abraham. This was all."[36] Herndon had clearly pulled in his horns, either because of the uncertainty he felt about the facts, the pressure he felt from Robert Todd Lincoln and the public, or both. Although he remained committed to getting at the facts and resisting the claims of false testimony, his earlier bold commitment to providing readers with the necessary truth seems to have taken a diminished and more diplomatic form. Rather than spelling out the embarrassing but necessary truth in plain detail, Herndon suggests it would be sufficient to merely hint at the actual causes and conditions.

↬

In spite of his determination to go to Kentucky and then begin writing his biography in the summer of 1867, Herndon managed to do neither, and for what appears to be a combination of reasons his project of writing Lincoln's biography languished. With the death of his father the same year, Herndon inherited a large farm north of Springfield and used the opportunity to escape the practice of law, which he had come to hate, and establish himself as a gentleman farmer. All of this activity and refocusing of attention was more than a distraction from the biography. It was also a welcome opportunity to escape the dilemma in which Herndon found or had placed himself. Briefly stated, it was that although Herndon believed he had discovered some of the important causes and contributing factors to Lincoln's distinctive character, the American public did not want to hear them. It was already enamored of a Lincoln who Herndon knew to be a falsified image of the real man. But in spite of the relevance and the significance of what Herndon had discovered, to say nothing of its truth, even Lincoln's dearest friends and

supporters preferred the sanitized Lincoln and regarded it as their duty
to resist Herndon's unwanted revelations in the interest of preserving
Lincoln's reputation. In these circumstances, Herndon recognized that
his attempts to elevate Lincoln by telling the necessary truths would
only be seen as degrading and that he would be resisted by Lincoln's
friends and reviled by the public for bringing them forth.

There is some evidence that Herndon had already begun to think that
his principal contribution to Lincoln biography might ultimately be not
writing a book but rather assembling and preserving the mass of testimony and information contained in what he called his "Lincoln
Record." In early March 1867 he hinted as much to Hart and expressed
concern for the safety of his archival treasure: "My records of Mr. Lincoln shall go down the files of time," he wrote Hart in March, "if I have
to send them to England, Russia, unless confiscated by false men and
burned before landing, etc."[37] Two years later, in serious financial distress, Herndon sold the copies John G. Springer had made of his "Lincoln Record" to Ward Hill Lamon, who turned them over to a ghostwriter, Chauncey F. Black.

The resulting biography proved something of a trial run for many of
Herndon's necessary truths, for it contained an unvarnished and sometimes undiscriminating version, not entirely sympathetic to Lincoln, of
what Herndon's informants had told him. Because Black did not see his
role as rationalizing the embarrassing aspects of the testimony, as Herndon had proposed to do, he exercised little diplomacy or discretion in
presenting sensitive material, with the result that when it appeared in
1872 even the publisher was offended by the book. It was roundly con-
demned as hostile, sensational, and in bad taste. Predictably, Lincoln's
close friends liked it little more than the general public. O. H. Browning wrote to Isaac Arnold, "It contains many things which I regret to
see in print. Admitting them to be true, their publication was, to say
the least, injudicious. Many things which are stated in the book were
not necessary to the elucidation, or full comprehension, of Mr Lincoln's
character, and should have been omitted."[38]

Herndon, of course, did not agree, and he defended Lamon's book as
reasonably accurate and far in advance of the shamelessly hagiograhic
competition. Friends warned Robert Todd Lincoln not to even look into
Lamon's biography, which he claimed not to have done until many years
later when he wished to cite chapter and verse in a letter telling Lamon off. It would have come as no surprise to Herndon that Robert cited, as a flagrant affront to his father and his family, a passage raising
embarrassing questions about the relationship of Thomas Lincoln and

Nancy Hanks.[39] What might have surprised Herndon was that Robert apparently held him equally responsible with Lamon for the offending passage, which he later referred to as the "Lamon-Herndon slander."[40] Blaming Herndon for Lamon's revelations eventually seems to have had the effect of blurring the question of authorship in Robert's mind, so that in a 1918 letter to his aunt, Emily Helm, he referred to Lamon's biography as Herndon's first book.[41]

Partly in response to his distress at the efforts of Herndon and Lamon, Robert lent support to the major biography of his father undertaken by John G. Nicolay and John Hay by giving them access to the family papers. When the biography began to appear serially in *The Century* magazine in 1886, Herndon proved as perceptive about Robert's role as Robert had been about Herndon's own efforts twenty years earlier. "Nicolay and Hay handle things with silken gloves and a camel-hair pencil," Herndon observed. "They do not write with an iron pen." Moreover, he sensed the reason: "They are writing the Life of Lincoln under the surveillance of Bob Lincoln. Nicolay and Hay, in my opinion, are afraid of Bob. He gives them materials and they play hush."[42]

There is little doubt that Herndon was right about the operative arrangements, for as David C. Mearns concluded, "It is evident that Robert Lincoln either required or was granted the right to edit, amend, or cancel any use of the papers which he disapproved."[43] Although it is undoubtedly true that Robert did seek to limit the exposure of his father's personal life, being particularly sensitive about the early years and anything affecting his mother, it must be said in his defense that his view of what constituted "necessary" biographical truth was not simply special pleading but was unquestionably the generally accepted view of his age. Almost without exception, those who advised Herndon on the subject counseled against the kind of bold truth-telling that he originally favored. Lincoln's friend and fellow circuit attorney Leonard Swett cautioned Herndon, "Now while I would have your history true I would not have it too rigid[.] There's a skeleton in every house. . . . Lincoln's Character will bear a close scrutiny but even with him you must not let your Efforts run in the line of develloping his weaknesses."[44]

Swett had participated in a heavy-handed effort to censor Lamon's book before its publication, and by the phrase "develloping his weaknesses" he undoubtedly had in mind the embarrassing and unflattering things that had appeared there. At the end of his letter, Swett wrote, "I would like to have you write me what the skeleton was with Lincoln. What gave him that peculiar melancholy? What cancer had he inside? You may send it by express and as soon as I read it, *I will express it back to you.* I always thought there was something but never knew what."[45] Swett's assumptions here provide a useful contrast to Herndon's that Lincoln must have had a skeleton in his closet (the secret cause of his melancholy) that Herndon knew about, and also that such necessarily embarrassing information could harmlessly circulate among Lincoln's friends but should otherwise remain a secret. Herndon's doctrine of necessary truth, by contrast, operated on an entirely different principle in which the necessity for disclosure was based not on the sensitive nature of the facts but rather on the bearing the information had on an understanding of Lincoln's distinctive character and accomplishments.

By the time his long-delayed biography was being put together in collaboration with Jesse W. Weik in the 1880s, Herndon had mellowed considerably and, especially in the hope of producing a popular and more saleable book, was willing to moderate his impulses and accommodate the public's sensibilities. When their book was already in proof, he wrote to his collaborator, "No one will get mad because we suppress Nancy Hank's illegitimacy or unchastity, if true, but thousands will go crazy, wrathy, furious, wild, etc., if we insert such suggestion."[46] It is doubtful that he ever changed his mind about the doctrine of necessary truth, but he had resigned himself to the notion that, at least in his own time, some things needed to be touched on very lightly or alluded to indirectly and others must be passed over in silence.

Posterity, it seems fair to say, has been well served by Herndon's precocious and, at the time, disreputable notion of necessary truth. Although it caused his biography to be derailed in the 1860s, it led him to gather and pursue information that other biographers would have thought inappropriate, irrelevant, or not worth the trouble. After he sold copies of his material to Lamon and temporarily retired from the role of biographer, he told Lamon, "When I was getting up the records, people tried to induce me *to state only what Mr. Lincoln was* and not what *he was not.*" Here Herndon is referring to the efforts by Lincoln's friends to enforce a biographical silence on such matters as Lincoln's religion, for they all knew that the martyred president was not a believing or practicing Christian. But, Herndon continued, "I kept on in pursuit of my original idea, determined to give the world light, if I could. I think that to state only what a man *was* only presents half the man."[47] Much of the material he collected did not even find a place in Herndon's own biography, but as he rightly anticipated it has survived in his "Lincoln Record" to serve future generations—generations with different standards about what constitutes relevant or necessary information and interested not just in the public and more presentable Lincoln but in the other half of the man.

NOTES

1. Robert Todd Lincoln to Francis James Child, April 27, 1865, in *The Lincoln Papers*, ed. David C. Mearns (Garden City: Doubleday, 1948), 1:45.

2. Cited in John S. Goff, *Robert Todd Lincoln: A Man in His Own Right* (Norman: University of Oklahoma Press, 1969), 84, 85.

3. William H. Herndon to Josiah G. Holland, May 26, 1865, Holland Papers, New York Public Library.

4. William H. Herndon to Josiah G. Holland, June 8, 1865, Holland Papers, New York Public Library.

5. David Donald, *Lincoln's Herndon: A Biography* (1948, repr. New York: DaCapo Press, 1989), 170.

6. William H. Herndon to Charles H. Hart, April 13, 1866, in *The Hidden Lincoln: From the Letters and Papers of William H. Herndon*, ed. Emanuel Hertz (New York: Viking Press, 1938), 32.

7. William H. Herndon to Charles H. Hart, June 29, 1866, in *The Hidden Lincoln*, ed. Hertz, 32–33.

8. Ibid., 33.

9. This is related in the opening pages of his biography, but the most detailed account of the episode is in William H. Herndon to Ward Hill Lamon, March 6, 1870, in *The Hidden Lincoln*, ed. Hertz, 73–74.

10. For Herndon's reasons for thinking that Caroline Dall, a Boston writer, might preempt him with the Ann Rutledge story, see Donald, *Lincoln's Herndon*, 221–23.

11. William H. Herndon to Charles H. Hart, Nov. 16, 1866, in *The Hidden Lincoln*, ed. Hertz, 36.

12. Francis B. Carpenter to William H. Herndon, Dec. 4, 1866, Herndon-Weik Collection, Manuscript Division, Library of Congress (hereafter cited as H-W), quoted in Donald, *Lincoln's Herndon*, 230.

13. Ibid., 335–36.

14. John Y. Simon, "Abraham Lincoln and Ann Rutledge," *Journal of the Abraham Lincoln Association* 11 (1990): 15.

15. William H. Herndon to Isaac N. Arnold, Nov. 20, 1866, H-W, printed in *The Hidden Lincoln*, ed. Hertz, 36.

16. Ibid., 36–37.

17. Ibid., 38.

18. Ibid., 38–39.

19. William H. Herndon to Charles H. Hart, Nov. 26, 1866, Hart Papers, Huntington Library, printed in *The Hidden Lincoln*, ed. Hertz, 40, 41.

20. William H. Herndon to Francis B. Carpenter, Dec. 11, 1866, in *The Hidden Lincoln*, ed. Hertz, 47.

21. Robert Todd Lincoln to David Davis, Nov. 19, 1866, quoted in Goff, *Robert Todd Lincoln*, 84.

22. Robert Todd Lincoln to David Davis, Jan. 25, 1866, quoted in Willard L. King, *Lincoln's Manager: David Davis* (Cambridge: Harvard University Press, 1960), 238.

23. Robert Todd Lincoln to David Davis, Nov. 19, 1866. Text interpolated from passages from this letter quoted in Goff, *Robert Todd Lincoln*, 84, and in King, *Lincoln's Manager*, 239.

24. Herndon's recollection is in an undated letter to Jesse W. Weik, quoted in *The Lincoln Papers*, ed. Mearns, 1:49–50.

25. Robert Todd Lincoln to William H. Herndon, Dec. 13, 1866, H-W.

26. Robert Todd Lincoln to William H. Herndon, Dec. 24, 1866, H-W.

27. Robert Todd Lincoln to William H. Herndon, Dec. 27, 1866, H-W.

28. William H. Herndon to Isaac N. Arnold, Nov. 20, 1866, in *The Hidden Lincoln*, ed. Hertz, 37–38.

29. William H. Herndon to Charles H. Hart, Dec. 12, 1866, in *The Hidden Lincoln*, ed. Hertz, 49.

30. William H. Herndon to Charles H. Hart, Dec. 28, 1866, in *The Hidden Lincoln*, ed. Hertz, 51.

31. Ibid., 52.

32. William H. Herndon to Ward Hill Lamon, March 6, 1870, in *The Hidden Lincoln*, ed. Hertz, 73–74.

33. Ibid., 74.

34. William H. Herndon to Charles H. Hart, Dec. 28, 1866, in *The Hidden Lincoln*, ed. Hertz, 52.

35. William H. Herndon to Charles H. Hart, Jan. 12, 1867, in *The Hidden Lincoln*, ed. Hertz, 53.

36. Ibid., 53–54.

37. William H. Herndon to Charles H. Hart, March 2, 1867, in *The Hidden Lincoln*, ed. Hertz, 54.

38. O. H. Browning to Isaac N. Arnold, Nov. 25, 1872, Arnold Papers, Chicago Historical Society.

39. Robert Todd Lincoln to Ward Hill Lamon, May 20, 1883, Lamon Papers, Huntington Library.

40. Robert Todd Lincoln to H. C. Whitney, Sept. 18, 1886, Robert Todd Lincoln Papers, Chicago Historical Society.

41. Robert Todd Lincoln to Emily Helm, July 26, 1918, Robert Todd Lincoln Papers, Chicago Historical Society.

42. William H. Herndon quoted in *The Lincoln Papers*, ed. Mearns, 1:76.

43. Ibid., 1:70.

44. Leonard Swett to William H. Herndon, Feb. 14, 1866, H-W.

45. Ibid.

46. William H. Herndon to Jesse W. Weik, Dec. 1, 1888, in *The Hidden Lincoln*, ed. Hertz, 227.

47. William H. Herndon to Ward Hill Lamon, March 6, 1870, in *The Hidden Lincoln*, ed. Hertz, 70–71.

PART THREE

New Perspectives on Lincoln

— 4 —

Abraham Lincoln versus Peter Cartwright

From the time Abraham Lincoln first came to Illinois in 1830, he found himself on the opposite side of the political fence from Peter Cartwright, the well-known Methodist circuit rider who freely mixed politics with moral reform and religion from frontier pulpits. They had crossed paths in the Illinois legislature in the 1830s, but their most memorable conjunction was as opponents in an 1846 congressional election, which Lincoln won handily. Late in the campaign, Lincoln found himself having to combat a rumor that he was an "infidel," or unbeliever, a charge uncomfortably close to the truth and that he was unable to meet openly without some fine hair-splitting. If Peter Cartwright was responsible for these discomforting rumors, he may have thought of it as the evening an old score.

In canvassing Abraham Lincoln's friends and acquaintances for information about his years in New Salem, William H. Herndon turned up a number of unexpected and surprising stories about his great law partner's early life. Some he was able to confirm and develop more fully by securing supporting testimony or documentation, but corroboration for others eluded him. One intriguing story that he was unable to substantiate came to him in two versions. The first was in a letter from Caleb Carman, who had known Lincoln even before he arrived at New Salem: "Lincoln once rote an Artical against Peter Cartwrgh which was a good one[.] the name Sined to it was Diotrefus[.] you may Bet it used the old man very Ruff[.] it was a hard one[.] it was Published in the Beardstown Cronicle by Francis Earns[.] Simeon Francis would not publish in the Sangamon Journal[.]"[1] Shortly thereafter, Herndon received a letter from John McNamar, another former New Salem resident, who wrote:

> Mr Lincoln wrote a first rate Notice of the Revd Peter Cartwright, before he left here . . . the article alluding to Mr Cartwright obtained a good deal of notoriety from the fact that Mr Hill rather inocently I should think, signed the article with his own name and published it and consequently Received the Skinning that old Peter administered in a public speech at Salem shortly after, I think Lincoln must have enjoyed the joke rather Hugely, I think you can find the article in the Journal somewhere from 33 to 36.[2]

Although Herndon apparently never located it, such a newspaper article does exist, and, if authentic, its date qualifies it as the earliest surviving example of political satire from the hand of Abraham Lincoln.

Before turning to the problem of authenticity and the text itself, it may be useful to take a closer look at the information Herndon was offered. Although Carman and McNamar appear to be referring to the same incident, there are notable differences in their stories—about the newspaper involved and about the name signed to the article—and the possibility exists that these informants were referring to two different incidents. But what is most striking about these two recollections is their close agreement on the central facts of an incident previously unremarked in Lincoln biography: that when living in New Salem, Lincoln delighted his neighbors by writing, under another name, a satiric newspaper piece at the expense of the famous Methodist preacher Peter Cartwright.

The *Sangamo Journal*, founded and edited by Simeon Francis, is well known as the leading Whig newspaper of Lincoln's political arena and is commonly believed to have printed many anonymous and pseudonymous articles by Lincoln. It is clear from Herndon's notes for his biography that he ransacked the pages of the *Journal* for material relating to Lincoln and presumably would have found the piece on Peter Cartwright had it been there.[3] Research notes in the papers of Herndon's collaborator Jesse W. Weik suggest that he also tried his hand at following up the same leads.[4] But in all likelihood neither Herndon nor Weik had access to backfiles of the obscure early Beardstown paper published from 1833 to 1835 by Francis Arenz, the *Beardstown Chronicle and Illinois Military Bounty Land Advertiser*. It was there, in the issue of November 1, 1834, that the attack on Peter Cartwright signed by Samuel Hill appeared.[5]

Testimony about the distant past is often dubious with respect to details, even if the substance or central facts are faithfully recalled, and precise accuracy may often be a matter of circumstance. Thus Caleb Carman, because he remembered why the article did not appear in the *Journal,* was right about the newspaper although wrong about the signature.[6] And McNamar, who was out of the state at the time the incident occurred and was reporting what he had heard (and perhaps seen) after the fact, was wrong about the newspaper, because he assumed it must have been Simeon Francis's *Sangamo Journal.* But he remembered correctly that Samuel Hill's name was signed to the article because it earned his former business partner a public "skinning" at the hands of Peter Cartwright. A more perfect example of complementary, cross-correcting testimony is hard to imagine.

The Cast of Characters

In the fall of 1834, when the incident took place, Abraham Lincoln had been living in and around New Salem for three years, having arrived in the late summer of 1831. After working as a store clerk for Denton Offutt until the following spring, he served in the Black Hawk War for about three months and, upon his return to New Salem in late July, ran unsuccessfully for the legislature. Thereafter he became a partner in an unsuccessful store with William Berry, worked at odd jobs, took over the postmastership of New Salem from Hill, and taught himself enough from books to perform the duties of deputy county surveyor. At the time the attack on Peter Cartwright was written in September 1834, Lincoln was probably working in Samuel Hill's store and had been elected only a few weeks earlier to his first term in the lower house of the Illinois General Assembly.[7]

Peter Cartwright had been a successful candidate against Lincoln in 1832 and, although not a candidate for reelection in 1834, was considered a formidable political protagonist of the Jacksonian persuasion. But his chief claim to fame was his standing as the foremost Methodist circuit rider in pioneer Illinois. In a fearless frontier ministry, preaching the gospel to a farflung constituency unreached and unreachable by conventional, college-trained ministers, Cartwright was a legend in his time. A powerful man who could not be intimidated by frontier roughs and who could intimidate those who opposed him, Cartwright had engaged his conspicuous talents as a speaker and activist as freely in politics as in religion. His biographer Robert Bray observes, "Throughout his career Cartwright either could not or would not clearly distinguish church from state, religion from civic life, preaching from politicking—especially when he was concurrently doing both himself."[8] It was this trait that seems to have made him particularly resented by anti-Jacksonian political opponents such as Abraham Lincoln.

Lincoln and Cartwright were political antagonists from the first time they met, which was apparently in the summer of 1830, a year before Lincoln came to New Salem. William Butler described how Lincoln, although working as a farmhand and "very shabbily dressed," stood up to Cartwright when he came through Island Grove electioneering. "A discussion soon arose between him and Cartwright, and my first special attention was attracted to Lincoln by the way in which he met the great preacher in his arguments, and the extensive acquaintance he showed with the politics of the State—in fact he quite beat him in the argument."[9]

While living in and around New Salem working as a store clerk and surveyor, Lincoln would have had frequent personal contact with Cartwright from the time he arrived, for "Uncle Peter" lived only six miles away and came to town frequently to trade, preach, or talk politics. T. G. Onstot, who had lived as a boy in New Salem, later wrote, "He was a man of great force of character and whether as preacher or politician, generally carried his point; ... He had great conversational powers, coupled with keen wit. He could interest a crowd as well as any man I ever saw."[10] Not only was Cartwright an effective political speaker, but he also apparently boasted that he could command the support of a loyal Methodist "militia" in political contests, something that clearly infuriated his opponents.[11]

Samuel Hill was New Salem's earliest and most successful merchant. He is described by a local historian as "a small, slender man of irascible temperament. He couldn't drive a horse without fighting him, and so his wife drove whenever they went riding together."[12] Onstot said Hill "was not a man of much physical strength himself, but was in the habit of taking some delight in whipping any person that might be offensive to him."[13] In cases where he could not whip his antagonist, he was said to have hired others to do it for him. Although he lost his postmastership to Lincoln in 1833, they were still friends and, in these years at least, political allies. Hill told his son John that he and others had promoted Lincoln's early candidacy for the legislature along bipartisan lines in order to get the region surrounding New Salem set off from Sangamon County.[14] John Hill also reported what Herndon heard elsewhere, that Lincoln had written a controversial treatise on religion while working in Hill's store and that his employer had thrown it in the fire, presumably to forestall the personal and political damage that would have ensued upon publication.[15]

Hill's store was described as "headquarters for all political discussions.

The farmers would congregate there and discuss the questions of the day. Peter Cartright, who was a politician then as well as a preacher, would spend hours on the porch, and by his wit and sallies keep the audience in an uproar of laughter, and the man who undertook to badger Uncle Peter always came out second best."[16] None of this pleased the irritable storekeeper. "It was when Cartright was at his best," according to Onstot, "that Hill conceived a dislike for him, but no bully ever took the job of whipping him from Hill."[17] Eventually, an outright feud irrupted between the two men, and Cartwright began to abuse Hill publicly in front of his own store. "He would come and sit for hours and laugh and talk about Hill, while Hill stayed indoors. He was describing one day to a crowd how he viewed Hill's soul. He said he had some doubts whether he had a soul till one day he put a quarter of a dollar on Hill's lips, when his soul came guggling up to get the piece of silver."[18]

Francis Arenz, the editor and proprietor of the *Beardstown Chronicle*, emigrated from Germany as a young man and located on the Illinois frontier to make his fortune. First a pioneer merchant in the boom town of Galena, he became one of the founders of Beardstown on the Illinois River in the early 1830s, speculating in land and town lots, operating a general store, and establishing a newspaper.[19] A tireless promoter of schemes to benefit his community, Arenz regularly frequented the sessions of the state legislature as a lobbyist and was active as a Whig politician. To foster navigation of the Sangamon River, Arenz promoted a private company to build a canal between Beardstown, at the mouth of the river, and Miller's Ferry, a location some twelve miles north of New Salem.[20] Abraham Lincoln had endorsed just such a scheme in first announcing his candidacy in 1832, and in his first term in the legislature he helped gain a charter for Arenz's canal company (Herndon identified the project as "Abes pet") and soon thereafter platted a town at the site of Miller's Ferry for a group of investors and entered forty acres of nearby land in his own name.[21] In later years, John T. Stuart, a Whig and former member of Congress, and Abraham Lincoln would recommend Arenz in glowing terms for a federal appointment.[22]

The Common Schools and the "Moral Waste"

A minor character in this incident, but nonetheless the catalytic agent, was Ashford Smith, printer for the *Pioneer and Western Baptist*, a sectarian paper edited and published at Rock Spring by the prominent Baptist churchman, educator, and politician John Mason Peck.[23] Smith was apparently alarmed by what Cartwright had written in the May 30,

1834, issue of the Methodist periodical *Christian Advocate and Journal* about the recruitment of eastern teachers for the common schools of Illinois. Appearing in a letter reporting on his missionary activities on the circuit, Cartwright's call for Methodist teachers and a denominational effort to promote common schools sounded to Baptist ears like a bold Methodist attempt to control or dominate public education. To call attention to this perceived threat, Smith printed Cartwright's letter in a handbill that seems to have been distributed generally in the Sangamon County region. The beginning of Cartwright's letter—as reprinted in Smith's handbill—figured prominently in the attack printed in the *Beardstown Chronicle*: "This second report of the present conference year of the Fort Edwards, Henderson river, and Rock Island missions, under my superintendence, is made with gratitude to God for the success that crowns our little efforts in these regions of moral desolation." And here is what Cartwright's letter had to say on the subject of teachers for the common schools:

> And now let me ask through the medium of the Christian Advocate and Journal, could we not, who live in the "far off West," obtain some pious young men and young women from the older States and Conferences, under the influence of our own church, with good literary qualifications, to teach common schools in this State, [Illinois.][24] There is a vast opening here for school teachers. We greatly need them. I am confident that I could give employment to more than 100 immediately, in my district, and perhaps 500 in the State. It would afford the presiding elders and circuit preachers great pleasure, every where, to lend their aid in getting up schools for such teachers, if they could be prevailed upon to come.
>
> We expect our conference to form itself into a common school education society. All we lack is the right sort of teachers. These teachers would greatly aid our missionary efforts, train the rising generation, and do a good part for themselves in a pecuniary point of view.[25]

Cartwright's appeal for teachers "under the influence of our own church" to come out from the East prompted Ashford Smith to inquire in the section of the handbill labeled "Remarks" whether the aim was not to "advance the missionary efforts, and the support of a speculative clergy? Is this not enough to make the parson hang his sham'd face, decline as a candidate for office, and hunt a place to hide himself from the free people of Sangamon County?"

In fact, the subject of common schools and the need to have an organized system of public education was just coming to the fore in Illinois, and a call had been recently issued for a state convention on the topic. Abraham Lincoln would be named a delegate from Sangamon

County to this convention, and the topic would receive considerable attention in the upcoming session of the legislature.[26] Before the summer was out, Cartwright was made aware that he had inadvertently stirred up a vocal public reaction when Smith's handbills publicized his call for common school teachers. At least partly in response to this public reaction, Cartwright sent a letter to the *Sangamo Journal*, which printed it on August 30, 1834, under the heading "The Valley of the Mississippi, or the Moral Waste. NO. 1." It follows in full:

Fellow Citizens:

Permit me, through the medium of one of your public Journals, to state a few things on a subject of vital importance to the whole community. For a number of years past, the character of the citizens of the *Valley* of *Mississippi*, has been assailed and slandered, to an extent never surpassed, in any civilized country. We have been represented as totally destitute of all kinds of Literature, without religion, immoral, intemperate, rude, uncultivated in our manners, denying the obligation of the Sabbath for civil or religious purposes, destitute of any Evangelical Preachers; and, notwithstanding there have been, and still are, hundreds of ministers of the Gospel, of the different religious denominations, who preach with great acceptibility to listening thousands of deeply attentive hearers, yet we have been, and still are, represented, as in a perishing condition for want of *competent Evangelical ministers* of the *Gospel*. It is true, a great many of those ministers of the gospel who preach, and command, respect as preachers, by all classes of our community, did not graduate in a college in some of the older states, and it is also true, that many of them never went through a regular theological course of reading and study, as is taught in those Literary institutions that have theological departments appended to them: but at the same time, they are better pulpit orators, and their minds are richly stored with a knowledge of the Holy Scriptures, and their sermons are attended with the power and omnipotence of truth to the salvation of thousands.—And, notwithstanding this *Valley of the Mississippi* has furnished some of the ablest statesmen and orators that ever graced the Legislative Halls of Congress, good jurists, sound, practical and successful Physicians, and able, intelligent, learned, Gentlemen of the Bar, and many Gentlemen that have stood pre-eminent in the Literary world, yet when we read the foul, false, and slanderous productions of a certain set of hired and mercenary men, whose letters have been published in many of the religious periodicals, on this continent, you would suppose the citizens of the Valley, and especially of the state of Illinois, were a perfect band of ignorant, lawless, *Goths or Vandals*, or something worse.

Who are these mighty men that write about the poor heathens in this Valley? are they not generally found in the ranks of the political and religious aristocrats of the day? Have not the theological seminaries produced more men designed for the ministry, than can be employed by the churches in the older states? and is it not a fact that *American and national societies* have been gotten up in those states in order to place those young men at the head of them, in order to secure to them a good sound four or five hundred dollars salary? and is it not evident to all informed observers, that the devil might get all the *poor, ignorant,* Heathens, in this Valley if *they* did not get the money?

And these very men, after coming among us, and begging thousands of dollars for those *national societies,* then turn right round and abuse, and misrepresent the talents, worth and intelligence of the *"Far off West:"* and is this course not intended to move on the sympathies of their brethren in the older states, in order to get more money from them into their own pockets, as agents? Now, I put this question to the sober judgment of every christian and enlightened gentleman, whether this conduct is fair, truthful or honest? and whether these men ought not to be rebuked by an insulted and abused community? Now, after these very men have come on, and settled down in some flourishing town, or growing settlement, with their salaries made sure to them with all their travelling expenses, is it then right to circulate a subscription for their benefit? and after they have appealed to the best feelings of an uninformed and abused community and obtained their money for their national societies and agents, is it then right to slander and misrepresent them?

Does it not come with an ill grace from these very sectarian *national agents,* to cry "sectarianism," "sectarianism," "persecution," "persecution," when any other church opposes their monopolizing plan, and thinks the preferable way is, to carry on these benevolent societies by the churches in their individual or denominational capacity?

Mr. Smith, the Editor of the Pioneer, or some other scribbler in that paper, has thought proper to sound an alarm, by quoting and commenting on a part of a letter written by me to the Editor of the Christian Advocate and Journal, which letter invited teachers from the older states and conferences, to teach in common schools in this state. If the Editor of the Advocate had published all my letter, then no man but an advocate for *national* societies could reasonably have objected: nor do I see any reasonable ground for objection any how.[27] I did not ask for methodist teachers, and when I asked for those under the influence of our own church, I only meant those that were opposed to *American or national societies,* and in favor of each church carrying on these benevolent activities in its own proper name, without any amalgamation or combination. Now, where was the harm in this? This I believe to be right. I do not think proper to notice the author any further at this time, but I may in some future number, say a little more to this Gentleman.

And if any Editor or individual thinks proper to reply to these hasty remarks, I wish to come out in a tangible form, and with a proper name, and in some future number I may give some further remarks on the subject.

PETER CARTWRIGHT
Pleasant Plains, Aug. the 24th, 1834

The Reply

To most readers of the time, this probably appeared a reasonable defense, and Cartwright seemed confident that he could handle any writer bold enough "to come out in a tangible form, and with a proper name." But to someone with a keen eye for logical inconsistencies, a talent for satire, and a political animus toward Peter Cartwright, the conjunction of the *Advocate* letter and the "Moral Waste" letter represented an irresistible opportunity to hoist Uncle Peter by his own petard. Here is the reply that appeared in Francis Arenz's *Beardstown Chronicle* on November 1, 1834:

For the Beardstown Chronicle.
New Salem, Sept. 7th, 1834
Mr. Editor:
In the Journal of August 30th, I see an article headed the "Valley of the Mississippi, or the Moral Waste, No. 1," and signed "Peter Cartwright," to which the writer seems to invite a reply from any editor or individual.

Now, if I could possibly conceive that this article was written with a view to aid the true religion in any shape, I should not meddle with it; or, if I could conceive that it was intended to vindicate the character of the "West," I should be the last to censure it. But being thoroughly satisfied that it is wholly a political manœuvre, and being equally well satisfied that the author is a most abondoned hypocrite (I will not say in religion — for of this I pretend to know nothing — but) in politics, I venture to handle it without restraint.

The first sentence in the article that I shall notice is in the following words: "For a number of years past, the character of the citizens of the Valley of the Mississippi, has been assailed and slandered to an extent never surpassed in any civilized country.["] Now, as to the truth of this charge of slander, I know but little. This much, however, I do know—that whenever an eastern man becomes a candidate for office in this country, this general charge of slander is resorted to, with a view to prejudice men against him. But I must confess that I have never known but one man fairly proved guilty of the charge; and that man was a western man—and no other than Peter Cartwright. He was proved guilty in the following manner:—

Some time last summer, the letter to which he alludes in his "Moral Waste," was discovered in the Christian Advocate Journal, bearing his signature. In this letter, speaking of this country, he says:—"This land of moral desolation." This letter was published in handbill form, and circulated in great numbers throughout Sangamon county, was posted up on the doors of stores and groceries, and even read in public companies of which he formed a part, and, so far as I can learn, the authorship was never disavowed by him. I have not the letter before me, and therefore cannot make many or long quotations from it; but the short one I have made I know is correct, and I well recollect that the whole tenor of the letter was in perfect unison with it.

The next sentence that I shall notice is in these words: "Who are these mighty men that write about the poor heathens in this Valley?" To this I answer that I cannot say who they all are; but the world has positive evidence that Peter Cartwright is one of them.

Again he says, "Are they not generally found in the ranks of the political and religious aristocrats of the day."

To this I cannot give a direct answer. However, if uncle Peter be a fair sample of the clan, I should say they are.

Again he says, "Is is it not evident to all informed observers that the devil might get all the poor ignorant heathens in this Valley if they did not get the money." To this I incline to answer yes. I beleive the people in this country are in some degree priest ridden. I also believe, and if I am not badly mistaken "all informed observers" will concur in the belief that Peter Cartwright bestrides, more than any four men in the northwestern part of the State. He

He has one of the largest and best improved farms in Sangamon county, with other property in proportion. And how has he got it? Only by the contributions he has been able to levy upon and collect from a priest ridden church. It will not do to say he has earned it "by the sweat of his brow;" for although he may sometimes labor, all know that he spends the greater part of his time in preaching and electioneering.

And then to hear him in electioneering times publicly boasting of mustering his militia, (alluding to the Methodist Church) and marching and counter-marching them in favor of, or against this or that candidate—why, this is not only hard riding, but it is riding clear off the track, stumps, logs and blackjack brush, notwithstanding. For a church or community to be priest ridden by a man who will take their money and treat them kindly in return is bad enough in all conscience; but to be ridden by one who is continually exposing them to ridicule by making a public boast of his power to hoodwink them, is insufferable.

Again, he says, "Now I put this question to the sober judgment of every Christian and enlightened gentleman, whether this conduct is fair, truthful, or honest? and whether these men ought not to be rebuked by an insulted and abused community?" In answer to this, I should say, that as a general punishment, I think those men ought to be rebuked as uncle Peter recommends: but in his particular case, I would recommend some more sanguinary punishment; for such punishments as rebuke will be forever lost upon one of such superlative hardihood and as he possesses—he has been more than rebuked these twenty years.

Again he says, "Now after these men have come on, settled down in some, flourishing town or growing settlement with their salaries made sure to them, with all their travelling expenses, is it then right to circulate a subscription for their benefit? and after they have appealed to the best feelings of an *uninformed* and abused community, and obtained their money for their national societies and agents, is it then right to slander and misrepresent them?" What, in the name of common sense, is it of which uncle Peter is complaining? He has been quarrelling with—nobody knows whom—half down the column of a newspaper, because, as he says, somebody has misrepresented this community by calling it ignorant, &c; when suddenly forgetting himself, he calls this same community an *"uninformed* and abused community." — That he should be heard saying things that he does not believe himself, I do not wonder at; but that after his long dealing in duplicity, he should be found unable to travel half way down the column of a newspaper without crossing his own trail is passing strange. Speaking of his Advocate letter in his "Moral Waste," Cartwright says, "I did not ask for Methodist teachers, and when I asked for those under the influence of our own church, I only meant those that were opposed to American or National societies, &c."

If any of Cartwright's real friends have a blush left, now is the time to use it. He did not ask for Methodist teachers! Will any man risk his reputation for common sense by pretending to believe this? Mark the circumstances. He was writing to the editor of the only Methodist periodical published in the nation—a paper seldomly opened by any but Methodists—so much so that although the letter had been published some considerable time, and the paper had many subscribers in Sangamon county, so far as I can learn, no eye, save that of a Methodist ever beheld it till the editor of the Pioneer, through the medium of his exchange list, I suppose, discovered it and republished a part of it.

Does this look like a general invitation to all who were opposed to American or National Societies? — To me it appears a general invitation to particular individuals—something of a public call made in a private way.

But this is not all—"These teachers were asked of the older States conferences"—mark the word *conferences.* Now I may be mistaken, but if I am not, no church except the methodist has the word conference in its whole technical vocabulary. I will here venture a legal opinion: If asking for methodist teachers were a crime of the magnitude of homicide, none of Cartwright's gentlemen of the bar, could be found able, intelligent and learned enough to save *his* neck from the halter—(no insinuations that the said neck ever deserved such a fate.) as I have before said, I have not the Advocate letter before me, neither can I recollect what Cartwright said in it about American and National societies, or whether he said any thing. I am, however confident he said nothing against them; and I well recollect, he, in terms congratulated the editor upon a late accession of members to the Temperance Society.

A few more words and I shall have done. The sum totum of this matter is this: None has a greater thirst for political distinction than Peter Cartwright. When he wrote his Advocate letter he had no intention that any western man, save probably a few of his militia should see it: but, unfortunately, it was discovered. This was a trying time with Peter. He saw, as any man might have seen, that the effect of this letter was fastening itself upon his political prospects with the benumbing embrace of an incubus, and weighing them down with the weight of a mountain. Then came his "Moral Waste," which is nothing more nor less than an effort to shake off the effect of the Advocate letter. But it is a failure. He will have to shake again.

Poor ghost of ambition! He must have two sets of opinions, one for his religious, and one for his political friends; and to plat them together smoothly, presents a task to which his feverish brain is incompetent. — Let the Advocate letter and the "Moral Waste, No. 1" be presented to an intelligent stranger, and be told that they are the productions of the same man, and he will be much puzzled to decide whether the auther is greater fool or knave; although he may readily see that he has but few rivals in either capacity.

SAMUEL HILL.

Lincoln or Hill?

Even in the rough-and-tumble world of frontier politics, this letter constitutes a scathing personal attack on Peter Cartwright. In the words of Caleb Carman, "It used the old man very Ruff," and the prime question that confronts us is whether or not it should be considered the work of Abraham Lincoln or Samuel Hill. In signing his own name to the letter, Samuel Hill not only paid the price of being the recipient of Cartwright's wrath and public "skinning" but also apparently had to pay to have the letter published in the first place. On the back page (4) of the issue carrying the letter appeared a notice: "On the first side of todays paper will be found a cammunication, signed *Samuel Hill*, addressed to the Rev. P. Cartwright. It is inserted by request and paid for as an advertisement. We place such like articles under contribution, in order to prevent a too frequent recurrence." By acknowledging that the letter signed by Hill had been paid for as though it were an advertisement, the editor made clear that publishing this kind of personal attack was exceptional and not to be encouraged.

Although paying to have the letter published could suggest Hill's authorship, it also lends color, if not weight, to Caleb Carman's contention in his letter to Herndon that the piece, written by Lincoln, was rejected by Simeon Francis, the editor of the *Sangamo Journal*, where Cartwright's "Moral Waste" had appeared. Certainly the lateness of the letter's appearance, nearly two months after its composition, supports Carman's story that it had been submitted, turned down, and resubmitted elsewhere.

But Hill's undoubted determination to have the letter published is a consideration that, in the question of authorship, could cut both ways. Although indicating that he went to trouble and expense to have the attack reach the press, Hill's signing his own name might also reflect the fact that such a printed riposte was the only form of personal reprisal available to him. No other example of Hill's literary abilities, if any, is known, but he did have a reputation for having others do battle with opponents who were too much for him.[28] And none of the local historians of New Salem who recorded Hill's feud with Cartwright spoke of his capacity for getting back at the famous preacher in print. Hill could be sure that he would get a "skinning" from Cartwright when the letter appeared, but as one who had to suffer Cartwright's abuse anyhow, he had very little to lose. In the absence of evidence that Hill was either capable of the satire in the *Chronicle* letter or given credit for it by others, the case for his authorship comes down to his signature on the letter.

The arguments for Lincoln's authorship, on the other hand, are manifold. In the first instance, there is the positive testimony of two witnesses—Caleb Carman and John McNamar—that Lincoln did write such a letter. Both appear as responsible witnesses in the other testimony they gave Herndon, both had known Lincoln and his New Salem environment well, and neither had any known reason to deceive. From the proximity of the dates on which they wrote to Herndon, one might suspect that Carman and McNamar had been conferring or comparing old New Salem stories thirty years after the fact, and this might in turn raise a suspicion that instead of confirming stories, what we have here is one repeating a story he heard from the other. But even if they had been conferring, the fact that each volunteered his story to Herndon in the distinctive form in which he remembered it argues against the likelihood of one simply borrowing from the other.

Why, if Lincoln wrote the letter, would he not have signed his own name? Even if Hill published the letter to get back at Cartwright it seems wholly unlikely that Lincoln would have signed his own name in any event. It would have been unprecedented for Lincoln to have put his name on a piece written for political effect; although he is reputed to have written prodigiously for Francis's *Sangamo Journal*, nothing of this kind has been found over his own name.[29] Nor is this at all surprising. Anonymous and pseudonymous pieces were the norm for political disputation, and exceptions were relatively rare. By the same token, signing one's own name, particularly in the case of an abusive piece like the one in question, invited the imputation of a personal, rather than a political, motive. Because Peter Cartwright was a minister of the Gospel, Hill could be fairly certain that he would be repaid with no more than verbal abuse, but many of Hill and Lincoln's contemporaries in public life would have felt called upon by such a letter to issue a challenge. For ridicule a good deal less venomous, James Shields did just that eight years later, because he believed Abraham Lincoln to be the author of the pseudonymous "Lost Township" letters.[30]

If Hill is not known to have been a satirist, the opposite is true of Lincoln. He was writing satirical pieces at the expense of his Indiana neighbors as a teenager, and such was his success that Herndon found people who recalled and could recite fragments from some of them thirty-five years later.[31] Lincoln was proud enough of his Indiana satire during his New Salem years to share some of it with his friend, William G. Greene.[32] His closest Springfield friend, Joshua F. Speed, carried an indelible memory of Lincoln's withering reply to an attack by one of the Democrats' leading orators, George Forquer, in the election of 1836. His reported speeches in the legislature show an unmistakable talent for one-upmanship, and on the stump his powers of ridicule could be devastating, as Jesse B. Thomas, Jr., famously discovered in the campaign of 1840.[33] Robert Bray has shown that Lincoln's literary gifts endowed him with "the power to hurt," a power that he invoked frequently in the early years of his political career.[34]

The text of the letter itself presents further evidence at least consistent with Lincoln's authorship. Its personal vindictiveness, which Lincoln's partisan neighbors found so effective, is likely to prove somewhat distasteful to modern readers and is certainly out of character with the generous and forbearing man who led the nation as president through the Civil War. But the letter comes from a much earlier time and exhibits an earlier and much rougher version of the man. Although the work is hardly a masterpiece, as bare-knuckled frontier satire it deserves to be judged reasonably successful of its kind. It clearly lacks the suppleness and natural quality of Lincoln's best performances in this vein, such as his masterful send-up of Lewis Cass on the floor of the U.S. House of Representatives in 1848, but it nonetheless displays wit and lands some very solid blows.[35]

When, for example, he writes, "Why, this is not only hard riding, but it is riding clear off the track, stumps, logs and blackjack brush, notwithstanding," he scores doubly—by effectively employing the sure-fire device of exaggeration and by exuberantly following his metaphor into what was, for his frontier audience, familiar territory. Or when he offers his legal opinion—"If asking for methodist teachers were a crime of the magnitude of homicide, none of Cartwright's gentlemen of the bar, could be found able, intelligent and learned enough to save *his* neck from the halter"—he deftly sketches in a few words a comic scene that his audience can readily visualize: a hapless Uncle Peter arraigned before the bar of justice.

The most conspicuously Lincolnian aspect of the letter is surely its logical method. Perhaps the quality most remarked in his mental make-up by those who knew him, apart from his melancholy, was the logical cast of Lincoln's mind. Clearly, the underlying strategy of the letter is to show that Cartwright is guilty of precisely the thing he finds so offensive in others.[36] Making a great show of castigating those who slander the western country as inhabited by "a perfect band of ignorant, lawless, *Goths or Vandals*" in one letter, Cartwright is caught referring to "these regions of moral desolation" in another. The great appeal of this tactic lies in making one's opponent serve as his own accuser and presenting the argument in such a way that the opponent's own words pronounce judgment upon himself. Lincoln practiced the technique to perfection, most famously in the debates with Douglas in 1858, but it had long been a deadly part of his arsenal. The Cartwright piece is readily conceivable as an early example of his art.[37]

The single passage in the letter most indicative of Lincoln's authorship is perhaps this: "Poor ghost of ambition! He must have two sets of opinions, one for his religious, and one for his political friends; and to plat them together smoothly, presents a task to which his feverish brain is incompetent." The ingenious imagery of platting is as effective as it is unusual, but its occurrence here is perhaps not so surprising if composed by an author who had been spending much of his time learning how to survey land and reconcile the stubbornly disparate plats of neighboring landholders.

The Upshot

The attack on Peter Cartwright in the *Beardstown Chronicle* in November 1834, although signed and paid for by Samuel Hill, is far more likely to have come from the pen of the young Abraham Lincoln. Hill had motive and opportunity, but there is no indication that he had the requisite literary facility. Lincoln had all three, plus experience, and there seems little reason to doubt that he was acknowledged as the author by certain of his New Salem friends.

The possibility that Hill hired Lincoln to write the letter would accord with what we know about Hill but would run counter to everything we know about Lincoln. If one were to speculate on the basis of what is known, a plausible scenario might be that Lincoln, seeing that Cartwright had tripped himself up in the "Moral Waste No. 1," wrote the letter with the intention of publishing it in the *Sangamo Journal* under a pseudonym but was turned down by Simeon Francis on the grounds that the letter was too directly personal. Unwilling to publish it as his own, Lincoln may then have permitted or arranged for Samuel Hill, whose store was said in these days to have been his "headquarters" and who was anxious for a means to repay Cartwright's insults, to have it published over his own name in the paper of a man who would prove Lincoln's friend and political ally, Francis Arenz.[38] Arenz, for his part, agreed to publish if a real name were to be affixed to the letter and it could be treated as a paid advertisement.

The letter is interesting as an example of frontier political satire and invective and doubly interesting as an early example of the satiric and rhetorical skills of Abraham Lincoln. Although lacking in smoothness and polish, and perhaps written as much to punish as to amuse and instruct, the letter has sufficient energy and Lincolnian verve to count as revealing apprentice work from the hand of a man who would eventually become a literary master.

NOTES

1. Caleb Carman to William H. Herndon, Nov. 30, 1866, Herndon-Weik Collection, Manuscript Division, Library of Congress (hereafter cited as H-W).

2. John McNamar to William H. Herndon, Dec. 1, 1866, H-W.

3. See the many citations and extracts from the *Sangamo Journal* in the material Herndon sold to Ward Hill Lamon, especially LN2408, vols. 2 and 3, Huntington Library.

4. See Weik's notes in the Jesse W. Weik Papers, Illinois State Historical Library.

5. *Beardstown Chronicle and Illinois Military Bounty Land Advertiser,* edited by Francis Arenz, Nov. 1, 1834, 1. Only eleven issues of the paper are known

to have survived. I have used the microfilm of these surviving issues produced by the Illinois State Historical Library.

6. This assumes, of course, that no article attacking Peter Cartwright and signed "Diotrefus" exists.

7. On Abraham Lincoln working for Hill, see Harvey Lee Ross, *The Early Pioneers and Pioneer Events of the State of Illinois* (1899, repr. Havana, Ill.: The Church of Jesus Christ of Latter-Day Saints, 1986), 96–97; Thomas P. Reep, *Lincoln at New Salem* (Petersburg: Old Salem League, 1927), 61; and John Hill to Ida M. Tarbell, Feb. 6, 1896, Ida M. Tarbell Papers, Allegheny College Library.

8. Robert Bray, "The Cartwright-Lincoln Acquaintance," *The Old Northwest* 13 (Summer 1987): 113. Bray is at work on a full-length biography of Cartwright.

9. John G. Nicolay interview, June 13, 1875, John Hay Papers, Brown University Library. I am grateful to Michael Burlingame for generously sharing these interviews.

10. T. G. Onstot, *Pioneers of Menard and Mason Counties* (1902, repr. Havana, Ill.: The Church of Jesus Christ of Latter-Day Saints, 1986), 103. In this same passage, Onstot says he was "well acquainted with Peter Cartright, and this acquaintance dates as far back as I can recollect."

11. Cartwright's "militia" is described as "a group of some 400 men he could count on for support in any political contest." Bray, "The Cartwright-Lincoln Acquaintance," 116.

12. Reep, *Lincoln at New Salem*, 104.

13. Onstot, *Pioneers of Menard and Mason Counties*, 114.

14. John Hill to Ida M. Tarbell, Feb. 6, 1896, Ida M. Tarbell Papers, Allegheny College Library. Menard County, with Petersburg as its seat, was set off from Sangamon County in 1839.

15. Ibid. For Herndon's informants on the burned manuscript, see Hardin Bale, May 29, 1865 (William H. Herndon interview) and John Hill to William H. Herndon, June 27, 1865, H-W.

16. Onstot, *Pioneers of Menard and Mason Counties*, 152.

17. Ibid., 114.

18. Ibid.

19. Information on the life and career of Arenz is taken from J. Henry Shaw, *Historical Sketch of Cass County, Illinois* (Beardstown: Cass County Messenger, 1876), supplemented by *History of Cass County, Illinois*, ed. William Henry Perrin (Chicago: O. L. Baskin, 1882) and *History of Cass County*, ed. Charles Æ. Martin (Chicago: Munsell Publishing, 1915).

20. Perrin, *History of Cass County, Illinois*, 150–51.

21. "Communication to the People of Sangamon County," in *The Collected Works of Abraham Lincoln*, ed. Roy P. Basler, asst. eds. Marion D. Pratt and Lloyd A. Dunlap (New Brunswick: Rutgers University Press, 1953–55), 1:6–7 (hereafter cited as *Collected Works*). See Herndon's listing of notable legislative actions during Lincoln's tenure in the legislature, which includes "Sangamon River Bill—'The Beardstown and Sangamon Canal Co.' (Abes Pet)," Lamon Papers, LN2408, 2:373, Huntington Library. For Lincoln's plat of the town of Huron near Miller's Ferry, see *Collected Works*, 1:48ff.

22. *Collected Works*, 2:103. The editor's note says that Arenz was duly "appointed as 'bearer of dispatches to Prussia and Austria.'"

23. I am grateful to Terence A. Tanner for information about Arenz and the *Beardstown Chronicle*, as well as about Smith, Peck, and the *Pioneer*, and for giving me the benefit of his extensive knowledge of early Illinois newspapers.

24. Brackets appear in the original text.

25. *Rev. Peter Cartwright's Letter* [Rock Spring, 1834]. See Cecil K. Byrd, *A Bibliography of Illinois Imprints, 1814–58* (Chicago: University of Chicago Press, 1966), no. 245. The only known copy of the handbill is in the Illinois State Historical Library. Byrd tentatively locates the printer in Springfield and dates the handbill from 1835, but the Cartwright and *Beardstown Chronicle* letters make clear that the press was that of the *Pioneer and Western Baptist*, located in Rock Spring, and the date was 1834. I am grateful to Robert Bray for sharing a transcript of the *Christian Advocate*'s text of the letter.

26. See *Proceedings of the Illinois Education Convention: Held in the State House at Vandalia, December 5th and 6th, 1834, with an Address to the People of Illinois, and a Memorial to the Legislature, on Common Schools* (Rock Spring: Printed at the Pioneer Office, 1834). For Lincoln's selection as delegate, see *Lincoln Day by Day: A Chronology, 1809–1865*, ed. Earl Schenck Miers and William Baringer (Washington: Lincoln Sesquicentennial Commission, 1960), 1:41.

27. In spite of Cartwright's objection, the handbill's text of his letter seems to be complete.

28. Onstot recounts the story, repeated by Reep, of Hill hiring John Ferguson to fight Jack Armstrong for him. See *Pioneers of Menard and Mason Counties*, 114.

29. For Lincoln's reputation as a writer for the *Sangamo Journal*, see Robert S. Harper, *Lincoln and the Press* (New York: McGraw-Hill, 1951), 2ff.

30. For the details of the Shields challenge, see Albert J. Beveridge, *Abraham Lincoln, 1809–1858* (Boston: Houghton Mifflin, 1928), 1:334–53.

31. See Herndon's interviews and correspondence with Lincoln's Indiana neighbors Nathaniel Grigsby, Joseph C. Richardson, and especially Elizabeth Crawford, who dictated fragments from memory, in S. A. Crawford to William H. Herndon, Jan. 4, 1866, H-W. Crawford's account is published in *The Hidden Lincoln: From the Letters and Papers of William H. Herndon*, ed. Emanuel Hertz (New York: Viking Press, 1938), 285–87.

32. See W. G. Greene to William H. Herndon, Jan. 23, 1866, H-W.

33. For an example of his satiric gifts on the floor of the legislature, see Lincoln's reply to Usher F. Linder, *Collected Works*, 1:61–70; for his "skinning" of Thomas, see William H. Herndon and Jesse W. Weik, *Herndon's Life of Lincoln*, ed. Paul M. Angle (Cleveland: World Publishing, 1949), 159–60.

34. See Robert Bray, "'The Power to Hurt': Lincoln's Early Use of Satire and Invective," *Journal of the Abraham Lincoln Association* 16 (Winter 1995): 39–58. I am grateful to Robert Bray for the opportunity to study his findings in advance of publication.

35. *Collected Works*, 1:501–16.

36. For a discussion of this point and for a sharply critical appraisal of Lincoln's logical tactics, see Bray, "'The Power to Hurt.'"

37. For example, he turned the tables on Douglas at Galesburg by showing that if, as Douglas charged, Lincoln's supporters tried to broaden their base by organizing meetings without mention of party, Douglas's followers were assiduously doing the same thing. *Collected Works*, 3:221.

38. Lincoln "went to work for Saml Hill goods brought from St Louis—even after became surveyor made Hill's house headquarters." Jesse W. Weik interview with Travis Elmore, memorandum book, Jesse W. Weik Papers, Illinois State Historical Library.

——— 5 ———

Abraham Lincoln, Ann Rutledge, and the Evidence of Herndon's Informants

The Ann Rutledge story has always sounded like nineteenth-century popular fiction. The most beautiful girl in the village becomes engaged to a rich storekeeper, who admits he has been living under an assumed name and who says he will marry her when he returns from a visit to his aged parents. When he stops writing and shows no sign of returning after two years, the deserted girl accepts the advances of the poor-but-honest postmaster, who has loved her secretly all along. She agrees to marry him, and they plan a bright future, including college for her and a legal career for him, only to have death intervene at the height of their happiness and cancel all their vows. When William H. Herndon came across the Ann Rutledge story unexpectedly after Abraham Lincoln's death, it gradually took possession of his nineteenth-century soul. He came to believe he had found in the tragedy of Lincoln's first romance at least a partial answer to the mystery of his great law partner's chronic melancholy, namely that the loss of Ann Rutledge had given a permanent wound to his spirit and altered his outlook on life. This theory he laid on in extravagant terms in a lecture in November 1866 and later incorporated in a more measured and moderate form some twenty-three years later in his biography, *Herndon's Lincoln*.[1]

It was perhaps inevitable that such a story should wear out its welcome, threatening, as it does, to reduce Lincoln's deep inner life—if not the key to his greatness—to a romantic cliché. Novels and popular biographies could not resist the theme that was stated most memorably in Edgar Lee Masters's epitaph for Ann Rutledge in *Spoon River Anthology:*

Out of me unworthy and unknown
The vibrations of deathless music:
"With malice toward none, with charity for all."
Out of me the forgiveness of millions toward millions
And the beneficent face of a nation
Shining with justice and truth.[2]

For the rising generation of twentieth-century Lincoln scholars, the last straw seems to have been Carl Sandburg's *The Prairie Years*, published in 1926, in which the hero's amorous feelings toward the fair Ann are rendered in mawkish scenes and trembling soliloquies. The following year the young Paul M. Angle attacked the Ann Rutledge story as "one of the great myths of American history."[3] All of the evidence in support of it, he argued, was after the fact, with no contemporary evidence of any kind having been produced. He charged Herndon with having chosen his evidence selectively, ignoring and suppressing testimony that cast doubt on the story, and accepting as authentic testimony he should have regarded as suspect. Moreover, Herndon had heedlessly given credence to the doubtful tale of Lincoln's near insanity after the death of Ann Rutledge.

This repudiation of the Ann Rutledge story as a critical event in Lincoln's life, reinforced by Angle's sensational exposure a few years later of an Ann Rutledge hoax, found favor with Lincoln scholars, but there remained one difficulty.[4] The documents upon which Herndon had based his account were not generally available for examination. This was a consideration of some importance in that the position taken by Angle and others was in large part a critique of Herndon's use of evidence they themselves had not seen. Other than Herndon's collaborator Jesse W. Weik, the only scholar to have full access to this prodigious mass of unique source material was Albert J. Beveridge, who, in writing before Angle's attack, relied on the Herndon documents extensively in his account of Lincoln's New Salem years and had apparently found nothing to fault Herndon's factual rendering of the Ann Rutledge story.[5] Thus, when the Library of Congress acquired the Herndon documents in 1941 and made them available to researchers, it was fitting, if not inevitable, that the authoritative "sifting of the Ann Rutledge evidence" should have been undertaken by the most imposing Lincoln scholar of the day, J. G. Randall, whose analysis of the Herndon documents appears as an appendix to the first part of his study of Lincoln's presidency. This was, he admitted, "something of a digression." "Yet," he noted, "the popular writing has created a stock picture, and the true state of the evidence requires attention."[6] Like Angle, Randall did not attempt to disguise his belief that the Ann Rutledge story, in having "usurped the spotlight," had worked great mischief in the understanding of Abraham Lincoln.

Although much more detailed and fully worked out, Randall's objections to Herndon's evidence are essentially Angle's: that Herndon adduced no contemporary evidence to support his conclusions, that he chose selectively from conflicting testimony, and that he credited dubious and unreliable witnesses. In addition, Randall lays great stress on the problematic character of the evidence, which largely consists of older people's recollections of what happened thirty years before. Randall accomplishes what Angle had been unable to do without full access to the Herndon documents: closely analyzes the letters and interviews of many of the key informants, points out contradictions and inconsistencies, and calls attention to the indirect and hearsay character of some of the testimony. His clear-cut conclusion is that the story of the love affair between Lincoln and Ann Rutledge and Lincoln's subsequent temporary derangement must be regarded as "unproved" and that, as such, "it does not belong in a recital of those Lincoln episodes which one presents as unquestioned reality."[7]

Randall's appendix formed the capstone contribution to the effort to discredit the Ann Rutledge story as history, an effort whose success among historians has been virtually complete. Lincoln's first love affair was thus effectively proscribed, and in the nearly half century that has elapsed no reputable Lincoln biographer has seen fit to treat the Ann Rutledge story seriously. A clear indication of the profound effect these strictures have had is the chastened version of the Ann Rutledge story given by Carl Sandburg in the one-volume edition of his biography published in 1954. In the acknowledgments, he pays tribute to the scholars who "made a strong case that the [Lincoln-Rutledge] 'romance' rested on conjecture and assumption while the often related grief and borderline insanity of Lincoln at her death were improbable."[8] In a completely rewritten account of the New Salem period, Sandburg drops the mawkish interior monologues and substitutes circumspect passages such as: "It was certain that Ann Rutledge and Lincoln knew each other and he took an interest in her; probably they formed some mutual attachment not made clear to the community; possibly they loved each other and her hand went into his long fingers whose bones told her of refuge and security. They were the only two persons who could tell what secret they shared, if any."[9]

↩

But is the Ann Rutledge story, as we have been telling ourselves all these years, mostly a myth—or, as Louis A. Warren has termed it, "pure fiction"?[10] In a paper first presented before the Abraham Lincoln Symposium in 1988, John Y. Simon argued persuasively that the critique under review, although it "exposed the shaky underpinnings of any detailed account of the [Lincoln-Rutledge] relationship," has been carried too far. "This commendable correction of the historical record, once valuable, now requires reappraisal, especially as it provoked an overreaction."[11] Simon traces the public career of the Ann Rutledge story from its first appearance in Herndon's 1866 lecture and shows that by mingling evidence with speculation, embellishing the story of Lincoln's derangement, and tastelessly offending Mary Todd Lincoln, Herndon "grossly mishandled a major incident in the Lincoln story," from which "neither Herndon's reputation nor that of Ann Rutledge ever recovered."[12] He concludes that in spite of Herndon's blunders and the caveats and misgivings of doubting historians, "the reality of the story appears certain," and that Ann "should take her proper place in Lincoln biography."[13]

The discussion that follows comes at the problem from a different direction. It is based on a study of the evidence provided by Herndon's informants, the letters and interviews relating to the Ann Rutledge affair in the Herndon-Weik Collection at the Library of Congress.[14] At the heart of the controversy, as Simon has shown, is the role of Herndon himself, but beyond that is the standing of the testimony of Herndon's informants. Of Herndon, it has been alleged that he was not an impartial investigator, that he coached his witnesses and guided their responses with leading questions, and that he was assiduous only in the pursuit of answers and information that suited him. David Donald, who, in the 1940s, was one of the first (and apparently the last) to survey the Herndon documents for their Ann Rutledge testimony, helped perpetuate the notion that the romance was little short of a collaborative fabrication: "One letter of inquiry followed another, and the more often old men and women repeated their tales the surer they became of the whole story. The hundreds of papers, letters, and interviews on the Ann Rutledge theme preserved in the Herndon-Weik Collection show that the legend grew in color and in detail and that over the years the story crystallized from a floating rumor into a fixed romance."[15] Randall and his wife, Ruth Painter Randall, are especially hard on Herndon as an avowed enemy of Mary Todd Lincoln and are disposed to see his rendering of the Ann Rutledge affair as a deliberate affront in this regard.[16]

Herndon's informants, the former residents of the New Salem neighborhood who offered their recollections of the Ann Rutledge romance, have fared little better. It is charged that their testimony is generally suspect because they were eager to associate themselves with the early career of a great man, that they were therefore easily led to say what his biographer wanted to hear, that their testimony is contradictory and inconclusive, and that they could not be expected to recall with clarity events that had happened thirty years earlier. Randall, who is generally condescending about Herndon's informants, pointedly praises one of them, George Spears, for what he calls the "refreshing candor" with which Spears admitted that he did not remember much about the events in question. The clear implication is that other witnesses suffered from a similar inability but lacked the candor to admit it.

Some of these charges were made by critics, such as Angle, who did not have access to the documents and were basing their conclusions on portions of the testimony that had appeared in print, on Herndon's tarnished reputation, and on speculation about how and when he developed his information. But strictly on the basis of the documents themselves and what they reveal, it is difficult to fault Herndon as an investigator. They show that his efforts, which began about a month after Lincoln was assassinated, were prompt and prodigious.[17] Within four months, he had opened a correspondence with Lincoln's relatives, with his earliest acquaintances and his oldest friends, and with informants at the scenes of his childhood in Kentucky and Indiana. He had also traveled to Chicago to interview Lincoln's cousins, John and Dennis Hanks, to Coles County to interview his stepmother and other relatives, and to Spencer County, Indiana, to question the people with whom Lincoln had grown up. Amid this flurry of investigative activity that was aimed at the whole span of Lincoln's life, Herndon did not neglect the people who knew Lincoln in New Salem. He traveled to Petersburg to interview residents still on the scene, and he corresponded frequently with them and with others who had moved away. Herndon kept up this pattern of energetic, dedicated investigation for nearly two years, and although his efforts eventually languished, he was still taking interviews about Ann Rutledge as late as 1887.[18] The resulting archive, a cache of primary material containing thousands of documents, is the richest source of information extant on Lincoln's life and is still far from being exhausted.

When Herndon first heard the story of Lincoln's romance with Ann Rutledge, within days of beginning his inquiries, he naturally pursued it with other informants, but the responses from this period indicate that he was more interested in other matters, such as Lincoln's early movements and his reading. Herndon's cousin, J. Rowan Herndon, who had known Lincoln well in New Salem, sent a torrent of information in response to Herndon's first letter in May 1865, but it was not until the prospective biographer's fourth letter several weeks later that he got around to sounding out his cousin about Lincoln and women. Rowan replied, "You ask about him as Regard women. They all Liked him and [he] liked them as well[.] There was a Miss Rutlege i have know Dout he would have maried iff she had of Lived But Deth Prevented."[19] This indirect way of raising the question initially with his informants is indicative of Herndon's approach. Writing six months later to his father-in-law in Petersburg, G. U. Miles, who acted as a kind of research assistant, he directed, "If you ever see Mrs Armstrong please get out of her all the facts in reference to Mr. Lincolns life when in Menard — what he did — what he said — when he said it where he said it — before whom — How he lived — his manners — customs — habits — sports, frolics — fun — his sadness — his wit; his humor. What he read — when he read it — How he read — and what and who he loved. etc. etc. and in short all she may know about him in mind — heart — soul — body."[20] These examples show what becomes clear when one reviews the documents, that Herndon's initial approach to informants was typically open-ended, and although it may have prompted informants to respond on certain subjects, it was not calculated to elicit preconceived answers. As Beveridge said of the material, "Everywhere it is obvious that Herndon is intent on telling the truth himself and on getting the truth from those who could give personal, first-hand information."[21]

This is not to say that Herndon did not eventually pursue the Ann Rutledge story with vigor and resourcefulness. But the character of his investigation has often been misrepresented by his critics, who have sometimes assumed that he knew little or nothing of the Ann Rutledge affair until the fall of 1866 and that, once he got wind of it, became obsessed by it.[22] Both of these conceptions are wrong. Herndon learned of the romance in late May 1865, possibly in an interview on the twenty-ninth with Hardin Bale in Petersburg.[23] Although he would accumulate information on the affair for many months, the documents suggest that he did not begin to bear down on the matter until early in 1866, when he inquired about it specifically.[24] By March 23, his father-in-law, sending testimony from Petersburg, would write, "the above Statements I think you may rely on but if you Should undertake to write a history of my life after I am dead I dont want you to inquire So close into my Early courtships as you do of Mr Lincolns."[25]

Herndon had the advantage of knowing the people involved: "I knew Miss Rutledge myself, as well as her father and other members of the family, and have been personally acquainted with every one of the score or more of witnesses whom I at one time or another interviewed on this delicate subject."[26] But at the same time, Herndon was an able and experienced lawyer and was not naive where witnesses were concerned.

The responses of his informants show again and again that Herndon checked the information he was gathering, particularly when he noted discrepancies, by trying it out on other informants. Not surprisingly, they frequently disputed each other's recollections. William G. Greene disputed Mentor Graham's claim to have taught Lincoln as a student and advanced his own claim to have loaned Lincoln books with which to study grammar and surveying. James Short in turn disputed this, stating that Greene's father was a drinking and illiterate man and had no books in his house. And so on. Ironically, following up in this way has earned Herndon the accusation of leading his witnesses, while the disputes among the informants have contributed to their testimony being called a "mass of confused and contradictory evidence."[27]

↵

Herndon's reputation as an honest man—as, indeed, a man with a passion for the truth—has been affirmed in all quarters and is not in dispute.[28] But he did love to analyze and speculate, and he undoubtedly had a romantic disposition to which the Ann Rutledge story appealed and which led him, especially in his 1866 lecture, to expand on the story and rhapsodize shamelessly on the lasting effects of the romance on Abraham Lincoln. His informants, although not responsible for most of Herndon's speculations, have suffered because of them. Angle complained that Herndon's testimony "comes either from a member of the Rutledge family—naturally interested in making the attachment between Ann and the martyred President as intimate as possible—or from a one-time resident of New Salem, interested in fastening all possible glamour to that forgotten village."[29] Angle had not seen the documents when he wrote this, but one who had seen them said much the same. "Old-timers dug back into their store of gossip to reproduce, verbatim, conversations held with Lincoln fully thirty years before (and in some cases fifty years before). It was a kind of local contest to see who could remember the most."[30] These characterizations are manifestly unfair. In fact, Herndon's informants were, for the most part, reasonably circumspect in what they said and ready to acknowledge the limits of their own knowledge. Although, as Herndon knew, a few of his informants were suspiciously facile and self-important in their testimony, most seemed to be straightforward and reliable witnesses who exhibit no purpose to exaggerate or deceive.[31]

To be sure, the recollections of the New Salem informants are fragmentary and impressionistic. They remember that Lincoln was a great reader, a good storyteller, and a good wrestler and that he was a store clerk, postmaster, and elected to the state legislature. They remember Lincoln's wrestling match and subsequent friendship with Jack Armstrong and that he was elected captain of a company of volunteers in the Black Hawk War. They recall that Lincoln was great friends with Jack Kelso and that they loved to recite Burns and Shakespeare and that Lincoln studied first grammar and surveying and then the law. One of the things they remember and comment on is that he courted Ann Rutledge, who was engaged at the time to another man, and that he went a little crazy at her death.

The condescending treatment of Herndon's informants as unreliable witnesses is a curious business, for even the critics find it impossible not to rely on them. For example, J. G. Randall accepts John McNamar as "Ann's fiancé" not because there is contemporary documentary evidence to this effect but because Herndon's informants seemed to agree that this was the case.[32] But he is reluctant to accept Lincoln's courtship of Ann or his excessive grief and apparent derangement at her death in spite of the fact that these were just as clearly affirmed by the same group of witnesses. He characterizes the Ann Rutledge testimony as "some *pro,* some *con,* some inconclusive, all of it long delayed reminiscence, much of it second- or third-hand, part of it consisting of inference or supposition as to what 'must have been' true."[33] But even if these charges are strictly true, does this warrant the conclusion Randall wants us to accept—that Herndon's evidence is a hopeless hodgepodge from which no historical reality can reliably be drawn?

What is most notable in the case of the Ann Rutledge affair—the objections of Angle, Randall, and Donald notwithstanding—is that there is remarkably little disagreement among the informants on the basic elements of the story. Reduced to three essential questions, these may be represented as follows: 1. Did Lincoln love or court Ann Rutledge? 2. Did Lincoln grieve excessively at Ann's death? and 3. Did they have an understanding about marriage? In order to gauge the evidence in terms of these questions, the testimony of all Herndon's informants who mentioned the Ann Rutledge story has been reviewed, and a "yes," "no," or "no opinion" has been assigned for each question (Table 1). The witnesses who testified about Ann Rutledge, including those whose testimony was forwarded to Herndon by others, number twenty-four.[34] It is obvious that some of these were clearly not testifying from firsthand knowledge. John Hill, for example, was not yet born when Ann died, and Lizzie Herndon Bell was only a small child. Others, such as B. F. Irwin, T. W. McNeely, and William Bennett, testified only about what they had heard from others. But most of the twenty-four were contemporaries of Lincoln, or older, were acquainted with Lincoln and Ann, and were well placed in the small circle of neighbors to know something about the events in question.

Table 1. Herndon's Informants on Lincoln and Ann Rutledge

Informant	Loved or Courted AR?	Grieved at AR's Death?	Understanding about Marriage?
Abell, Mrs. E. H.	No opinion	Yes	No opinion
Bale, Hardin	Yes	Yes	Yes
Bale, Mrs. Hardin	Yes	No opinion	No opinion
Bell, Lizzie	Yes	No opinion	No
Bennett, William	Yes	No opinion	Yes
Carman, Caleb	Yes	No opinion	Yes
Cogdal, Isaac	Yes	Yes	Yes
Graham, Mentor	Yes	Yes	Yes
Green, Mrs. Nancy	Yes	Yes	Yes
Greene, L. M.	Yes	Yes	Yes
Greene, William G.	Yes	Yes	Yes
Herndon, J. Rowan	Yes	No opinion	Yes
Hill, John	Yes	Yes	Yes
Hill, Mrs. Samuel	Yes	Yes	Yes
Hohimer, Henry	Yes	No opinion	Yes
Irwin, B. F.	Yes	Yes	Yes
Jones, John	Yes	Yes	Yes
McHenry, Henry	No opinion	Yes	No opinion
McNeely, T. W.	Yes	Yes	No opinion
Rutledge, J. McGrady	Yes	No opinion	Yes
Rutledge, John M.	Yes	Yes	Yes
Rutledge, Robert B.	Yes	Yes	Yes
Rutledge, Mrs. William	Yes	Yes	No
Short, James	Yes	Yes	No opinion

Sources: Herndon-Weik Collection, Library of Congress; Ward Hill Lamon Papers, Huntington Library.

As Simon has pointed out, none of these informants denied or expressed doubt that Lincoln loved or courted Ann Rutledge.[35] Moreover, all but two affirmed it directly or by implication. One of the two who failed to affirm it, Mrs. E. H. Abell, wrote to Herndon: "the Courtship between him and Miss Rutledge I can say but little[.] this much I do know he was staying with us at the time of her death it was a great shock to him and I never seen a man mourn for a companion more than he did for her[.] he made a remark one day when it was raining that he could not bare the idea of its raining on her Grave[.] that was the time the community said he was crazy[.] he was not crazy but he was very disponding a long time."[36] Mrs. Abell may have been reticent or uninformed about Lincoln's courtship of Ann, but she left no doubt that his feelings for her were very strong.[37] The tally for the first question—Did Lincoln love or court Ann Rutledge?—is "yes," twenty-two; "no," zero; and "no opinion," two.

The second question—Did Lincoln grieve excessively at Ann's death?—produces a similar result. No one denied the story of Lincoln's unusual behavior, although the informants who voiced an opinion differed about the severity of his reaction. Some claimed that he became temporarily deranged, others that his friends feared for his sanity, and others simply that he took Ann's death very hard. The reckoning here is "yes," seventeen; "no," zero; and "no opinion," seven.

The third question—Did Lincoln and Ann have an understanding about marriage?—is the only one about which there is actual disagreement, and the reason is not hard to understand. At the time of Lincoln's courtship of Ann, she was officially and publicly engaged to another man, John McNamar, who left town soon after their engagement. Ann's family reported that McNamar's long absence from New Salem, his failure to write to Ann, and the discovery that he had been operating under an assumed name caused Ann to accept Lincoln's attentions, which, in the words of Ann's brother Robert, "resulted in an engagement to marry, conditional to an honorable release from the contract with McNamar. There is no kind of doubt as to the existence of this engagement."[38] Few outside the Rutledge family, if any, knew about the understanding between Lincoln and Ann until after her death. James Short was probably typical of the close friends for whom Lincoln's extraordinary bereavement was a revelation: "the Rutledges lived about half a mile from me. Mr L. came over to see me & them every day or two. I did not know of any engagement or tender passages between Mr L and Miss R at the time. But after her death . . . he seemed to be so much affected and grieved so hardly that I then supposed there must have been something of the kind."[39] In these circumstances it is understandable that some residents, even one as well placed as Ann's aunt, Mrs. William Rutledge, would think that Ann really preferred the rich storekeeper, McNamar, and would have married him had she lived.[40] But she was the only one of Herndon's informants to say as much; the only other to dispute the engagement was Lizzie Bell, a child at the time, who was apparently repeating her mother's doubt that the two were "absolutely engaged."[41] Even with these two dissents, the totals for the third question—Did Lincoln and Ann have an understanding about marriage?—are "yes," sixteen; "no," two; and "no opinion," six.

The conclusion one must draw from this reckoning is that on the three basic points at issue in the Ann Rutledge affair—the existence of a courtship, the existence of an understanding about marriage, and Lincoln's excessive grief at the death of Ann Rutledge—the informants were overwhelmingly in agreement.

This tally of the opinions of Herndon's informants, decisive as it appears, gives equal weight to each informant and does nothing to help sort out those whose testimony is the most probative and thus most important. Nor is it possible, in many cases, to find out the basis of the informant's knowledge. Small communities are supposed to be hard places to keep secrets, but they are also notoriously rife with speculative gossip, and some of what Herndon collected is undoubtedly little more than this. But there are at least five witnesses who received information about the love affair between Ann Rutledge and Abraham Lincoln from a prime source—the principals themselves.

At least two informants received information directly from Ann: her brother, Robert B. Rutledge, and her cousin, James McGrady Rutledge. Critics of the story have come close to implying that members of the Rutledge family were, in and of themselves, unreliable witnesses, although this hardly seems warranted.[42] Far from trying to capitalize on Ann's connection to Lincoln, the Rutledges at first shied away from Herndon. When he approached James McGrady Rutledge, the cousin thought to know more about Ann's relations with Lincoln than anyone except her brother David, McGrady evaded him. Ann's brother Robert later advised Herndon to "correspond with [McGrady] and say to him that this is no longer a delicate question, inasmuch as it must of necessity become a matter of history, that I desire the whole truth to be recorded."[43] Apparently not even this could prompt McGrady Rutledge to answer Herndon's letters. Herndon probably had heard what McGrady would later write in his reminiscences, that he and Lincoln had lived together at Rutledge's tavern and that "While he was boarding there Lincoln became deeply in love with Ann."[44] Robert described McGrady to Herndon as "a cousin about [Ann's] age & who was in her confidence," which adds weight to what he reported to Robert: "Ann told me once in coming from a Camp Meeting on Rock creek, that engagements made too far ahead sometimes failed, that one had failed (meaning her engagement with McNamar) and gave me to understand, that as soon as certain studies were completed she and Lincoln would be married."[45] It was not until 1887 that Herndon caught up with the reluctant cousin, who gave him only a terse summary of what he knew. Herndon: "Do you know anything concerning the courtship and engagement of Abraham Lincoln and Ann Rutledge?" McGrady Rutledge: "Well I had an opportunity to know and I do know the facts. Abraham Lincoln and Ann Rutledge were engaged to be married. He came down and was with her during her last sickness and burial. Lincoln was studying law at Springfield Ill. Ann Rutledge concented to waite a year for their marriage after their engagement until Abraham

Lincoln was Admitted to the bar. And Ann Rutledge died within the year."[46]

When Herndon finally succeeded in making contact with Ann's immediate family more than a year after first hearing of the romance, it was her brother, Robert B. Rutledge, who agreed to cooperate. Rutledge acknowledged Herndon's letter of July 30, 1866, which he characterized as "Making inquiry as to my knowledge of the early history of our *Martered President.* . . . [It] will require some time to answer intelligably, as I will have to consult our Family Record, My Mother and elder Brother, who are in Van Buren Co Iowa."[47] Nearly three months later, Rutledge forwarded to Herndon a twelve-page statement drawn in part from the records and recollections of his family in the form of numbered answers to Herndon's queries. The beginning of his response to Herndon's eighth query tells us something about the man and how he regarded his responsibilities as an informant: "I cannot give you a satisfactory reply to many items embraced in this inquiry for the lack of dates or circumstances corroborating them. Many things said of him and done by him are indellibly fixed in my mind but the absence of the proper surroundings impels me to with hold them."[48]

The fourth query is about Ann: "You make some pertinent inquiries concerning my sister and the relations which existed between herself and Mr Lincoln." Rutledge's straightforward account of Ann's engagement to McNamar, her subsequent disenchantment and engagement to Lincoln, and the "terrible" effect of Ann's death on Lincoln's mind filled out and confirmed what Herndon had been hearing from other informants for more than a year. Rutledge made no attempt to swell the importance of his sister's relationship with Lincoln, and his description of her is rather modest: "My sister was esteemed the brightest mind of the family, was studious, devoted to her duties of whatever character, and possessed a remarkably amiable and lovable disposition. She had light hair and blue eyes."[49] He said nothing in his account of the cause of Ann's death, but when Herndon, in his next letter, tried out on him the theory he had heard repeated by some of the old neighbors, Rutledge demurred: "you suggest that the probable cause of Ann's sickness was her conflicts — Emotions &c., as to this I cannot say. I however have my own private convictions, the character of her sickness was brain fever."[50]

Robert's conscientious consultations with others, which he felt obliged to do to test his memory and augment the record, are objected to by Randall as violations of "the law of evidence," although he grants that "some investigators might not consider that his product was rendered less valuable by this consultation."[51] While he tries to suggest that

Robert was inconsistent and contradictory, that he was obsequious toward Herndon, and purports to be troubled by Rutledge's use of the term *conditional* for the engagement, Randall fails to find substantial fault with Robert's account, which he nevertheless tars as "dim and misty with the years."[52] Of McGrady's testimony through his brother Robert, Randall complains because of its indirectness: "Here is one person reporting what another person had written him concerning what that person recollected he had inferred from something Ann had casually said to him more than thirty-one years before!"[53] Of his direct testimony to Herndon, Randall says nothing.[54] On balance, there is little to object to in the responses of these deliberate, straightforward, and relatively modest witnesses.

If at least two reliable informants had knowledge of the love affair directly from Ann, at least three had knowledge of what happened from Lincoln himself. The first was Mentor Graham, who was Ann's schoolteacher and who helped Lincoln with his studies. He told Herndon: "Lincoln and [Ann] was Engaged — Lincoln told me so — She intimated to me the same: He Lincoln told me that he felt like committing Sucide after."[55] Although Randall minimizes Graham's testimony as a "meager" contribution, there is little reason to doubt this known friend and counselor of the young Lincoln.[56]

Another witness whose knowledge of the Ann Rutledge affair may be presumed to have come from Lincoln himself was Nancy Green, the wife of Lincoln's close friend Bowling Green. She told G. U. Miles that "Mr Lincoln was a regular suiter of Miss Ann Rutledge for between two & 3 years next up to august 1835 in which month Miss Rutledge died after a Short ilness that Lincoln took her death verry hard So much So that some thought his mind would become impared." She further confirmed what Herndon had heard elsewhere, that "in fear of it [i.e., of Lincoln's mind becoming impaired] Bolin Green [her husband] went to Salem after Lincoln brought him to his house and kept him a week or two & succeeded in cheering him Lincoln up though he was quite malencholy for months."[57] The close attachment of Lincoln to Bowling Green is well known, and if there is any cause to doubt the testimony of his wife, who helped care for Lincoln, it has not been advanced.

The third witness, Isaac Cogdal, claimed to have asked Lincoln directly about the Ann Rutledge affair in later years and received an answer. Angle and Randall argue that this counts against the credibility of his testimony, principally because of Lincoln's known reluctance to discuss personal matters, but they neglect two important considerations.[58] The first is that Cogdal was a longstanding personal and political friend of Lincoln's, a fellow Whig from Democratic Menard whose friendship went back to the New Salem days and who, Herndon attested, was intimate enough with Lincoln to discuss religious questions with him in his law office.[59] Randall tells us that Cogdal studied law and was granted a license in 1860, not long before the conversation took place, but he does not report that the man who advised him to study law and apparently offered him instruction was Abraham Lincoln.[60] The second thing overlooked in regard to Cogdal's testimony is the context in which it occurred. Cogdal told Herndon that Lincoln, as president-elect, had invited him to his office in the statehouse to talk about old times and had asked him pointedly about the Rutledges and other New Salem families. Cogdal's interview reads: "After we had spoken over old times . . . I then dared to ask him this question," and then he related his question and Lincoln's answer. Herndon, in taking down the interview, realized how critical the context was to the credibility of such an answer. He apparently queried Cogdal about the way in which his question was introduced into the conversation and recorded his response in the margin: "May I now in turn ask you a question Lincoln said Cogdall. Most assuredly. I will answer your question if a fair one with all my heart."[61]

As close friends of Lincoln, Cogdal and Herndon well knew that he did not customarily express himself on personal subjects. The wording of both Cogdal's descriptions of the moment—"I then dared to ask him" and "May I now in turn ask you a question Lincoln"—together with the remembered heartiness of Lincoln's reply, indicate Cogdal's awareness of the rare opportunity that had been given him to confront the reserved Lincoln on the subject of Ann Rutledge. Herndon's marginal addendum shows that he, too, was very much aware of how pertinent the context was to crediting the extraordinary candor of Lincoln's response. In his answer, Lincoln not only admitted to having been deeply in love with Ann Rutledge but also acknowledged, when pressed by Cogdal, that he "ran off the track" at her death. Although Herndon had already heard the story many times before, the last thing Cogdal remembered Lincoln saying contained something entirely new and seems to have made a particular impression on Herndon: "I did honestly — & truly love the girl & think often — often of her now."[62]

To Randall, Cogdal's testimony "seems artificial and made to order. It was given out after Lincoln's death; it presents him in an unlikely role; it puts in his mouth uncharacteristic sayings."[63] Perhaps so, but this was not testimony about something that happened in the "dim and misty" past; Cogdal was testifying just five or six years after the event, which was not an obscure encounter with an old friend but an extremely memorable one with the president-elect of the United States. And once

Lincoln's departure from his usual reserve in personal matters is accounted for, we have no more reason to doubt this testimony than did Herndon, who knew Cogdal as a man highly regarded in his community and an old friend of Lincoln's.[64]

⤸

The conclusion seems inescapable that the witnesses who had the best opportunity to know what transpired between Abraham Lincoln and Ann Rutledge tell essentially the same story as the other informants. In spite of the claim of critics that Herndon "collected sharply conflicting reminiscences on the Lincoln-Rutledge idyll," a review of the informants' letters and interviews fails to confirm it.[65] If the testimony on the basic elements of the Ann Rutledge story is thus overwhelming, as it assuredly is, why has the opposite view so roundly prevailed? John Y. Simon has offered some cogent insights into this curious state of affairs, one of which is that critics such as the Randalls have, in effect, "reclassified the romance as an accusation requiring proof, something of which Lincoln would be held innocent until proved guilty, rather than a biographical incident in which a preponderance of reliable evidence would prevail."[66] Simon's point is apt, for there can be little doubt that the key to understanding the banishment of the Ann Rutledge story from Lincoln biography is not simply the historical evidence itself but the standards by which the leading critic, J. G. Randall, insisted that the evidence be judged.

In choosing to address the question of standards, it is by no means conceded that the criticism of Herndon's evidence that has prevailed for more than sixty years has been always fair, even-handed, or accurate. On the contrary, there is much to dispute. There is Angle, for example, who had not seen anything like the full evidence in 1927 but wrote as though he had. His characterization of Herndon's testimony shows how limited his knowledge was: "The Rutledge-New Salem testimony consists of letters written to Herndon soon after the publication of his lecture, and of signed statements collected by friends at his request."[67] Most of Herndon's testimony, much of it consisting of personal interviews he conducted, was assembled well before the lecture. Nor is Angle at pains to exercise care in his characterization of Herndon's evidence: "some thought it amounted to nothing, others felt that Ann cared just as much for McNamar as for Lincoln, while 'Uncle' Jimmy Short . . . wrote that he had never heard of anything of the kind!"[68] There is no testimony that the love affair amounted to nothing. The only testimony that Ann cared just as much for McNamar is qualified by the phrase "to appearances," by which Mrs. Nancy Green clearly meant "as far as outsiders were able to judge by the way things appeared."[69] And Uncle Jimmy's testimony shows that he *did* believe in the romance; he came to this belief, he testified, when he saw the effect Ann's death had on Lincoln. Angle's failure to quote Uncle Jimmy's actual testimony is further explained by his eagerness to discredit what he calls "the 'disastrous effect' legend."[70]

In the light of more than sixty years' hindsight, it seems clear that Angle's position was way out in front of his evidence and that his essay ultimately demonstrated little more than his eagerness to endorse an idea whose time had come. Like Lee on the attack, his aggressive seizure of the moment more than made up for his lack of resources. J. G. Randall's "Sifting of the Ann Rutledge Evidence," written nearly twenty years later, is of an altogether different character. More comprehensive in its scope, it is widely recognized as the most authoritative treatment of the evidence and therefore the prime document in the debunking of the Ann Rutledge story. Randall gives notice at the outset that he has taken up the subject "not for any intrinsic importance at all, but because historical criticism finds here a challenge and a needful task."[71] It is clear from the start that he means to deal not only with the evidence but also with broader issues involved in the proper and legitimate use of historical evidence, and he begins with the problem of reminiscence.

> Historians must use reminiscence, but they must do so critically. Even close-up evidence is fallible. When it comes through the mists of many years, some of it may be true, but a careful writer will check it with known facts. Contradictory reminiscences leave doubt about what is to be believed; unsupported memories are in themselves insufficient as proof; statements induced under suggestion, or psychological stimulus, as were some of the stories about Lincoln and Ann, call especially for careful appraisal. . . . When faulty memories are admitted, the resulting product becomes something other than history; it is no longer to be presented as a genuine record.[72]

Although this has the professorial tone of a lecture on historiography, there can be no doubt that it was intended to present a standard for separating history from nonhistory that the evidence given by Herndon's informants, all of which can readily be classified as reminiscence, cannot meet. The crux of the matter is that memories of participants or witnesses to historical events, being fallible, are not sufficient, in and of themselves, to constitute proof. Contemporary evidence or "known facts" must exist to check them against. Students of Herndon's documents know without reading further that, overwhelming as the Ann Rutledge evidence is, it cannot pass so stern a test.

Randall advances the view that "in the law of evidence . . . it is insisted that testimony ought to come straight," with the implication that testimony at second and third hand is automatically suspect, if not inadmissible. That is why he draws attention to Robert B. Rutledge's quoting a letter he had solicited from his cousin McGrady, even though what McGrady had to say seems critically relevant to the facts and events in question. In the same vein, it is why Randall finds it less noteworthy that John Jones was an eyewitness to Lincoln's regular visits to Ann Rutledge, and that he saw Lincoln in great distress after his last visit to Ann, than that this supposed eyewitness should qualify certain statements by indicating that he had them from others.[73] Just as Randall's evidentiary "law" seems modeled on the inadmissibility of hearsay in a court of law, his objection to what he calls "must have been" evidence seems to be based on the courtroom prohibition on questions calling for a conclusion on the part of a witness. James Short's inference that Lincoln took Ann's death so hard because he had been in love with her is thus a "must have been" conclusion. In a trial, Short could testify that he saw Lincoln come several miles to visit Ann's house every other day or so and that Lincoln appeared to be greatly distressed at her death, but Short's conclusion, which he freely gave to Herndon, would presumably be out of order.

In sum, Randall insists on an extremely high standard for proof: Evidence must be contemporary or confirmed by contemporary evidence; it must be firsthand and direct; it must not be elicited by leading questions; it must be consistent; and it must not include inferences drawn by witnesses. Evidence that fails these tests is less than adequate for proof and thus cannot establish historical reality. In requiring standards for proof not unlike those in a criminal trial, Randall tends to treat the Ann Rutledge story, as Simon suggests, like an accusation against Lincoln and one that must be proved beyond a reasonable doubt. This is what justifies his conclusion that the love affair of Lincoln and Ann Rutledge is "unproved" and that it therefore "does not belong in a recital of those Lincoln episodes which one presents as unquestioned reality."

So what does it matter, one may ask, if the standards for evidence are kept conspicuously high in judging the Ann Rutledge affair? Are we not then likely to arrive at a more accurate and reliable result? For reasons to question the appropriateness of such lofty standards one need look no further than the concrete details of Randall's own practice. In his analysis of the Ann Rutledge evidence, he objects to testimony given at second and third hand but uses it without complaint when it serves his purpose.[74] He objects to the use of hearsay but cannot resist mentioning Henry McHenry's statement that some residents thought that Lincoln's legal studies brought on his mental condition after Ann's death, even though no informant testified to this as his own belief.[75] And he is often "guilty" of accepting the testimony of a single witness even though it is unsupported. For example, on the basis of the unsupported testimony of John McNamar that he had placed a wooden marker on Ann's grave, Randall announces: "It was McNamar, not Lincoln, who marked Ann's grave. As to Lincoln's grief it has been seen that his alleged derangement of mind is without adequate substantiation; in the 'uncolumned air' of Herndon's lecture it is nothing more than fiction."[76] For Randall, one unsubstantiated word from McNamar is sufficient proof that McNamar carved Ann's marker, whereas the combined testimony of more than a dozen eyewitnesses cannot convince him that Lincoln's grief was unusual.

A contemporary letter written by Mathew S. Marsh shortly after Ann's death "establishes the fact that Lincoln was attending to his postmaster duties as usual," although Marsh said Lincoln was absent from the post office and could be expected, in violation of postal regulations, to frank the letter.[77] Randall thus allows himself a "must have been" inference that he would have found objectionable in Uncle Jimmy Short. Randall, of course, is not a witness, but in the Ann Rutledge dispute he presents himself less as a historian in search of the truth than as an advocate doggedly defending a position. In the early pages of *Lincoln the President*, Randall the historian draws extensively on Herndon's informants and depends on them for the documentation of Lincoln's personal and political background. There he does not confine himself to testimony that can be checked with contemporary sources or "known facts," nor does he balk at accepting as historical incidents about which the evidence is conflicting.

That Randall's own practice is at odds with the standards he himself laid down for judging the Ann Rutledge evidence is hardly surprising. Historical scholarship, for whatever similarities it might bear to trying a case in a court of law, is a different kind of enterprise and employs different methods. Observing the evidentiary safeguards of a criminal trial would, after all, bring a substantial portion of historical inquiry to a halt, for much of what we want to know about the past simply cannot be established on these terms. Abraham Lincoln's early life is a perfect example. Virtually everything we know about Lincoln as a child and as a young man—his incessant reading and self-education, his storytelling, his honesty, and his interest in politics—comes exclusively from the recollections of those who knew him. Noncontemporary, subjective, often unable to be confirmed even by the recollections of others, to say nothing of contemporary documents, this evidence is sheer

reminiscence. Even Lincoln's autobiographical statements fall squarely into this category, and although he was known for his honesty, he
was, in the most extensive and valuable of these statements, represent-
ing himself and his personal history for political purposes.[78] Randall's
caveats about such evidence and the admixture of error and bias it may
contain are certainly justified, but historians or biographers have no
alternative but to find a way to work with it and, indeed, with anything
that may be indicative of the truth.

Consider as a parallel episode to the Ann Rutledge affair Lincoln's
famous wrestling match with Jack Armstrong, the leader of the Clary's
Grove boys. The event has been seen as important not only for its role
in establishing the young newcomer at New Salem but, as Beveridge and
others have observed, in the launching of Lincoln's political career. From
the same group of informants who told him about Ann Rutledge, Herndon collected several versions of the event, some of which were wholly incompatible. One version had Armstrong taking unfair advantage
of Lincoln, who took it in such good part that he won the admiration
of Armstrong and his followers.[79] Herndon and Weik favored a version
in which Lincoln believed he had been fouled and angrily shook Armstrong by the throat.[80] Beveridge inclined toward the account of Henry
McHenry, one of the Clary's Grove boys, in which Lincoln and Jack
agreed that neither could throw the other and shook hands.[81] Benjamin
Thomas opted for a version printed by William Dean Howells in which
the Clary's Grove boys threatened to intercede when their champion
began to get the worst of it, at which point Lincoln offered to fight them
all one at a time.[82] Although it is true that there is no contemporary
evidence of Lincoln's match with Jack Armstrong, several old residents
did claim to have seen it. And although it is true that Henry Clark,
James Short, Henry McHenry, and Robert B. Rutledge disagreed substantially about what happened in the match, they did agree, as Beveridge
has noted, "that it ended in such fashion as to win the friendship of
Armstrong and the allegiance of his band."[83]

If we treat this episode as Randall treats the Ann Rutledge affair, we
must declare the evidence hopelessly contradictory and find Lincoln
innocent of wrestling Jack Armstrong. The famous match might be
granted the status of folklore, but, as Randall writes of the Ann Rutledge story, it would "not belong in a recital of those Lincoln episodes
which one presents as unquestioned reality." But Beveridge sees in the
conflicting accounts of the wrestling match some critical points of
agreement. His approach, in which the discrepancies are not allowed to
overshadow more important considerations, preserves the incident as
an important part of the biographical record. To accept the essentials

of the Jack Armstrong story as proved—which Randall does—and dispute the basic elements of the Ann Rutledge story as "unproved" is to operate with a double standard.[84] More important, of course, it works to withhold from consideration an incident in Lincoln's early life, which is at least as important.

John Y. Simon has sensibly suggested that the Ann Rutledge story should be regarded not as an "accusation requiring proof" but as "a biographical incident in which a preponderance of reliable evidence would prevail." This calls to mind Herndon's story of Lincoln pleading a case in Coles County in which the jury returned for further elucidation of the phrase *preponderance of evidence*. After the explanations of the judge and the opposing attorney only added to the confusion, Lincoln asked the jury to picture a pair of scales such as they were used to seeing in stores and think of the evidence introduced by each side as being placed in the scales and weighed. If either side had even the slightest bit more evidence than the other, he told them, it would cause one side of the scales to go down, and that would determine the preponderance of evidence.[85] The jury understood, and Lincoln won. In the case of Ann Rutledge, it is utterly clear where the preponderance of evidence lies, but it hardly follows, as his defenders seem to have feared, that Lincoln is thereby the loser. The restoration of his love affair with Ann Rutledge to Lincoln's biography must be regarded as a positive gain for all who seek to understand the man and the circumstances that brought him forth.

NOTES

1. Herndon's lecture, "Abraham Lincoln. Miss Ann Rutledge. New Salem. Pioneering, and THE POEM," delivered on November 16, 1866, and distributed as a broadside, has been reprinted in *Lincoln and Ann Rutledge and the Pioneers of New Salem* (Herrin, Ill.: Trovillion Private Press, 1945). His biography, coauthored with Jesse W. Weik, appeared in 1889.

2. Edgar Lee Masters, *Spoon River Anthology: An Annotated Edition*, ed. John E. Hallwas (1915, repr. Urbana: University of Illinois Press, 1992), 288.

3. Paul M. Angle, "Lincoln's First Love?" *Lincoln Centennial Association Bulletin*, Dec. 1, 1927, 1.

4. See, for example, Benjamin Thomas, *Lincoln's New Salem* (1934, repr. Chicago: Americana House, 1961); Roy P. Basler, *The Lincoln Legend: A Study in Changing Conceptions* (Boston: Houghton Mifflin, 1935), 147–63; and Louis A. Warren, "The Ann Rutledge Myth," *The Lincoln Kinsman* 35 (May 1941): 1–8.

5. See the massive documentation of Lincoln's New Salem years, almost exclusively from Herndon's documents, in Albert J. Beveridge, *Abraham Lin-*

coln, 1809–1858 (Boston: Houghton Mifflin, 1928), 1:100–159. Beveridge did not live to complete his biography, but his letters to Angle responding favorably to his thesis written just before his death suggest that he may have altered his opinion had he lived. This correspondence is in the Albert J. Beveridge Papers, Library of Congress.

6. J. G. Randall, "Sifting the Ann Rutledge Evidence," appendix to *Lincoln the President: Springfield to Gettysburg* (New York: Dodd, Mead, 1945), 2:321.

7. Randall, "Sifting the Ann Rutledge Evidence," 341.

8. Carl Sandburg, *Abraham Lincoln: The Prairie Years and the War Years.* 1 vol. (New York: Harcourt, Brace, 1954), 743.

9. Sandburg, *Abraham Lincoln,* 44. This is reminiscent of Paul Angle's summary: "Certainly Ann Rutledge and Lincoln knew each other; probably they formed a mutual attachment; possibly they were in love. But the evidence on which the story has heretofore been based is certainly far from conclusive." Angle, "Lincoln's First Love?" 6.

10. Louis A. Warren quoted in John Y. Simon, "Abraham Lincoln and Ann Rutledge," *Journal of the Abraham Lincoln Association* 11 (1990): 19. My study of Herndon's informants was well along when I first learned of Simon's paper through the friendly offices of Roger D. Bridges. I am grateful to John Y. Simon for generously making a revised draft of his pioneering essay available in advance of publication.

11. Simon, "Abraham Lincoln and Ann Rutledge," 28.

12. Ibid., 15.

13. Ibid., 33.

14. The text of some of these documents was transcribed by John G. Springer in 1866 and is now in the Huntington Library. A small number of originals are in the Illinois State Historical Library. A fuller and more detailed examination of the evidence in the Ann Rutledge affair than is attempted here appeared some years after this essay was written in John Evangelist Walsh, *The Shadows Rise: Abraham Lincoln and the Ann Rutledge Legend* (Urbana: University of Illinois Press, 1993).

15. David Donald, *Lincoln's Herndon: A Biography* (1948, repr. New York: Da Capo Press, 1989), 187. This characterization ignores the fact that the story of the romance in all its essential features was common knowledge in Petersburg before Herndon had ever heard of it, as evidenced by the article "A Romance of Reality," written by John Hill and published in the Menard *Axis* in 1862. Hill supplied Herndon with a copy of the article, which is now in the Herndon-Weik Collection, Manuscript Division, Library of Congress (hereafter cited as H-W). See Hill to William H. Herndon, June 6, 1865, H-W.

16. Simon, "Abraham Lincoln and Ann Rutledge," 19–28.

17. Horace White's letter of May 22, 1865, H-W, refers to "yours of the 20th" and endorses Herndon as "peculiarly qualified . . . to be [Lincoln's] biographer."

18. See his interviews with Jasper Rutledge, Lizzie Herndon Bell, James McGrady Rutledge, and Henry Hohimer, all of which date from March 1887, and his letter about them to Jesse W. Weik (quoted in note 46).

19. J. R. Herndon to William H. Herndon, July 3, 1865, H-W.

20. William H. Herndon to G. U. Miles, Dec. 1, 1865, H-W.

21. Albert J. Beveridge, "Lincoln as His Partner Knew Him," *Literary Digest International Review* 1 (Sept. 1923): 33.

22. Angle assumes that Herndon first heard the story from John McNamar in October 1866. See Angle, "Lincoln's First Love?" 2.

23. Hardin Bale to William H. Herndon, May 29, 1865, H-W. This, like many of the early documents in the Herndon-Weik Collection, is in the form of a letter addressed to Herndon although in Herndon's own hand and signed by the informant. David Donald is surely correct in judging that these "should probably be understood as his memoranda of oral interviews, which were read back and approved by his informants." Donald, *Lincoln's Herndon,* 185n.

24. See letters of Henry McHenry, Jan. 8, 1866, and William G. Green, Jan. 23, 1866, H-W.

25. G. U. Miles to William H. Herndon, March 23, 1866, H-W.

26. William H. Herndon and Jesse W. Weik, *Herndon's Life of Lincoln,* ed. Paul M. Angle (Cleveland: World Publishing, 1949), 105.

27. Randall, "Sifting the Ann Rutledge Evidence," 324.

28. See Angle, "Lincoln's First Love?" 5; Albert J. Beveridge, quoted in Benjamin Thomas, *Portrait for Posterity: Lincoln and His Biographers* (New Brunswick: Rutgers University Press, 1947), 250; Randall, "Sifting the Ann Rutledge Evidence," 339; and Donald, *Lincoln's Herndon,* 347.

29. Angle, "Lincoln's First Love?" 5.

30. Donald, *Lincoln's Herndon,* 353.

31. Herndon was especially wary of William G. ("Slicky Bill") Greene and Dennis F. Hanks.

32. Randall, "Sifting the Ann Rutledge Evidence," 331, see also 324 and 341.

33. Ibid., 333.

34. This count must regarded as minimal and may not be complete. For example, Herndon refers in his biography to a remark of A. Y. Ellis about Lincoln and Ann Rutledge, but I have not found it in Ellis's letters. See Herndon and Weik, *Herndon's Life of Lincoln,* 110.

35. "Loved" is used here in the overt sense, as opposed to worshipping from afar. This is lumped with "courted" to avoid verbal distinctions that are not substantive. Some responses are scored by implication. Informants who testify that they believed the couple engaged to be married ("yes" to the second question) are counted as "yes" to the first question also.

36. Mrs. E. H. Abell to William H. Herndon, Feb. 15, 1867, H-W.

37. Henry McHenry, the only other informant whose affirmation of the courtship is not explicit, reported that there were two theories in the neighborhood about Lincoln's behavior after Ann's death. One was that he was studying too hard at the law; the other that he was grieving over Ann. McHenry said he subscribed to the latter view. Henry McHenry to William H. Herndon, Jan. 8, 1866, H-W.

38. R. B. Rutledge to William H. Herndon, [Oct. 1866], H-W.

39. William H. Herndon interview with James Short, July 7, 1865, H-W. This response is tallied as a "yes" to the second question (about Lincoln's grief) and

as a "yes" by implication to the first question (about Lincoln's love for Ann) but a "no opinion" on the question of an engagement.

40. G. U. Miles to William H. Herndon, March 23, 1866, H-W. In this letter, Miles reported that Mrs. Samuel Hill thought "that Lincoln would have got her had She lived," but in her undated interview with Herndon she said, "if McNamar had got back from NY before Anns death that she would have married McNamar." These two views are not strictly incompatible but may show a vacillation on her part.

41. William H. Herndon interview with Lizzie Herndon Bell, [March 1887], H-W.

42. Angle, "Lincoln's First Love?" 5.

43. See R. B. Rutledge to William H. Herndon, Nov. 21, 1866, H-W: "He [James McGrady Rutledge] says you and Mr. Cogsdell talked with him on this subject, but he did not tell you as much, as he thot you had a design in it." For McGrady's reputed knowledge of the Lincoln-Rutledge affair, see Thomas P. Reep, *Lincoln at New Salem* (Petersburg: Old Salem Lincoln League, 1927), 32.

44. Fern Nance Pond, ed., "The Memoirs of James McGrady Rutledge 1814–1899," *Journal of the Illinois State Historical Society* 29 (April-Jan. 1937–38): 88.

45. R. B. Rutledge to William H. Herndon, Nov. 21, 1866, H-W.

46. William H. Herndon interview with James M. Rutledge, undated, H-W. The conjectural date assigned by the Library of Congress, March 1887, seems correct. The handwriting of the manuscript looks clearer and more precise than Herndon's and may represent the hand of Jesse W. Weik, to whom Herndon addressed a letter on April 22, 1887: "Inclosed you will find some evidence which I took down in writing when I was at Menard. You had better copy the pencil writing before it rubs out: it is important, as I think on the Ann Rutledge question, and it may be on others." The reference is presumably to the interviews with Jasper Rutledge, Caleb Carman, and Lizzie Bell, which are still in Herndon's pencil, and that of James McGrady Rutledge, which has been copied in ink.

47. R. B. Rutledge to William H. Herndon, Aug. 5, 1866, H-W. The family apparently agreed to speak with one voice on the subject of Ann, for in addition to his lack of success with McGrady Rutledge, Herndon had little luck getting additional information from another brother, John, although he made several attempts. Ann's sister, Nancy Rutledge Prewitt, retold the family version many years later, adding a few details not reported by Robert. See the article by Margaret Flindt transcribed from the Chicago *Inter Ocean*, Feb. 10, 1899, in "Memoire of the Rutledge Family of New Salem, Illinois," comp. Jane E. Hamand (Decatur: Decatur Lincoln Memorial Collection, Nov. 1921). A typescript copy is on deposit at the Library of Congress. I am grateful to James Gilreath of the Rare Book and Special Collections Division for assistance in locating this document.

48. R. B. Rutledge to William H. Herndon, [Oct. 1866], H-W. Rutledge's letter is replete with information and anecdotes about Lincoln at New Salem and is relied upon extensively by Beveridge in his biography.

49. Ibid.

50. R. B. Rutledge to William H. Herndon, Nov. 18, 1866, H-W. For informants offering this interpretation, see the undated interviews with Mrs. Hardin Bale (Ann "died as it were of grief") and Mrs. Samuel Hill ("Anns sickness was caused by her complications").

51. Randall, "Sifting the Ann Rutledge Evidence," 329.

52. Robert first used the word *conditional* to describe the understanding that there would be no official "engagement" until Ann had notified McNamar of her decision. He later admitted that suggesting that the engagement of Lincoln and Ann depended upon contacting the lost McNamar was misleading and declared it "not conditional." See R. B. Rutledge to William H. Herndon, Nov. 18, 1866, H-W; Randall, "Sifting the Ann Rutledge Evidence," 330.

53. Ibid., 328.

54. This is possibly because the transcript does not appear with the other letters and interviews on the microfilm, which was made before the documents were given foliation numbers and placed in the current order. I am grateful to Oliver Orr of the Manuscript Division, Library of Congress, for assistance in examining the Herndon-Weik Collection.

55. Interview with Mentor Graham, April 2, 1866, H-W.

56. Randall calls attention to the cautionary note Herndon wrote on the margin of his interview with Graham's daughter, Lizzie Bell, describing them both as "cranky—flighty—at times nearly non copus mentis—but good & honest." "Sifting the Ann Rutledge Evidence," 326. But this characterization (written no earlier than 1887) is a obviously a two-edged sword.

57. G. U. Miles to William H. Herndon, March 23, 1866, H-W.

58. See Angle, who tries to dismiss Cogdal as a "mediocre lawyer" with no claim on Lincoln's friendship, "Lincoln's First Love?" 6–7, and Randall, "Sifting the Ann Rutledge Evidence," 333–35. Simon successfully answers other objections, such as the circumstance of Cogdal calling Lincoln "Abe" at a time when he was always called "Lincoln." New Salem residents knew, and frequently referred to Lincoln in their testimony, as "Abe."

59. See Herndon's parenthetical note in their second undated interview, H-W.

60. See the biographical account of Cogdal, almost certainly from data he supplied, in [R. D. Miller], *History of Mason and Menard Counties* (Chicago: O. L. Baskin, 1879), 749. Randall cites this source.

61. Interview with Isaac Cogdal, undated, H-W.

62. Ibid. This is surely the germ of Herndon's theory, expounded in his November 16, 1866, lecture, that Lincoln never got over Ann Rutledge's death and brooded on her all his life.

63. Randall, "Sifting the Ann Rutledge Evidence," 335.

64. For Cogdal's standing in his community, see T. G. Onstot, *Pioneers of Menard and Mason Counties* (1902, repr. Havana, Ill.: Church of Jesus Christ of Latter-Day Saints, 1986), 231.

65. Donald, *Lincoln's Herndon,* 316. This depends on what is allowed as "sharply" and "conflicting." The variety of testimony that Donald mentions does not seem to me to exhibit serious conflict about the basic elements of the story.

66. Simon, "Abraham Lincoln and Ann Rutledge," 27.

67. Angle, "Lincoln's First Love?" 7.

68. Ibid., 6.

69. See G. U. Miles to William H. Herndon, March 23, 1866, H-W. Randall's discussion also fails to consider Mrs. Green's qualification.

70. Angle, "Lincoln's First Love?" 7.

71. Randall, "Sifting the Ann Rutledge Evidence," 321.

72. Ibid., 325.

73. Ibid., 328n.

74. See his use of the testimony of Mrs. Nancy Green and Mrs. William Rutledge as given in G. U. Miles's letter to William H. Herndon, ibid., 331.

75. Ibid., 332.

76. Ibid., 340.

77. Ibid., 335. Only Randall's predisposition prompts him to see this letter as casting doubt on the story of Lincoln's excessive grief; it can just as readily be seen as supporting it.

78. For the two most notable statements, those prepared for Jesse W. Fell and John L. Scripps, see *The Collected Works of Abraham Lincoln,* ed. Roy P. Basler, asst. eds. Marion D. Pratt and Lloyd A. Dunlap (New Brunswick: Rutgers University Press, 1953), 3:511–12, 4:60–68.

79. See James Short to William H. Herndon, July 7, 1865, H-W.

80. Herndon and Weik, *Herndon's Life of Lincoln,* 70.

81. Beveridge, *Abraham Lincoln,* 1:111. Beveridge's text names Rowan Herndon as the source of the account he favors, but this is in error and should be Henry McHenry.

82. Thomas, *Lincoln's New Salem,* 65–66. Howells's version was based on interviews by James Quay Howard with John T. Stuart, William G. Greene, and Royal Clary. See David C. Mearns, ed., *The Lincoln Papers* (Garden City: Doubleday, 1948), 1:152–57, for Greene and Clary; for Stuart's account, see the manuscript in the Abraham Lincoln Papers, Library of Congress. Thomas notes that Lincoln let this version stand uncorrected in the copy of Howells's campaign biography he annotated for Samuel Parks. The assumption that whatever Lincoln left uncorrected may be relied upon as accurate is extremely dubious, not only in light of the known errors Lincoln thus "authorized" but also in light of the distinctly political context in which the corrections were sought and rendered.

83. Beveridge, *Abraham Lincoln,* 1:111.

84. Randall, *Lincoln the President,* 1:31n.

85. See William H. Herndon to Jesse W. Weik, Nov. 11, 1885, H-W.

──── 6 ────

Abraham Lincoln and
"That Fatal First of January"

Abraham Lincoln's courtship of Mary Todd, although one of the most colorful and dramatic episodes in his early life, is also one of the least understood. What obscures this critical chapter in Lincoln's maturation and emergence, and in turn hampers our ability to assess its character and importance, is the fragmentary and incoherent form in which the story of the courtship has come down to us. The crux of the problem of what happened to Lincoln during the course of his courtship is the mysterious broken engagement. Lincoln became engaged to Mary Todd in 1840, but by "that fatal first of January, 1841" the engagement had been abruptly broken. How it came to be broken, by whom, and under what circumstances have long been subjects of speculation, but much of the mystery still remains. What follows is an attempt to shed light on the broken engagement, and thus on Lincoln's development, by relating the testimony of the most knowledgeable witnesses to Lincoln's own letters and other contemporary evidence.

The biographer with the best opportunities for determining what happened in the broken engagement, William H. Herndon, ingloriously failed, for he ultimately opted for an account of the affair that does not stand up. After questioning many witnesses and puzzling over the problem for several years, he decided to accept as true the story of Lincoln's failure to appear at his own wedding on the "fatal first of January" 1841.[1] Although some later biographers were still to give it credence, by 1900 Ida M. Tarbell had effectively undermined its credibility by showing that of the surviving friends and relatives—some of the very people who were presumably left waiting with Mary at the altar—none had ever heard of such a thing, and all denounced it as false.[2]

Paul M. Angle tackled the broken engagement in collaborating with Carl Sandburg on *Mary Lincoln: Wife and Widow*, making it the subject of a special appendix, but he lacked full access to the letters and interviews of Herndon's informants (whom he mistrusted) and tried, with inconclusive results, to clarify the picture through reliance on contemporary letters.[3] The most detailed investigation of Lincoln's courtship was made by Ruth Painter Randall.[4] Her rationale of the courtship was part of a highly partisan and self-conscious effort to rescue the character and reputation of Mary Todd Lincoln, but in spite of a prodigious program of research her account is essentially that of Mary's family as first put forward by Elizabeth Edwards and later refined by Frances Wallace, Albert S. Edwards, and Katherine Helm: that Lincoln loved Mary from the beginning and that she returned his love; that because of family opposition and Lincoln's doubts about his ability to make Mary a suitable husband their engagement was broken through a confrontation on January 1, 1841, and a letter of release sent by Mary shortly thereafter; and that in spite of an estrangement of a year and a half, the residual love on both sides eventually triumphed over these obstacles, resulting in the quickly arranged marriage on November 4, 1842.[5] This family version is difficult to reconcile with the testimony of competent witnesses, but for Ruth Randall it was a classic American love story "where a girl of the aristocracy remained loyal to her lover of log-cabin origin, meeting him secretly and defying family opposition to her marrying a man 'on a different social plane.'"[6]

Randall's account of the broken engagement in her biography of Mary Todd Lincoln has long been considered standard, if not definitive, but as Charles B. Strozier has urged, her "explanation of Lincoln's motivation is naive." He calls her smiling version of this troubled courtship "Romeo and Juliet, American style" in that it "posits an external force [the family's disapproval] to explain Lincoln's breaking the engagement."[7] Strozier has argued forcefully that Lincoln's broken engagement is related to his "inner conflicts over intimacy [which] cannot be fully grasped by examining his courtship of Mary Todd." This provocative thesis may have dampened the incentive for a reexamination of the factual history of the courtship, for Strozier accepted Randall's account of the factual details as "not likely to be surpassed."[8] But while acquiescing in Randall's factual account of what happened, Strozier opened up an original and fruitful venue by emphasizing the critical role played by Lincoln's friend Joshua F. Speed, "whose patient friendship during these crucial years first aggravated Lincoln's conflicts, then served as the vehicle for their resolution."[9] The present discussion, accordingly, takes as its starting point Joshua Speed's own account of the broken engagement.

～

Joshua Speed was a well-to-do and well-educated young Kentuckian, a friend of Mary Todd and her Springfield circle, and by all accounts the closest friend Abraham Lincoln ever had. Even Herndon, who yielded to no one in overall knowledge of Lincoln, conceded, on the basis of what Speed told him and the copies of Speed's letters from Lincoln, that Speed had Lincoln's confidence in something he rarely discussed with others: his relations with women. "Lincoln loved this man [Speed] more than any one dead or living; and it may truthfully be said that Lincoln 'poured out his whole soul['] to Speed in his love scrapes with Miss Todd."[10]

In sending Herndon copies of Lincoln's letters to him from this period, Speed explained that a special relationship had existed between himself and Lincoln in the matter of courtship. "In the winter of 40 & 41, he was very unhappy about his engagement to his wife — Not being entirely satisfied that his *heart* was going with his hand. How much he suffered then on that account none know so well as myself. He disclosed his whole heart to me."[11] We have no reason to doubt what Speed says, and for confirmation we have Lincoln's explicit acknowledgment that Speed knew the intimate details of his ordeal. Referring to the personal difficulties surrounding his courtship as a failure "to keep my resolves when they are made," Lincoln wrote to Speed in July 1842: "In that ability, you know, I once prided myself as the only, or at least the chief, gem of my character; that gem I lost — how, and when, you know too well."[12]

What was it that Speed knew? This was the question Herndon asked in an interview with Speed, and his response deserves careful attention. In the original manuscript in the Herndon-Weik Collection, Herndon's notes on what Speed told him about the broken engagement are recorded in two separate, undated entries on different sheets of paper but marked by Herndon with carets, indicating that the two were part of the same narrative and intended to be woven together. The first is as follows:

J. F. Speed
    In 1840 Lincoln went into the southern partt of the state as Election Canvasser debator Speaker — Here first wrote his *Mary* — She darted after him — wrote him — Lincoln — seeing an other girl — & finding he did not love his wife wrote a letter saying he did not love her — ~~Speed saw the letter~~ — tell the Conversation — between Lin-

coln & Speed — Went to see "Mary" — told her that he did not love
her — She rose — and said "the deciever shall be decieved wo is me,"
alluding to a young man she fooled — Lincoln drew her down on his
knee kissed her — & parted — He going one way & she an other —
Lincoln did love Miss Edwards — "Mary" saw it — told Lincoln the
reason of his change of mind — heart & soul — released him — Lincoln went crazy — had to remove razors from his room—take away
all knives and other such dangerous things — &c — it was terrible —
was during the Special session of the Ills Legislature in *1840* Lincoln
married her for honor — feeling his honor bound to her —[13]

This is what Herndon first wrote, apparently at white heat, either as
Speed spoke or as Herndon remembered his testimony. The second part
is written on a separate sheet and apparently represents Herndon's effort to "tell the Conversation—between Lincoln & Speed" about the
proposed letter to Mary Todd:

Speed saw the letter to "Mary" written by Mr Lincoln. Speed tried
to persuade Lincoln to burn it up. Lincoln said — "Speed I always
knew you were an obstinate man. If you won't deliver it I will get
some one to do it. I should not deliver it nor give it to you to be delivered: Words are forgotten — Misunderstood — passed by — not
noticed in a private Conversation — but once put your words in writing and they stand as a living & eternal monument against you. If you
think you have *will* & manhood enough to go and see her and speak
to her what you say in that letter, you may do that. Lincoln did go
and see her — did tell her &c — Speed said — Lincoln tell me what
you said and did" — Lincoln told him — Speed said — The last thing
is a bad lick, but it cannot now be helped — Lincoln kept his promises and did not go to her for months — they got together somehow.[14]

It is clear that this second part was intended to go into the narrative
at the point where Herndon had written, and then struck out, "Speed
saw the letter"; these are the first words of the second passage, and the
first passage is marked at that place with a caret.[15] But simply insert-
ing the second passage at the point indicated has the unfortunate effect
of confusing the chronology, because the second passage, which was
originally intended to "tell the conversation" of Speed and Lincoln,
actually continues the narrative beyond the time of the conversation
and thus, when inserted as indicated, gets ahead of the story. If we attempt to rectify this editorially, by putting the narrated events from the
second passage in sequence, we arrive at the following (the second-pas-
sage material is italicized):

J. F. Speed
   In 1840 Lincoln went into the southern partt of the state as Elec-

tion Canvasser debator Speaker — Here first wrote his *Mary* — She darted after him — wrote him — Lincoln — seeing an other girl — & finding he did not love his wife wrote a letter saying he did not love her — *Speed saw the letter to "Mary" written by Mr Lincoln. Speed tried to persuade Lincoln to burn it up. Lincoln said — "Speed I always knew you were an obstinate man. If you won't deliver it I will get some one to do it. I should not deliver it nor give it to you to be delivered: Words are forgotten — Misunderstood — passed by — not noticed in a private Conversation — but once put your words in writing and they stand as a living & eternal monument against you. If you think you have <u>will</u> & manhood enough to go and see her and speak to her what you say in that letter, you may do that. Lincoln did go and see her —* ... told her that he did not love her — She rose — and said "the deciever shall be deciewed wo is me," alluding to a young man she fooled — Lincoln drew her down on his knee kissed her — & parted — He going one way & she an other — *Speed said —* ["]*Lincoln tell me what you said and did" — Lincoln told him — Speed said — The last thing is a bad lick, but it cannot now be helped* — Lincoln did love Miss Edwards — "Mary" saw it — told Lincoln the reason of his change of mind — heart & soul — released him — Lincoln went crazy — had to remove razors from his room — take away all knives and other such dangerous things — &c — it was terrible — was during the Special session of the Ills Legislature in 1840 *Lincoln kept his promises and did not go to see her for months — they got together somehow.* — Lincoln married her for honor — feeling his honor bound to her —[16]

This seems to represent Herndon's intention, as nearly as it can be inferred, and has the fortunate effect of resolving the chronological discrepancies.[17] Here then, in Herndon's abbreviated and sometimes telegraphic report, is what Speed told him about Lincoln's courtship: Lincoln took up with Mary by letter during his campaign excursion into Egypt (in August and September of 1840), and she responded eagerly. Through his interest in another woman he discovered that he did not love Mary. He wrote this in a letter to Mary but was persuaded by Speed to tell her its import in person. When he confronted her, she reproached herself and wept, at which point he comforted and kissed her, a gesture that Speed put down as a "bad lick." Later, seeing that Lincoln was in love with Matilda Edwards, Mary confronted him, told him she knew how things stood, and released him. This happened during the special session of the legislature in 1840 (November 23 to December 5) and caused Lincoln to go crazy and appear suicidal. Having made a promise (either to himself, to Mary, or to the Edwards family), he did not call on her for many months. When he finally married her, it was to satisfy

his sense of honor, presumably because he felt bound by the commitment he had originally made.

↬

Speed's version of what happened between Lincoln and Mary Todd contains at least two elements that stand out as striking departures from
the versions of Ruth Randall and most authoritative biographers. The
first is the date of the confrontation with Mary that precipitated Lincoln's temporary derangement. The documentary record of Lincoln's
prolonged bout with the "hypo" in January 1841, of which his own letters are a telling part, has suggested to all biographers from Herndon
onward that any suicidal behavior must have come then. But Speed, his
closest friend and confidant, is quite specific that the break with Mary
and the consequent "crazy spell" happened during the special session
of the legislature, which he correctly places in 1840. We shall return to
the matter of chronology in due course. The second thing that stands
out in Speed's account is the critical role played by Lincoln's feelings
for Matilda Edwards in his relations with Mary Todd. Matilda was the
eighteen-year-old daughter of the prominent Whig politician Cyrus
Edwards of Alton, who had brought his daughter along with him in mid-
November when he came to Springfield to attend the upcoming sessions
of the legislature.[18] She stayed in the home of her cousin, Ninian W.
Edwards, the same household in which Mary Todd was living, and she
remained there for many months.[19]

Ninian W. Edwards was also Mary Todd's brother-in-law, and his
version of what brought about the broken engagement accords with
Speed's. As the head of the household to which Mary Todd belonged,
and one who considered himself responsible for her welfare, he was in
a position to know a good deal of what went on between Mary and Lincoln, especially from Mary's point of view. Herndon's notes on his interview with Edwards are given in full:

> Says — Sept 22d 1865 — That during Lincoln's Courtship with Miss
> Todd — afterwards Lincoln's wife — that he, Lincoln, fell in Love with
> a Miss Edwards — daughter of Cyrus Edwards, who was brother of
> Govr N. W. Edwards — Matilda Edwards was her name: she subse-
> quently became the wife of Mr. Strong of Alton. Lincoln did not ever
> by act or deed directly or indirectly hint or speak of it to Miss Edwards:
> she became aware of this — Lincoln's affections — the Lincoln and
> Todd engagement was broken off in consequence of it — Miss Todd
> released Lincoln from the Contract, leaving Lincoln the privilege of
> renewing it (poor fellow H.) if he wished — Lincoln in his conflicts
> of duty — honor and his love went as crazy as a *Loon* — was taken to

Kentucky — by Speed — or went to Speed's — was kept there till he recovered finally — (unfortunate man! H) He was cured — Edwards admits that he wanted Speed to marry Miss Edwards and Lincoln Miss Todd: He gave me policy reasons for it — the substance of which I give in an other place[20] — Matilda Edwards refused Speed — (J. F. Speed of Louisville Ky) as she refused S. A. Douglas — she refused Douglas on the grounds of his bad morals. Lincoln did not attend the Legislature in 1841 & 2 for this reason — so is Mrs Wm Butler correct as to her suspicions.[21]

When taking down this interview, which came fairly early in his investigations, Herndon affected not to have heard of Matilda Edwards, but he was eventually to hear a good deal more.[22] Elizabeth Edwards, the wife of Ninian and the elder sister of Mary Todd, had her own version of what happened. Her testimony Herndon took down in unusual detail. No doubt this was because Elizabeth Edwards was in an even better position to know what was going on between Lincoln and Mary, inasmuch as she had been something of a mother to her younger sister and had taken a close interest in her affairs. Elizabeth was particularly at pains to explain her own and her husband's role in the affair, first encouraging and then discouraging the match, and her account contained an even more startling assertion.

I Knew Mr L well — he was a cold Man — had no affection — was not Social — was abstracted — thoughtful. I Knew he was a great man long years Since — Knew he was a rising Man and nothing Else modifying this, desired Mary at first to Marry L. Could not hold a lengthy Conversation with a lady — was not sufficiently Educated & intelligent in the female line to do so — He was charmed with Mary's wit and fascinated with her quick sagacity — her will — her nature — and Culture — I have happened in the room where they were sitting often & often and Mary led the Conversation — Lincoln would listen & gaze on her as if drawn by some Superior power, irresistably So: he listened — never Scarcely Said a word. I did not in a little time think that Mr L. & Mary were Suitable to Each other & so Said to Mary. Mary was quick, lively, gay — frivalous it may be, Social and loved glitter Show & pomp & power. She was an Extremely Ambitious woman and in Ky often & often Contended that She was destined to be the wife of some future President — Said it in my presence in Springfield and Said it in Earnest. Mr Speed Came to See Miss Matilda Edwards — left & went to Ky — Miss Edwards Staying. Mr Lincoln loved Mary — he went Crazy in my own opinion — not because he loved Miss Edwards as Said, but because he wanted to marry and doubted his ability & Capacity to please and support a wife. Lincoln & Mary were Engaged — Every thing was ready & prepared for the marriage — Even to the Supper &c —. Mr L failed to meet his Engagement — Cause insanity. In his lunacy he declared he hated Mary and loved Miss Edwds. This is true, yet it was not his real feelings. A Crazy man hates those he loves when at himself — often — often is this the Case. The world had it that Mr L backed out. and this placed Mary in a peculiar Situation & to set herself right and to free Mr Lincoln's mind She wrote a letter to Mr L Stating that She would release him from his Engagements. Mr Edwards & myself after the first Crush of things told Mary & Lincoln that they had better not Ever marry — that their natures, mind — Education — raising &c were So different they Could not live happy as husband & wife — had better never think of the Subject again However all at once we heard that Mr L & Mary had Secret meetings at Mr S. Francis' — Editor of the Spfgd Journal. Mary Said the reason this was So — the Cause why it was — that the world — woman & man were uncertain & slippery and that it was best to keep the secret Courtship from all Eyes & Ears. Mrs Mrs L told Mr L that though She had released him in the letter Spoken of — yet She Said that She would hold the question an open one — that is that She had not Changed her mind, but felt as always. The whole of the year year the Crazy Spell Miss Edwards was at our house[23] — Say for a year. I asked Miss Edwards — Subsequently Mrs Strong if Mr Lincoln Ever Mentioned the subject of his love to her. Miss Edwards Said — "On my word he never mentioned Such a Subject to me: he never even Stooped to pay me a Compliment."[24]

Ninian and Elizabeth Edwards clearly had different interpretations of Matilda Edwards's role in what occurred between Lincoln and Mary Todd in the winter of 1840–41, but they agreed that Matilda and Lincoln's supposed love for her had been spoken of.[25] For Ninian, Lincoln's "affections" for Matilda were the cause of the broken engagement, and he probably regarded Lincoln's telling Mary that he loved Matilda as the precipitating factor. For Elizabeth, this outburst was merely a manifestation of Lincoln's insanity. They agreed that Mary gave Lincoln an open-ended release and that he went crazy, but although Ninian's account seems to support Speed's in having the lunacy come after the release, Elizabeth clearly believed the release came by letter after Lincoln's derangement.

What struck Herndon most forcefully in Elizabeth Edwards's testimony was, of course, the sensational story of Lincoln's failure to appear at his own wedding. Herndon may have been skeptical at first, but Mrs. Edwards repeated her story independently to his collaborator, Jesse W. Weik, and Herndon eventually decided to accept it.[26] The decision had important consequences: it not only skewed his entire conception of the courtship, but it also eventually cost him much in the way of credibility as a biographer.

In addition to the testimony of Speed and the Edwardses, Herndon heard about the role of Matilda Edwards from yet another well-placed member of Lincoln's early Springfield circle, James H. Matheny, who was chosen to stand up with Lincoln when he finally married Mary Todd. Some of the details of Matheny's testimony must have horrified Ninian and Elizabeth Edwards when they appeared in Ward Hill Lamon's biography in 1872, but Matheny's testimony corroborates important parts of Ninian's testimony and supports Speed's belief that the ultimate reason Lincoln married Mary Todd was to preserve his honor.[27] In recording his interview with Matheny, Herndon noted:

> That Lincoln and himself in 1842 were very friendly — That Lincoln came to him one evening and said — Jim — "I shall have to marry that girl." Matheny says that on the same evening Mr & Mrs Lincoln were married — That Lincoln looked and acted as if he were going to the slaughter —: That Lincoln often told him directly & indirectly that he was driven into the marriage — said it was concocted & planned by the Edwards family —: that Miss Todd — afterwards Mrs Lincoln told L. that he was in honor bound to marry her —: That Lincoln was crazy for a week or so — not knowing what to do —: that he loved Miss Matilda Edwards and went to see her and not Mrs. Lincoln — Miss Todd.
> Matheny further says that soon after the race — the political friendly race between Baker & Lincoln — which was in 1846 or 7 and after Lincoln was married that Lincoln took him — Matheny to the woods and there and then said in reference to L's marriage *in the aristocracy* — "Jim — I am now and always shall be the same Abe Lincoln that I always was" — Lincoln said this with great Emphasis — The cause of this was that in the Baker & Lincoln race it had been charged that L had married in the aristocracy — had married in the Edwards — Todd & Stuart family.[28]

Herndon's notes suggest a credible context for Lincoln's having spoken candidly to Matheny on so personal and presumably so painful a subject—the galling imputation that he had married for social position "in the aristocracy" when he had actually been maneuvered into a commitment he could not honorably evade. At the same time, it should be noted that Lincoln had a political motive for putting this construction on his marriage, for Matheny was one of a group of young Sangamon County Whigs who resented the aristocratic wing of the party and whose support was apparently shifting from Lincoln to Edward D. Baker.[29] Matheny's other testimony shows that he was not an admirer of Mary Todd, but he seems to be clear in stating that Lincoln told him on several occasions that the Edwards family—presumably Ninian and Elizabeth—had connived at his engagement and that afterward Mary told

Lincoln that "he was honor bound to marry her." He also seems clear that Lincoln told him he had loved and wished to court Matilda Edwards, not Mary Todd.

Those familiar with these witnesses and their relationships to Lincoln will realize that there are things that need to be taken into account. The Edwardses, whose political and personal relations with Lincoln were often strained and who were still chafing at their treatment during Lincoln's presidency when they gave their testimony, were presumably well aware of the charge to which Matheny referred: that Lincoln married into their family for social position. In their testimony, the Edwardses were at pains to emphasize their discouragement of the match, although when he spoke to Herndon alone Ninian had admitted that he originally wanted Lincoln to marry his sister-in-law for "policy reasons." For his part, Lincoln may well have come to see this original encouragement in a different light and thus told Matheny that he had been lured into an engagement that Mary had subsequently told him he could not bow out of with honor. Sensitivity to this charge, along with the rumors that Lincoln had backed out, were surely reasons the Edwardses both stressed Mary's letter of release and its generous, open-ended character.

But the point here is that the four principal accounts of the courtship Herndon collected—those of Joshua F. Speed, Ninian W. Edwards, Elizabeth Todd Edwards, and James H. Matheny—all implicate Lincoln's feelings for Matilda Edwards as a prime factor in the breaking of the engagement. And what is noteworthy about all this testimony naming Matilda Edwards is that it cannot be classified as gossip.[30] All of these informants were either intimates of Lincoln or close relatives of Mary. They are presumably describing for Herndon what they witnessed and were told by the principals themselves, as opposed to what was speculated by others. And although they have varying perspectives and interpretations of what they saw and heard, all of the informants indicate that Lincoln's attraction for Matilda Edwards was a factor in the broken engagement of Lincoln and Mary Todd. Even Elizabeth Edwards, who thought Lincoln did not love Matilda, acknowledged that he told Mary he did.

Although recent biographies of Lincoln or Mary Todd fail even to mention the name of Matilda Edwards, there is a surprising amount of other evidence that supports the testimony that Lincoln had romantic inclinations toward her and that she was at least a passive player in what one contemporary called "the Mary Todd 'embrigglement'."[31] Herndon himself was for several years persuaded of its truth, with the result that Chauncey Black adopted this interpretation in scripting Ward Hill Lamon's biography.[32] A niece of Matilda's, Alice Edwards Quigley, bore witness to the tradition in her family: "Tradition tells us that Lincoln and Douglas were both in love with her."[33] Ninian W. Edwards's son, Albert S. Edwards, also reported that his "family thought that Lincoln was much taken with Matilda, but nothing came of it beyond story-telling and fun-making."[34] Sarah Rickard, herself the object of Lincoln's attentions during this period, remembered something similar.[35]

There were, as Ruth Randall acknowledges, indications in Spring-field's gossip that Matilda Edwards was accounted the cause of Lincoln and Mary's breakup. An example appears in the tradition handed down in the Springfield family of Octavia Roberts, in which Matilda's rela-tionship to Ninian W. Edwards (she was his cousin) has been confused. Roberts, who interviewed many people who had known the Lincolns, wrote: "That [Lincoln's] attraction for [Mary Todd] suddenly ceased all the world knows, but the reasons given for his change of heart differ. My Grandmother, who was Mrs. Lincoln's contemporary, always told her family that it was owing to the visit of Ninian Edward's own sis-ter, who was a beautiful girl, and won Lincoln's love."[36]

But in addition to family traditions and gossip, there is also the in-dependent testimony of two people close to Lincoln and Mary Todd: Mrs. Benjamin S. Edwards and Orville H. Browning. Mrs. Edwards was the wife of Ninian W. Edwards's brother and thus a member of the fam-ily circle. She attended the wedding and is one of the persons who in-sisted to Ida M. Tarbell that the aborted wedding ceremony described in Herndon's biography could not have taken place. She also wrote to Tarbell that Lincoln, at the time of his engagement to Mary Todd, was *"deeply* in love with Matilda Edwards."[37] Orville H. Browning, who was closely associated with Lincoln at the bar and as a fellow Whig legisla-tor, described the affair at length for John G. Nicolay. Mary, according to Browning, "had taken a fancy to Mr. Lincoln and I always thought she did most of the courting until they became engaged." But after their engagement, Browning affirmed, Lincoln "fell desperately in love with [Matilda Edwards], and proposed to her, but she rejected him." During this period, Browning reported, "Miss Todd used to sit down with me, and talk to me sometimes till midnight, about this affair of hers with Mr. Lincoln. In these conversations I think it came out, that Mr. Lin-coln had perhaps on one occasion told Miss Todd that he loved Matil-da Edwards, and no doubt his conscience was greatly worked up by the supposed pain and injury which this avowal had inflicted upon her."[38]

Recollections are valuable, and in the case of Lincoln's early life, indispensable, but the strongest historical evidence is a contemporary document. One such document that strikingly confirms the recollections of Speed, Ninian W. Edwards, Matheny, and the others is a letter from Jane D. Bell in Springfield to Ann Bell in Danville, Kentucky, dated January 27, 1841, which reads in part:

> Miss Todd is flourishing largely. She has a great many Beaus.
>
> You ask me how she and Mr. Lincoln are getting along. Poor fellow, he is in rather a bad way. Just at present though he is on the mend now as he was out on Monday for the first time for a month dying with love they say. The Doctors say he came within an inch of being a perfect lunatic for life. He was perfectly crazy for some time, not able to attend to his business at all. They say he don't look like the same person. It seems he had addressed Mary Todd and she accepted him and they had been engaged some time when a Miss Edwards of Alton came here, and he fell desperately in love with her and found he was not so much attached to Mary as he thought. He says if he had it in his power he would not have one feature in her face altered, he thinks she is so perfect (that is, Miss E.) He and Mr. Speed have spent the most of their time at Edwards this winter and Lincoln could never bear to leave Miss Edward's side in company. Some of his friends thought he was acting very wrong and very imprudently and told him so and he went crazy on the strength of it so the story goes and that is all I know . . . [torn off] No one but Speed . . . [torn off][39]

Although Jane D. Bell did not claim to offer a firsthand account or even to know more than a few details, her source of information seems to be close to Lincoln's circle of friends, the coterie that frequented the Edwards home. Ruth Painter Randall scorns the testimony in this letter as mere gossip, citing the expression "they say" as indicative of its being little more than "wagging tongues." But Jane D. Bell would appear to have been much better connected in such matters than the typical Springfield gossip. She was another Kentuckian, related by marriage to James Bell, the proprietor of James Bell and Company, over whose store Lincoln shared a bed with Bell's first cousin and business partner, Joshua F. Speed.[40] Writing to the sister of James Bell, Jane D. Bell was not so much spreading idle gossip as responding, as the letter clearly shows, to a request for information about the status of a match that must have been of particular interest to Kentuckians—that of the upstart politician Abraham Lincoln and the aristocratic Kentucky belle Mary Todd. Her source is not named, but it seems likely that the most intimate details of the story she sketched were known, in the words of her fragmentary sentence, to "no one but Speed."

↪

Jane D. Bell's pointed reference to the admonitions of Lincoln's friends concerning his behavior points to an issue that requires attention—the possibility that Speed and Lincoln were both in love with Matilda Edwards at the same time. Speed's account is silent on the subject, but both Ninian and Elizabeth Edwards testified explicitly that Speed courted Matilda, and Ninian told Herndon that Speed went so far as to propose marriage and was refused. Elizabeth's testimony even hints that his lack of success with Matilda had something to do with his decision to return to Kentucky: "Mr. Speed came to see Miss Matilda Edwards — left & went to Ky — Miss Edwards staying." Speed himself, although he did not name the woman involved, described his feelings as a failed suitor in a letter to his sister in March 1841 and talked about leaving Illinois for Kentucky.[41] But perhaps the most vivid and telling proof of Speed's pursuit of Matilda Edwards in the winter of 1840 and 1841 is found in another contemporary document: a letter Mary Todd wrote about two weeks before the "fatal" first of January 1841. In the letter, Mary briefed her close friend, Mercy Levering, on the newest arrival on the Springfield social scene: "I know you would be pleased with Matilda Edwards, a lovelier girl I never saw. Mr Speed's ever changing heart I suspect is about offering its young affections at her shrine, with some others."[42] "With some others" confirms what Mary had written earlier and others were to remark: that Matilda had many admirers.

If such testimony may be credited, Speed and Lincoln did both love Matilda Edwards. Whether they were both in love with her at the same time returns us to the first point raised by Speed's account of Lincoln's broken engagement: its chronology. Herndon's ultimate decision to accept Elizabeth Edwards's version of the broken engagement seems to have affected his entire conception of the courtship and caused him to ignore much of what Speed and others had told him, including the recurring testimony about the role of Matilda Edwards.[43] Although he and Weik say little about the chronology of the courtship in their biography, Herndon had blocked one out in a manuscript drafted in the 1880s, "Lincoln and Mary Todd." Here he worked backward from the supposed wedding day, January 1, 1841, and reasoned that the letter to Mary Todd "was handed to Speed about August 1840 probably a little before."

What might be called the accepted chronology of the courtship, inasmuch as virtually every modern biographer employs it, features an extended acquaintance and courtship beginning in 1839, an engagement sometime in 1840, an incident involving another suitor that provokes a jealous reaction from Lincoln, and a confrontation on the first day of January 1841 that sunders the engagement. When we compare this to the account given by Joshua Speed, whose familiarity with the facts was attested by Lincoln himself, we are presented with a very different picture. Speed implies that Lincoln first made romantic overtures to Mary by mail during his electioneering trip to southern Illinois in August and September 1840. Because Lincoln left for the circuit almost immediately upon returning from his electioneering junket in September, he and Mary could have had very few days together before the special session of the legislature, which opened November 23.[44] The session only lasted two weeks and was marked at the end by Lincoln's famous leap from the church window on the final day, December 5. Speed says that it was during this special session that Lincoln had his final interview with Mary Todd and subsequently went crazy and became suicidal, at least four weeks before the first of January 1841. Of course, Speed could have been mistaken, or he could have confused the special session with the regular one that began two days later on December 7. But he does make a point of its being the special session, presumably in order to distinguish it from the regular one and place the incident more precisely in time, and he does date it correctly in 1840. And, surprising as it may seem, this dating fits very well with the other testimony and contemporary evidence.

If Speed's dating is accurate, the events he recounted happened in a fairly short period. Except for two brief stopovers between trips, Lincoln was absent from Springfield between August 18 and November 7 or 8. Matilda Edwards probably arrived about a week later. In Herndon's notes, Speed says that "Lincoln — seeing an other girl — & finding he did not love his wife wrote a letter saying he did not love her." It would seem an obvious inference that Matilda Edwards, whom Speed later named and said Lincoln did love, was the other girl to whom Lincoln was attracted, especially in light of the testimony. According to Speed, Lincoln's first confrontation with Mary, when he told her he did not love her and Mary reproached herself and wept, failed of its intention and actually had the opposite effect of renewing the engagement.[45] But a second confrontation, Speed told Herndon, in which Mary acknowledged Lincoln's love for Matilda, brought the engagement to an end.

Speed's account of the second confrontation is encapsulated in Herndon's notes thus: "Lincoln did love Miss Edwards — 'Mary' saw it — told Lincoln the reason of his change of mind — heart & soul — released him." Speed here has Mary confront Lincoln with his love for Matilda Edwards, but it is quite possible that her remarks about Matilda may have come in response to something offered by Lincoln. There is a persistent and widespread tradition that Mary's flagrant attentions to another suitor—most likely Stephen A. Douglas or Edwin B. Webb—were the cause of an angry remonstrance by Lincoln at their last interview.[46] Although Speed's and Ninian Edwards's testimony suggests that she may have given Lincoln his release at this second encounter, Matheny testified that Lincoln told him of a confrontation in which Mary told him "that he was in honor bound to marry her." But all three informants told Herndon that the breakup precipitated in Lincoln a spell of temporary insanity, which, by Speed's dating, would have had to occur no later than December 5, 1840.

There was certainly a good deal of talk at the time and subsequently about Lincoln's attentions to Matilda Edwards, and although Ninian and Elizabeth Edwards admitted that Lincoln mentioned her name during the course of the breakup, they both insisted that he never addressed her directly in romantic terms. (It is, of course, an indicative circumstance that Elizabeth felt called upon to ask her about it.) Indeed, Matilda's reported denial has been offered as proof that Lincoln could not have been a serious admirer whose partiality brought about the end of his engagement.[47] Matilda was, by all accounts, a beautiful young woman whose presence in Springfield was immediately felt. One of the most revealing documents that confirms this state of affairs is Mary's December 1840 letter to Mercy Levering. Internal references date the letter about December 15, 1840, or ten days after the special session of the legislature ended. Speed's version of what happened between Lincoln and Mary casts the letter in a new light. If Lincoln and Mary had already broken their engagement during the special session, then some long-standing puzzles about the letter, written ten days later, are explained. Mary's letter reads in part:

> Mr Edwards has a cousin from Alton spending the winter with us, a most interesting young lady, her fascinations, have drawn a concourse of beaux & company round us, occasionaly, I *feel as Miss Whitney,* we have too much of such useless commodities, you know it takes some time for habit to render us familiar with what we are not greatly accustomed to — Could you step in upon us some evenings in these 'western wilds,' you would be astonished at the change, time has wrought on the hill, I would my Dearest, you now were with us, be assured your name is most frequently mentioned in our circle, words of mine are not necessary to assure you of the loss I have sustained in your society, on my return from Missouri, my time passed most heavily, I feel quite made up, in my present companion, a congenial spirit I assure you. I know you would be pleased with Matilda Edwards, a lovelier girl I never saw. Mr Speed's ever changing heart I suspect is about offering its young affections at her shrine, with some others, there is considerable acquisition in our society of marriagable gentlemen, unfortunately only 'birds of passage.' Mr Webb, a widower of modest merit, last winter is our *principal lion,* dances attendance very frequently.[48]

When she first introduces the subject of Matilda, Mary becomes vaguely defensive and circumspect; she wanders off the topic but later recovers, reintroducing Matilda by name and praising her. Students of this letter have been puzzled that Mary, although writing to Mercy about the recent and prospective marriages of mutual friends and joking about the "crime of matrimony," says nothing about her own engagement. In fact, in a long letter giving the news of her circle, she pointedly singles out Edwin B. Webb as "our *principal lion.*" His position as Mary's most attentive suitor becomes more interesting later on in the letter when she describes a prospective outing: "we have a pleasant jaunt in contemplation, to Jacksonville, next week there to spend a day or two, Mr Hardin & Browning are our leaders the van brought up by Miss E[dwards] my humble self, Webb, Lincoln & two or three others whom you know not."[49] Because the two leaders of this pleasant jaunt were married men, and Webb's attentions might be expected to be directed toward her, Mary seems to be anticipating the prospective pairing of Lincoln and Matilda Edwards.

Speed's version of the breakup provides a ready explanation for these supposed anomalies: Mary was no longer engaged to Lincoln and had been replaced in his affections by Matilda Edwards. She betrays no outright jealousy, nor would an overt display be expected, but the curious passage that apparently describes her reaction to Matilda's popularity—"occasionaly, I *feel as Miss Whitney,* we have too much of such useless commodities, you know it takes some time for habit to render us familiar with what we are not greatly accustomed to"—suggests that she was less than happy yielding the social spotlight to a newcomer. Whatever awkwardness she may have felt about Matilda, Mary represents her to Mercy Levering as "a congenial spirit" and a surpassingly lovely girl. Having said that Matilda had attracted "a concourse of beaux," Mary apparently felt obliged to tell Mercy just who among their circle had demonstrated romantic interest in this new sensation. She names Joshua Speed, whose "ever changing heart" she suspects is about to be committed, "with some others." The "others," according to Herndon's principal informants and other witnesses, included Abraham Lincoln.

Jane D. Bell's letter, written the following month, reports that Lincoln "and Mr. Speed have spent the most of their time at Edwards this winter and Lincoln could never bear to leave Miss Edward's side in company. Some of his friends thought he was acting very wrong and very imprudently and told him so and he went crazy on the strength of it." Lincoln's going crazy because his friends criticized him for imprudent behavior seems hardly credible, but this report takes on a different meaning when one considers that Lincoln and Speed, who slept in the same bed and were on the most intimate terms, were at this time both in love with the same woman. This meant that they were, inescapably, rivals for the attentions of Matilda Edwards and as such had to experience some degree of tension. Speed apparently did not mention any of this to Herndon, and whatever tension there was obviously did no permanent damage to their friendship, but Speed did describe a fairly heated argument over whether or not it was manly for Lincoln to send Mary Todd a letter rather than tell her face-to-face that he did not love her. Speed represents himself as having had Lincoln's best interests at heart, which may have been the case, but he does not relate what appears likely from other testimony—that Lincoln was trying to free himself from his engagement to Mary Todd in order to court the woman at whose shrine Speed would soon be observed offering his own affections.[50]

That Speed, in these circumstances, should reproach Lincoln for his unseemly attentions to Matilda Edwards—which surely must have been painful and humiliating to Mary Todd—is well within the realm of probability. And that Lincoln should react emotionally to a charge of ungentlemanly behavior from his closest friend, even as he was trying to live down the imputation that his change of heart was dishonorable, is plausible enough and consistent with what his friend Orville H. Browning told Nicolay: "I think that Mr. Lincoln's aberration of mind resulted entirely from the situation he thus got himself into—he was engaged to Miss Todd, and in love with Miss Edwards, and his conscience troubled him dreadfully for the supposed injustice he had done, and the supposed violation of his word which he had committed." In a letter to Speed written more than a year later, Lincoln apparently referred to this episode in justifying his prodding counsel about Speed's own love affair: "Perhaps this point [the constancy of Speed's love for Fanny Henning] is no longer a question with you, and my pertenacious dwelling upon it, is a rude intrusion upon your feelings. If so, you must pardon me. You know the Hell I have suffered on that point, and how tender I am upon it. You know I do not mean wrong."[51]

Ruth Randall argues that if Matilda Edwards had come between Lincoln and Mary Todd, the latter would not have remained her friend. Browning, in fact, told Nicolay that Mary "had very bitter feelings towards her rival Matilda Edwards." But what saved Matilda Edwards from a public display of jealous wrath from Mary Todd is reasonably discernible from the evidence. In the first place, Matilda did not appear to have been seriously interested in the Springfield beaux she attracted in such profusion. It is clear from her letter to her brother on November 30 that she welcomed the attentions of Newton D. Strong, who had accompanied her on the stage from Alton and whom she eventually married.[52] The letter further reveals that, unlike Mary Todd, she was decidedly unworldly.[53] Her cousin Ninian's pleading that she attend a ball she seems to have resisted on grounds of religious piety, and she was later said by Ninian to have rejected the advances of Stephen A. Douglas because of his bad morals, something Mary Todd was not heard to complain about. Speed was also said to have suffered rejection, but his active pursuit of Matilda in December 1840 may well have effectively blocked that of his more inhibited and self-conscious friend Abraham Lincoln.

Although upstaged by his socially accomplished rival in Springfield, Lincoln had at least one outing with Matilda that month in which Speed was not present. The excursion to Jacksonville mentioned in Mary Todd's letter to Mercy Levering came off as projected, as is evident in an unpublished letter from Matilda's father, Cyrus Edwards, in Springfield to his son Nelson in Alton: "Your Sister started with Miss Todd for Jacksonville on Thursday morning under the protection of Mr Hardin, accompanied by Gillespie, Lincoln, Webb and Brown of Vermilion. They will return on Monday. We miss them very much."[54] There was only one Thursday-to-Monday weekend in the latter half of December in which Lincoln might have been absent from Springfield: Christmas weekend from Thursday, December 24, to Monday, December 28.[55] Although Lincoln and Hardin were back in Springfield attending the legislature the following Tuesday, the postmark of Edwards's letter, which is dated the same Tuesday, December 29, suggests that Mary Todd and Matilda Edwards may have remained behind. If Cyrus Edwards meant that the young women who were so much missed were to be in Jacksonville until the Monday following the twenty-ninth, or January 4, then it is possible that Mary Todd was in Jacksonville on the "fatal first of January, 1841" and could not have had an acrimonious confrontation with Lincoln, who was in Springfield.

↜

Speed's version of what happened between Lincoln and Mary Todd, together with the evidence that he himself was in pursuit of Matilda Edwards, also puts some other contemporary documents in a different light. Mary's friend Mercy Levering was carrying on a romantic correspondence with a member of Mary's Springfield circle, James C. Conkling, whom she would soon marry. Their letters are a prime source of contemporary information about the affairs of Lincoln's Springfield, but they, too, have puzzling aspects. In first publishing excerpts from these letters, Paul M. Angle noted that they make it "obvious that the general impression among friends of the couple was that Lincoln had been jilted." Since a letter from Mary in June 1841 showed that she "was anxious that their former relations be resumed," and Lincoln's letter of

March 27, 1842, to Speed indicated "that the break between Lincoln and Mary Todd came on Lincoln's initiative," it was somewhat puzzling to Angle that these contemporary letters should "picture him quite clearly as a *rejected lover.*"[56]

That he is pictured in the letters as the victim of disappointment in love is beyond dispute. As Conkling wrote from Springfield to Mercy Levering on January 24, 1841:

> Last evening I spent upon the Hill [the site of the Edwards and Levering homes]. Mrs. L. informed me she had lately written you and had given you some particulars about Abraham, Joshua and Jacob [Mrs. Lawrason Levering writing about Lincoln, Speed, and Conkling (Jacob Faithful)]. Poor L! how are the mighty fallen! He was confined about a week, but though he now appears again he is reduced and emaciated in appearance and seems scarcely to possess strength enough to speak above a whisper. His case at present is truly deplorable but what prospect there may be for ultimate relief I cannot pretend to say I doubt not but he can declare 'That loving is a painful thrill, And not to love more painful still' but would not like to intimate that he has experienced 'That surely 'tis the worst of pain To love and not be loved again.'
>
> And Joshua too is about to leave. I know not what dreadful blow may be inflicted upon the interests of our State by his departure.[57]

The letters would be even more revealing had not Mercy Levering already written an account of the "particulars," as will be seen in her reply from Baltimore on February 7: "Yesterday I wrote a long letter to Bri__ [Mrs. Lawrason Levering] in answer to her particulars about Abraham, Joshua, and Jacob to which you refer. Poor A__ I fear his is a blighted heart! perhaps if he was as persevering as Mr. W__[58] he might be finally successful. And Joshua too, he has left the prairie state, really I think the citizens of S__ seem to be deserting it. But what more can one expect when the *Patriarchs* are beginning to move!"[59]

Conkling responded from Springfield on March 7:

> The Legislature have dispersed. Whether any persons regret it I cannot pretend to say. Miss Todd and her cousin Miss Edwards seemed to form the grand centre of attraction. Swarms of strangers who had little else to engage their attention hovered around them, to catch a *passing smile.* By the way, I do not think they were received, with even ordinary attention, if they did not obtain a *broad grin* or an *obstreporous laugh.* And L. poor hapless simple swain who loved most true but was not loved again — I suppose he will now endeavor to drown his cares among the intricacies and perplexities of the law.[60]

Read in the light of Speed's version of what happened and the evidence of his and Lincoln's mutual attraction to Matilda Edwards, these letters take on a very different meaning from the one offered by Angle and others. What Conkling and Levering were discussing involved not just Abraham but Joshua as well. And not just Mary Todd, but Matilda Edwards. The "particulars" are not revealed, but the outcome involves Lincoln's disappointment in love and subsequent despondency and Speed's decision to leave the state. If Lincoln and Mary had not kept company since early December 1840 and he had thereafter been attentive primarily to Matilda Edwards, and if, as Elizabeth Edwards testified, the word had gotten around Springfield that Lincoln had backed out on his engagement, it passes belief that Conkling and Levering could have connected his despondency in mid-January with rejection by Mary Todd. His depiction as a victim of disappointment in love in their letters could only have reference to what is spelled out explicitly in Browning's testimony and Jane D. Bell's letter of precisely the same period—his hapless pursuit of Matilda Edwards.

In fact, Conkling's letter points to a more complicated situation than simple rejection, which is what one would expect if several persons were involved. Of Lincoln's "deplorable" case Conkling says, "I doubt not but he can declare 'That loving is a painful thrill, And not to love more painful still' but would not like to intimate that he has experienced 'That surely 'tis the worst of pain To love and not be loved again.'" In other words, although he acknowledges that Lincoln had experienced the painful thrill of loving and not loving (falling in and out of love with Mary), Conkling doubts that Lincoln could claim that he did not know what it was to have his love returned (because Mary returned his love even though Matilda did not). Speed's involvement was presumably as the rival whose active courtship had frustrated the chances of his best friend but resulted in a more definitive form of rejection for himself. In the aftermath, both of these prominent young men were observed as having suffered a serious comedown but with differing results: Lincoln lapsed into despondency, and Speed resolved to sell his business and leave town.

↬

In tracking the critical phase of Lincoln's courtship, it becomes necessary to sort out the reports of Lincoln's temporary insanity. If Speed was right that Lincoln went crazy and became suicidal during the special session of the legislature, then there were at least two distinct episodes: a brief but violent one precipitated by the breakup with Mary Todd in late November or early December 1840 and a longer period of deep despondency that became noticeable and debilitating in January 1841. That the two were related or even parts of the same illness seems quite likely, especially in view of Speed's testimony that Lincoln wrote a long letter to Dr. Daniel Drake about his mental condition in "Decr 40 or early in January 41," a period that would appear to fall between the two episodes and that may well have been recalled by Speed on that basis.[61]

If the first episode occurred when Speed says it did, the contemporary record shows no evidence of it, for Lincoln's attendance at the special session of the legislature was nearly perfect and no document or testimony has come to light to confirm Speed's dating. But precisely the same may be said for the first day of January 1841, the date usually assigned for the onset of Lincoln's derangement, because the contemporary record shows no sign of anything unusual having occurred on that date. But this lack of contemporary evidence is perhaps only puzzling because an interested posterity has made so much of what would otherwise be rather obscure and distinctly private personal matters.

The second "crazy spell" is the one most often referred to, and it is well documented. During early January Lincoln began to miss rollcalls in the legislature, was finally reported ill, and was definitely absent from January 13 through January 18.[62] He referred to his "hypochondriaism" and unshakable depression in his own letters to his partner, John T. Stuart: "I am now the most miserable man living. If what I feel were equally distributed to the whole human family, there would not be one cheerful face on the earth. Whether I shall ever be better I can not tell; I awfully forebode I shall not."[63] The distraught Lincoln was described in Conkling's letter of January 24 as visibly altered: "reduced and emaciated in appearance and seems scarcely to possess strength enough to speak above a whisper."[64] Lyman Trumbull recalled that the Lincoln of this period (in language that is worth noting) "was engaged in love affairs which some of his friends feared had well-nigh unsettled his mental faculties."[65]

Apparently not all his associates thought of this January episode as desperate. H. W. Thornton, a fellow member of legislature, told Ida M. Tarbell, "Mr. Lincoln boarded at William Butler's, near to Dr. Henry's, where I boarded. The missing days [when Lincoln was absent from the legislature], from January 13th to 19th, Mr. Lincoln spent several hours each day at Dr. Henry's; a part of these days I remained with Mr. Lincoln. His most intimate friends had no fears of his injuring himself. He was very sad and melancholy, but being subject to these spells, nothing serious was apprehended."[66] Orville H. Browning, while admitting that the episode was not a trivial matter, stressed its temporary character: "As I now remember his derange[ment] lasted only about a week or such a matter. He was so much affected as to talk incoherently, and to be delirious to the extent of not knowing what he was doing. In the

course of a few days however it all passed off, leaving no trace whatever. I think it was only an intensification of his constitutional melancholy — his greater trials and embarrassments pressed him down to a
lower point than at other times."[67]

We have seen that Lincoln's "trials and embarrassments" were vaguely amusing to James C. Conkling and Mercy Levering, and contemporary letters show that some of his other acquaintances were lighthearted
about his situation. In late December 1840 John J. Hardin's family had
hosted the Jacksonville excursion party referred to earlier and must have
had some familiarity with how things stood regarding Lincoln, Mary
Todd, and Matilda Edwards. Very soon thereafter they came to make the
social rounds in Springfield, returning to Jacksonville on January 14,
about the time of Lincoln's seclusion. Writing back to her brother from
Jacksonville, John J. Hardin's sister, Martinette, expressed curiosity and
amusement: "We have been very much distressed, on Mr Lincolns account; hearing he had two Cat fits, and a Duck fit since we left. Is it
true? Do let us hear soon."[68] Hardin must have responded reassuringly,
because four days later his wife, Sarah, told her husband, "I am glad to
hear Lincoln has got over his cat fits we have concluded it was a very
unsatfactory way of terminating his romance[.]   he ought to have died
or gone crazy[.]   we are very much dissapointed indeed[.]   Jane Goudy
has made him the hero of a tale but she say it will never do for him to
get well."[69] The quip about dying or going crazy may have already made
the rounds, for John T. Stuart seems to have written something of the
sort to Lincoln in late January, to which Lincoln replied on February 3:
"You see by this, that I am neither dead nor quite crazy yet."[70]

Sarah Rickard reported in later life that her sister, Mrs. William Butler, took Lincoln into her home and cared for him during the worst of
his illness. "Mr Lincoln did not seem to recover, and my sister, who had
watched him closely, decided that he had something on his mind. At
last she decided upon a plan of action, and one day went into Mr. Lincoln's room, closed the door, and walking over to the bed, said: 'Now,
Abraham, what is the matter? Tell me all about it.' And he did. Suffering under the thought that he had treated Mary badly, knowing that she
loved him and that he did not love her, Mr. Lincoln was wearing his
very life away in an agony of remorse. He made no excuse for breaking
with Mary, but said, sadly, to my sister: 'Mrs. Butler, it would just kill
me to marry Mary Todd.'"[71]

Most modern biographers seem to agree with Paul M. Angle that
Lincoln's admission to Speed in 1842 that he continued to suffer for
having contributed to someone's unhappiness implies that it was he
who broke the engagement with Mary Todd. The nature of the evidence

makes it possible to argue the question either way or even to conclude that the engagement simply did not survive whatever occurred at the second confrontation, with neither party having decisively broken the engagement.[72] Recent biographers assume, as did Herndon, that the engagement was broken on the first day of January because of Lincoln's famous reference to "that fatal first of Jany. '41" in his letter to Speed.[73] But it is important to note that none of the witnesses said anything about this date, and there is evidence to suggest that Mary Todd may not even have been in Springfield on the first day of January. Placing the aborted wedding on that date is part of the speculative chronology worked out by Herndon, but it is no more speculative than the assumption of modern writers that the engagement of Lincoln and Mary Todd was broken off on that day.[74] In fact, the only thing that happened on January 1, 1841, that may well have had a bearing on the affair and for which there is firm evidence is Speed's liquidation of his interest in James Bell and Company's store.[75]

⤻

But if the "fatal first of January 1841" does not refer to the traumatic breaking of the engagement of Lincoln and Mary Todd, what does it refer to? For that we must go back to the letter and the context in which the phrase occurs. Lincoln's letter containing the famous phrase "that fatal first of Jany. '41" was written on March 27, 1842, nearly a month after Speed's marriage to Fanny Henning. In sending Herndon copies of Lincoln's remarkably revealing letters, Speed explained: "In the summer of 1841, I became engaged to my wife. He [Lincoln] was here on a visit when I courted her. And strange to say something of the same feeling which I regarded as so foolish in him took possession of me — and kept me very unhappy from the time of my engagement until I was married. This will explain the deep interest he manifested in his letters on my account."[76] Speed's unhappiness, which apparently amounted to a disposition to back out on his own engagement, is the subject of three letters from Lincoln to Speed before his marriage on February 15 and two more in the immediate aftermath.

In these intensely personal letters, Lincoln counsels Speed to put aside his doubts and see the marriage through, arguing that Speed's love of his fiancée was genuine, whereas his doubts and apprehensions merely transitory. The letter of March 27 containing the reference to "that fatal first of January" is Lincoln's response to Speed's acknowledgment a month after the wedding that he has weathered the storm and is "far happier than [he] ever expected to be." Lincoln's jubilation is so unbridled as to seem excessive and serves to demonstrate what has been obvious in his other letters, namely that Lincoln had been so deeply involved vicariously in the progress of Speed's ordeal that he experienced Speed's happiness (or lack of it) as his own. In an earlier letter, Lincoln had told Speed: "You well know that I do not feel my own sorrows much more keenly than I do yours, when I know of them."[77] When he received the much-anticipated letter from Speed confirming the fact of his marriage, Lincoln confessed: "I opened the [letter], with intense anxiety and trepidation — so much, that although it turned out better than I expected, I have hardly yet, at the distance of ten hours, become calm."[78]

This is the background and context for Lincoln's seemingly extravagant response to Speed on the subject of his marriage:

> But on that other subject, to me of the most intense interest, whether in joy or sorrow, I never had the power to withhold my sympathy from you. It can not be told, how it now thrills me with joy, to hear you say you are *'far happier than you ever expected to be.'* That much I know is enough. I know you too well to suppose your expectations were not, at least sometimes, extravagant; and if the reality exceeds them all, I say, enough, dear Lord. I am not going beyond the truth, when I tell you, that the short space it took me to read your last letter, gave me more pleasure, than the total sum of all I have enjoyed since that fatal first of Jany. '41.[79]

It is evident that Lincoln's allusion to "that fatal first of January" was intelligible to Speed. Although readers of this passage have assumed that Lincoln's phrase refers to a notable event in his own life, the context of the passage, and that of the entire series of letters up to this point, suggests that it refers to an event in the life of Speed. The predominant theme of this and the other letters is Lincoln's empathy—an extreme form of empathy in which the emotional polarity of one directly relates to that of the other. When Lincoln had been despondent and in the throes of an irresolvable dilemma about his situation in the winter of 1841, Speed had been his counselor. Speed tells of admonishing Lincoln "in his deepest gloom" that he must get a grip on himself or die.[80]

But just as Lincoln was finally showing signs of recovering in the sanctuary of Speed's home in Kentucky in the summer of 1841, Speed was entering into an engagement that almost immediately began to make him "very unhappy." Now the polarity reversed itself, and Lincoln became the mainstay and counselor of Speed. This state of affairs continued through the fall of 1841, because Lincoln remained, as he said, free of the "hypo," and Speed, who had accompanied him back to Springfield, became increasingly more apprehensive. Lincoln kept up a steady barrage of counsel and encouragement before and after the wedding until he finally received word in March that Speed was happier than he ever expected to be. The reference to "that fatal first of January" is problematical because its appearance in Lincoln's letter of March 27 marks the exact point at which the polarity is again reversed.

What has obscured the reference to "that fatal first of January," and obscures it still, is that it appears in the correspondence at precisely the point where Lincoln switches from celebrating and basking in Speed's good fortune to reflecting on the uncertain state of his own emotions. After the "fatal first of January" passage, the letter of March 27 continues: "Since then, [that is, since receiving Speed's letter] it seems to me, I should have been entirely happy, but for the never-absent idea, that there is *one* still unhappy whom I have contributed to make so. That still kills my soul. I can not but reproach myself, for even wishing to be happy while she is otherwise."[81] After months of absorption in Speed's anxieties, Lincoln acknowledged the inexorable presence and reemergence of his own.

In a shrewd characterization of the Lincoln-Speed relationship, Gary L. Williams observes that the two men had been trading off on the roles of doctor and patient and that this letter constitutes the turning point in the correspondence. Lincoln, who had been playing the doctor, "showed signs of renewed weakness," and in the next exchange of letters the roles were again reversed and Speed was again advising Lincoln.[82] Whatever figure one uses, emotional polarity or doctor and patient, it seems clear that the mention of "that fatal first of January" invoked, perhaps quite inadvertently, the specter of Lincoln's own troubled conscience. It is this invocation that suggests to the reader that Lincoln must have been referring to an event in his own life, and although it would be idle to suggest that the possibility is without merit, due account must be taken of the fact that the sentence to which the phrase belongs, and the letter itself—indeed, the entire correspondence up to that point—was not concerned with Lincoln's personal affairs or state of mind but was rather sharply focused on his emotional involvement on Speed's behalf. The critical sentence and phrase are cast in the spirit of sympathy that Lincoln, "whether in joy or sorrow," says he is powerless to withhold: "I am not going beyond the truth, when I tell you, that the short space it took me to read your last letter, gave me more pleasure, than the total sum of all I have enjoyed since that fatal first of Jany. '41."

Reinforcing the notion that the event referred to was an untoward event in the life of Speed is the strange case of Sarah Rickard. In sending copies of Lincoln's letters, Speed told Herndon: "I have eraced a name which I do not wish published. If I have failed to do it any where, strike it out when you come to it — That is the word Sarah."[83] There are three references to Sarah in the surviving correspondence, and although her name has been romantically connected to Lincoln, the references make it appear that there had been a relationship between Sarah and Speed.[84] This is especially evident in the last of the references, which comes shortly after the "fatal first of January" passage and in the context of Lincoln's continuing concern for his friend's fears and apprehensions:

> You know with what sleepless vigilance I have watched you, ever since the commencement of your affair; and altho' I am now almost confident it is useless, I can not forbear once more to say that I think it is even yet possible for your spirits to flag down and leave you miserable. If they should, dont fail to remember that they can not long remain so.
>
> One thing I can tell you which I know you will be glad to hear; and that is, that I have seen Sarah, and scrutinized her feelings as well as I could, and am fully convinced, she is far happier now, than she has been for the last fifteen months past.[85]

The context indicates that Sarah's feelings were still a matter of concern to Speed. Lincoln's references to Sarah, which Speed pointedly told Herndon to delete, suggest that he may have been acting in Speed's behalf, either as his emissary or his confidential agent. And in reporting on the state of her feelings, Lincoln refers to something that caused her pain or unhappiness fifteen months previously. This is another reference that is obviously intelligible to Speed, and it implies quite clearly that whatever happened to affect Sarah's feelings adversely in such a way as to be of continuing concern to Speed happened at the beginning of January 1841. It seems clear that the reference to "that fatal first of Jany. '41" and the reference that follows shortly to "fifteen months past" are certainly to the same time period and perhaps to the same date.[86] Does this imply that the "fatal first of January" refers to something that involved or affected Sarah Rickard?

A contemporary letter from Speed to William Butler may bear on the question. Butler and his wife Elizabeth reportedly took Lincoln in and cared for him in the depths of his despondency the previous January. And Sarah Rickard, for whom Lincoln seems at one time to have had a mild attraction, was the sister of Elizabeth Butler and frequently a member of the Butler household. In his letter to Butler, dated May 18, 1841, Speed wrote: "I am glad to hear from Mrs Butler that Lincoln is on the mend. Say to him that I have had but one attack since I left Springfield and that was on the river as I came here — I am not as happy as I could be and yet so much happier than I deserve to be that I think I ought to be satisfied —".[87] Here we see how their "hypochondriaism" was regarded by Speed and Lincoln as a bond between them, and we see further that Speed represents himself to Butler as being happier than he *deserved* to be. The reference was doubtless meaningful to Butler and may have referred to Speed's guilt over the unhappiness of his friend's sister-in-law. Could Speed have been in the same situation with Sarah as Lincoln was with Mary—having hurt her feelings by declaring his love for another? If so, it seems likely, if acutely ironic, that the "other" in both cases was Matilda Edwards.

Abraham Lincoln's courtship of Mary Todd remains an incomplete tableau, and the events surrounding the broken engagement still compose a mystery. But certain elements in the story are clarified in the evidence adduced above, and their significance may now be better understood. First, the accepted chronology of the courtship and Lincoln's "crazy spells" must be revised and the effects thereof on his behavior reassessed. For example, the actual breaking off of the engagement may now be seen as more closely related to the leap from the church window at the end of the special session than to Lincoln's collapse as an effective political leader in January 1841. Next, Lincoln's well-attested attraction for Matilda Edwards and its effect on his engagement to Mary Todd needs to be acknowledged and taken into account. This means, for example, that Ruth Painter Randall's Romeo and Juliet model will have to be drastically altered or dispensed with entirely. Third, a hitherto hidden element in Lincoln's emotional crisis—his romantic rivalry over Matilda Edwards with his closest friend, Joshua Speed—must now be weighed in the biographical balance. This has obvious implications for a psychological line of inquiry, such as that pursued by Strozier, for example, but should prove of interest and importance to all biographers. Finally, the provocative phrase "that fatal first of January" needs to be recognized as an ambiguous reference at the very least, and a problematical one at best, that may well relate less to Lincoln than to fateful developments in the life of his intimate friend Joshua Speed. These substantial changes in the accepted account of Lincoln's courtship may not yield all the answers that students of his early life and career are seeking, but they do present interesting new questions.

NOTES

1. Herndon's earliest theory regarding the broken engagement is detailed in the letter to Ward Hill Lamon, Feb. 25, 1870, in Lamon Papers, Huntington Library, printed in *The Hidden Lincoln: From the Letters and Papers of William H. Herndon,* ed. Emanuel Hertz (New York: Viking Press, 1938), 62–69. A later and much-altered version occurs in his manuscript account titled "Lincoln and

Mary Todd" in the Herndon-Weik Collection, Manuscript Division, Library of Congress (hereafter cited as H-W). His final version appears in the biography on which he collaborated with Jesse W. Weik, *Herndon's Life of Lincoln*, ed. Paul M. Angle (Cleveland: World Publishing, 1949), 166–71.

2. See Ida M. Tarbell, *The Life of Abraham Lincoln* (New York: Lincoln Memorial Association, 1900), 1:176–80. Albert J. Beveridge is the most prominent of later biographers to adopt Herndon's account of the aborted wedding.

3. See Angle's appendix in Carl Sandburg and Paul M. Angle, *Mary Lincoln: Wife and Widow* (New York: Harcourt, Brace, 1932), 329–50.

4. Ruth Painter Randall had three tries at it. She collaborated with her husband on the account given in J. G. Randall, *Lincoln the President: Springfield to Gettysburg* (New York: Dodd, Mead, 1945), 1:51–62; she went over the ground in great detail in a full-length biography, *Mary Lincoln: Biography of a Marriage* (Boston: Little, Brown, 1953), 36–51; and she retraced her steps in a popularized account, *The Courtship of Mr. Lincoln* (Boston: Little, Brown, 1957), 111–30.

5. Elizabeth Todd Edwards's account is given in two undated interviews with William H. Herndon, H-W; Frances Wallace's appears in *Lincoln's Marriage: Newspaper Interview . . . Springfield, Ill., Sept. 2, 1895* (Privately printed, 1917); Albert S. Edwards's is given in Walter B. Stevens, *A Reporter's Lincoln* (St. Louis: Missouri Historical Society, 1916), 73–79; and Katherine Helms's appears in her biography of her aunt, *The True Story of Mary, Wife of Lincoln* (New York: Harper and Brothers, 1928), 86–91.

6. Randall, *Mary Lincoln*, 64.

7. Charles B. Strozier, *Lincoln's Quest for Union: Public and Private Meanings* (Urbana: University of Illinois Press, 1987), 39.

8. Strozier, *Lincoln's Quest for Union*, 39.

9. Ibid., 41.

10. Herndon, "Lincoln and Mary Todd."

11. Joshua F. Speed to William Henry Herndon, Nov. 30, 1866, H-W.

12. Abraham Lincoln to Joshua F. Speed, July 4, 1842, in *The Collected Works of Abraham Lincoln*, ed. Roy P. Basler, asst. eds. Marion D. Pratt and Lloyd A. Dunlap (New Brunswick: Rutgers University Press, 1953), 1:289 (hereafter cited as *Collected Works*).

13. The passage "Lincoln went crazy . . . 1840" is written vertically on the same sheet in the left margin, with carets indicating its insertion point.

14. In his biography, Herndon expands on the exchange between Lincoln and Speed over the letter and fills in details about what transpired between them when Lincoln returned. See Herndon and Weik, *Herndon's Life of Lincoln*, 168–69.

15. Such an insertion is precisely what was done by the copyist, John G. Springer, in transcribing Herndon's "Lincoln Records," now part of the Ward Hill Lamon Papers at the Huntington Library.

16. Note that in this conflated version the crossed-out material, the instruction ("tell the conversation—between Lincoln & Speed"), and the overlapping phases ("did tell her &c —" and "Went to see 'Mary' —") have been eliminated.

17. Ruth Randall's failure to sort these matters properly leads her to accuse Herndon of deliberate misstatements. See Randall, *Mary Lincoln*, 45. In *Lincoln*

the President (1:59) she and James G. Randall hold that Speed's account as first put down in Herndon's notes has the release by Mary come in that same interview after Lincoln kissed her and is therefore at odds with that given by Herndon and Weik. But even as it stands in the manuscript, without the chronological matters adjusted, it is hard to see how Herndon's report on his interview with Speed can be read this way, for in his notes the statement about the release comes after the conclusion of the first interview ("He going one way & she an other —") and is clearly given as a result of Mary's later observation of Lincoln's attentions to Matilda Edwards.

18. The Edwards's arrival in Springfield must have occurred sometime before the opening of the special session of the legislature on November 23, 1840. Matilda's first letter home, addressed to her brother Nelson, is dated November 30 and describes her stagecoach ride from Alton, suggesting that she had only been in Springfield a short time. A photostat of the letter is in the Randall Papers, Library of Congress; it is quoted by Ruth Painter Randall in *The Courtship of Mr. Lincoln,* 69–70. For permission to examine the Randall Papers, I am grateful to David Donald and, for assistance in using them, to John R. Sellers.

19. See Elizabeth Todd Edwards's statement to Herndon on page 106.

20. This account does not seem to be in the Herndon-Weik Collection and has not been located.

21. Ninian W. Edwards interview with William H. Herndon, Sept. 22, 1865, H-W.

22. Although Herndon writes as though he had never heard of Matilda Edwards, this seems merely to be a style of reporting followed early in his investigations in which he affects to be an unknowing recorder of information. Note that he gives Speed's initials and even his address although he knew perfectly well to whom Edwards was referring. He wrote out some of his early interviews as though they were letters to himself and had the interviewees sign them.

23. Herndon originally wrote, "In about one year from the Crazy Spell."

24. Herndon's notes for this interview in the Herndon-Weik Collection are undated, but in the original edition of *Herndon's Lincoln* (227) it is dated January 10, 1866.

25. It is clear from his solo interview and from other testimony referred to later that Ninian W. Edwards disagreed with his wife's view of what happened but acquiesced in her version when they were interviewed together. Indirect confirmation of this comes from Mrs. John T. Stuart, who told Ida M. Tarbell, "The late Judge Broadwell told me that he had asked Mr. Ninian Edwards about [the aborted wedding ceremony], and Mr. Edwards told him that no such thing had ever taken place." Tarbell, *Life of Lincoln,* 1:177–78.

26. Herndon may have questioned Elizabeth Edwards again about this years later, although his notes, written after the interview on July 27, 1887 (H-W) make no mention of it. Weik's diary entry of his interview on December 20, 1883, is given in Beveridge, *Abraham Lincoln,* 1:313n-14n.

27. See Ward Hill Lamon, *The Life of Abraham Lincoln; From His Birth to His Inauguration as President* (Boston: James R. Osgood, 1872), 243. In addition

to selling copies of his Lincoln materials to Lamon in 1869, Herndon provided explanations and interpretations by letter that were incorporated into the biography by Lamon's ghostwriter, Chauncey Black.

28. James H. Mathey interview with William H. Herndon, dated May 3, 1866, H-W. Curiously, Matheny is the only witness to support Elizabeth Edwards's story of the aborted wedding. Weik said he spoke several times with Judge Matheny about the broken engagement and concluded that "the marriage was originally set for a day in the winter of 1840–41, probably New Year's Day, and Judge Matheney always insisted that he had been asked to serve as groomsman then." *The Real Lincoln*, 60.

29. Herndon spells out this circumstance explicitly in "Lincoln and Mary Todd."

30. Ruth Painter Randall's depiction of Ninian W. Edwards as merely retailing the Springfield gossip about his sister-in-law strains belief and is perhaps understandable only in terms of her undisguised wish to undermine his testimony. See Randall, *Mary Lincoln*, 49.

31. Attributed to "Uncle" Jesse Dubois in Milton Hay to John Hay, Feb. 8, 1887, in "Recollection of Lincoln: Three Letters of Intimate Friends," *Bulletin of the Abraham Lincoln Association* 25 (Dec. 1931): 9. An example of a well-received recent biography that ignores the testimony regarding Matilda Edwards, and Matilda herself, is Jean H. Baker, *Mary Todd Lincoln: A Biography* (New York: W. W. Norton, 1987).

32. See Lamon, *Life of Abraham Lincoln*, 239–41.

33. Reproduced in H. O. Knerr, "Abraham Lincoln and Matilda Edwards," mimeographed typescript (Allentown, Pa.: N.p.), Illinois State Historical Library.

34. Stevens, *A Reporter's Lincoln*, 75.

35. See the long interview with Sarah Rickard Barret and her husband, Richard F. Barret, reported by Nellie Crandall Sanford for the St. Louis *Globe-Democrat*. A clipping of the article, datelined "Kansas City, Missouri, February 9," without heading or page number but dated in pencil "1907," is in the files of the Lincoln Collection, Illinois State Historical Library.

36. Octavia Roberts, "We All Knew Abr'ham," *Abraham Lincoln Quarterly* 4 (March 1946): 27. The mistake of identifying Matilda as the sister of Ninian occurs in Ward Hill Lamon's biography and may have worked its way into Springfield traditions from that source. See Lamon, *Life of Abraham Lincoln*, 239.

37. Mrs. B. S. Edwards to Ida M. Tarbell, Oct. 8, 1895, Ida M. Tarbell Papers, Allegheny College Library.

38. "Conversation with Hon. O H Browning at Leland Hotel Springfield June 17th 1875," manuscript in Nicolay's hand, John Hay Papers, Brown University Library. I am indebted to Michael Burlingame for generously sharing his discovery of Nicolay's important interviews. In *Lincoln* (New York: Simon and Schuster, 1995), David Herbert Donald allows that "those who blamed Matilda Edwards for the rupture seem to have their information from Mary Todd" and that "there is no credible evidence that Lincoln was in love with Matilda Edwards" (612n). This seems to suggest that if Mary Todd blamed Matilda Edwards for the breakup it should not be believed and that none of the testimony of

Joshua F. Speed, Ninian W. Edwards, Elizabeth Todd Edwards, James H. Matheny, Orville H. Browning, Mrs. B. S. Edwards, or Jane D. Bell can claim credibility.

39. This text is taken from a copy of the letter supplied to John B. Clark of Lincoln Memorial University in 1948 by Mary B. E. (Mrs. Henry) Jackson, a relative of the writer of the letter, identified as Jane Hamilton Daviess Bell, and in turn copied and supplied to James G. Randall by R. Gerald McMurtry on November 7, 1950. Randall Papers, Manuscript Division, Library of Congress. The text varies slightly from the extract printed in the *Lincoln Herald* 50–51 (Dec. 1948–Feb. 1949): 47, which omits the final fragment. The original of this letter has not been located.

40. For an account of the relationship of Bell and Speed (their mothers were sisters), see George W. Frye, *Colonel Joshua Fry of Virginia and Some of His Descendants and Allied Families* (Cincinnati: N.p., 1966), 39, 103–4, 169–70. I am indebted to Thomas F. Schwartz and Jeffrey Douglas for assistance in establishing the relationship of Bell and Speed.

41. "I have been most anxiously in pursuit of one — and from all present appearances, if my philosophy be true I am to be most enviably felicitous, for I may have as much of the anticipation and pursuit as I please, but the possession I can hardly ever hope to realize." Joshua Speed to Eliza Speed, March 12, 1841, Illinois State Historical Library.

42. Mary Todd to Mercy Levering, Dec. [15?] 1840, in *Mary Todd Lincoln: Her Life and Letters*, ed. Justin G. Turner and Linda Levitt Turner (New York: Alfred A. Knopf, 1972), 20.

43. Herndon believed for some time what his informants had told him, that Lincoln's love for Matilda was a factor in the broken engagement, but he later acceded to Elizabeth Edwards's contention that it was not a factor and so left Matilda out of *Herndon's Lincoln*. See his statement in "Lincoln and Mary Todd."

44. See *Lincoln Day by Day: A Chronology, 1809–1865*, ed. Earl Schenck Miers and William E. Baringer (Washington: Lincoln Sesquicentennial Commission, 1960), 1:147.

45. Herndon quotes Speed as telling Lincoln, "You not only acted the fool, but your conduct was tantamount to a renewal of the engagement, and in decency you cannot back down now." Herndon and Weik, *Herndon's Life of Lincoln*, 169.

46. See, for example, Baker, *Mary Todd Lincoln*, 90–91.

47. Herndon in "Lincoln and Mary Todd," Angle, and Ruth Painter Randall all share this position.

48. Mary Todd to Mercy Levering, Dec. [15?], 1840, in *Mary Todd Lincoln*, ed. Turner and Turner, 20.

49. Ibid., 22.

50. Consider, in this light, Lincoln's remark to Speed eighteen months later: "I believe now that, had you understood my case at the time, as well as I understood yours afterwards, by the aid you would have given me, I should have sailed through clear." Abraham Lincoln to Joshua F. Speed, July 4, 1842, *Collected Works*, 1:289.

51. Abraham Lincoln to Joshua F. Speed, Feb. 3, 1842, *Collected Works*, 1:268.

52. "tell [Cal] that I praised her very much to Mr S and said nothing for myself except that I had very *Strong* attachments." Matilda Edwards to Nelson Edwards, Nov. 30, 1841, photostat in Randall Papers, Library of Congress.

53. See excerpts from this letter in Randall, *The Courtship of Mr. Lincoln*, 70.

54. Cyrus Edwards to Nelson G. Edwards, Dec. 1840. I am grateful to Mrs. R. H. Chrisco for permission to examine and quote from the Edwards family papers, now in the Knox College Library.

55. See Miers and Baringer, eds., *Lincoln Day by Day*, 1:149–50.

56. Sandburg and Angle, *Mary Lincoln*, 330, 331.

57. Ibid., 178–79.

58. This is usually taken to be Edwin B. Webb, Mary's most attentive suitor, but later references to "Mr. W__" in the correspondence make it appear that he was a persistent suitor of Mercy Levering's in Baltimore.

59. Sandburg and Angle, *Mary Lincoln*, 179–80.

60. Ibid., 180.

61. Joshua F. Speed to William Henry Herndon, Nov. 30, 1866, H-W.

62. Miers and Baringer, eds., *Lincoln Day by Day*, 1:151–52.

63. Abraham Lincoln to John T. Stuart, Jan. 20, 23, 1841, *Collected Works*, 1:228, 229.

64. James C. Conkling to Mercy Levering, Jan. 24, 1841, in Sandburg and Angle, *Mary Lincoln*, 179.

65. Horace White, *The Life of Lyman Trumbull* (New York: Houghton Mifflin, 1913), 427, quoted in Paul Simon, *Lincoln's Preparation for Greatness: The Illinois Legislative Years* (Urbana: University of Illinois Press, 1971), 238.

66. H. W. Thornton quoted in Tarbell, *Life of Lincoln*, 180. Thornton believed this refutes Herndon's report that Lincoln was suicidal, but it does not speak to the issue of suicidal behavior in November or early December.

67. Orville H. Browning, interview with John G. Nicolay. The last sentence is quoted in Nicolay and Hay's biography, where the details of Lincoln's romantic difficulties are entirely suppressed and his temporary insanity explained away. See John G. Nicolay and John Hay, *Abraham Lincoln: A History* (New York: Century, 1914), 1:187.

68. Martinette Hardin to John J. Hardin, Jan. 22, 1841, Hardin Family Papers, Chicago Historical Society. Martinette, known as "Netty," later married Alexander R. McKee, which is why the manuscript of this letter is misleadingly labeled and its contents attributed to "Martin McKee" by the editors of the *Collected Works* (1:229n) and subsequent writers. Ruth Painter Randall, for example, refers to the writer as a "slangy gentleman" in *The Courtship of Mr. Lincoln*, 114.

69. Sarah E. Hardin to John J. Hardin, Jan. 26, [1841], Hardin Family Papers, Chicago Historical Society. Jane Goudy was the daughter of the Jacksonville printer Robert Goudy and wrote verse romances, at least two of which were published by her brothers in 1842: *Minstrel: A Tale in Verse* and *Woman's Pride: A Metrical Romance*. I am grateful to Terence A. Tanner for this and much other useful information.

70. Abraham Lincoln to John T. Stuart, Feb. 3, 1841, in *The Collected Works of Abraham Lincoln: Supplement, 1832–1865*, ed. Roy P. Basler (Westport: Greenwood Press, 1974), 6.

71. For the source of this testimony, see note 35. There seems to be no reason to dispute this particular story, and the letter from Speed to William Butler cited in note 87 lends confirmation. But it should be noted that this provocative interview was given more than sixty-five years after the events described, and there is evidence that some of what Sarah Rickard Barrett told the reporter was very likely colored by, if not gleaned entirely from, Herndon's biography. Her account of the courtship, however, is entirely different from Herndon's.

72. At least one witness, A. Y. Ellis, testified that it was his understanding that Mary broke the engagement. He told Herndon: "I had it from good authority that after Mr. L. was engaged to be Married to his wife Mary. That she a short time before they were married backed out from her engagement with him; He was at the time a Member of the Legislature *then in Session* in your City; and her refusal to Comply actually made Mr. L Sick and Consequently went to bed and No one was allowed to see him but his friend Josh Speed & his friend the Doctor I think Henry. And that strong Brandy was administered to him freely for about one Week And I was also informed that his friend Speed brought about a reconcliation between them I was at that time in business with Bell & Speed under the Name of A Y Ellis &c & I Could only See Mr. Speed occationally." A. Y. Ellis to William H. Herndon, written on Herndon's letter to Ellis of March 24, 1866, H-W.

73. Abraham Lincoln to Joshua F. Speed, March 27, 1842, *Collected Works*, 1:282.

74. For example, the editors of the *Collected Works*, 1:282, confidently identify "that fatal first of Jany. '41" as "the date on which Lincoln asked to be released from his engagement to Mary Todd."

75. "I sold out to Hurst 1 Jany 1841. and came to Ky in the spring —." Joshua F. Speed to William H. Herndon, Sept. 17, 1866, H-W. This is cited by Strozier, who also cites a notice to this effect that appeared in the *Sangamo Journal* on Jan. 8, 1841. Strozier, *Lincoln's Quest for Union*, 242n.

76. Joshua F. Speed to William H. Herndon, Nov. 30, 1866, H-W.

77. Abraham Lincoln to Joshua F. Speed, Feb. 3, 1842, *Collected Works*, 1:267.

78. Abraham Lincoln to Joshua F. Speed, Feb. 25, 1842, *Collected Works*, 1:280.

79. Abraham Lincoln to Joshua F. Speed, March 27, 1842, *Collected Works*, 1:282.

80. Joshua F. Speed, *Reminiscences of Abraham Lincoln and Notes of a Visit to California. Two Lectures* (Louisville, 1884), 39.

81. Abraham Lincoln to Joshua F. Speed, March 27, 1842, *Collected Works*, 1:282.

82. Gary Lee Williams, "James and Joshua Speed: Lincoln's Kentucky Friends," Ph.D. diss., Duke University, 1971, 30.

83. Joshua F. Speed to William H. Herndon, Nov. 30, 1866, H-W.

84. I agree with Paul M. Angle, Ruth Painter Randall, and Gary L. Williams,

who argue that the references in these letters to Sarah suggest a romantic connection with Speed rather than Lincoln. Certainly Sarah's own account of Lincoln's attentions to her, which she gave to reporter Nellie Crandall Sanford at great length later in life (note 35) is entirely consistent with a friendly relationship that was attentive but only teasingly hinted at courtship.

85. Abraham Lincoln to Joshua F. Speed, March 27, 1842, *Collected Works*, 1:282.

86. Paul M. Angle points out these implications in Sandburg and Angle, *Mary Lincoln*, 346ff.

87. Joshua F. Speed to William Butler, May 18, 1841, William Butler Papers, Chicago Historical Society, photostat in the Illinois State Historical Library.

7

Abraham Lincoln and the
"Spirit of Mortal"

Abraham Lincoln was fond of poetry. As a young man, he memorized and recited the best-known poems of Robert Burns, admired Lord Byron, and cultivated a taste for Shakespeare that would last throughout his life. Perhaps more than any other president, the self-educated Lincoln invoked his familiarity with English verse, particularly the plays of Shakespeare, as a means of dealing with the pressures and burdens of office. But his favorite poem, which he would recite alongside passages from *Hamlet*, was so obscure that until the last months of his life he never knew it in an authoritative text or even knew the name of its author.

"Mortality" by the Scottish poet William Knox is better known by its first line—"O why should the spirit of mortal be proud?"—but it is safe to say it is only known or remembered at all in association with Abraham Lincoln. This was true even in Lincoln's lifetime, when he was sometimes identified as the poem's author, an attribution he found flattering. "Beyond all question, I am not the author," he wrote to a correspondent. "I would give all I am worth, and go in debt, to be able to write so fine a piece as I think that is."[1] Judging by the number of times he is reported to have praised it, recited it, and dictated or copied it out for friends during the last twenty years of his life, it seems reasonable to conclude with David C. Mearns that this obscure poem "had a special meaning for Abraham Lincoln."[2]

Lincoln's recitation of "Mortality" must have been extremely effective to judge by the reactions of witnesses. One of the most revealing accounts is provided by Francis B. Carpenter, who engaged Lincoln in literary conversation while painting his portrait in the White House. Carpenter described an evening spent in Lincoln's study when the president began talking about Shakespeare and then read several of his favorite passages, something he did often and with great effect. "Relapsing into a sadder strain," Carpenter wrote, "he laid the book aside, and leaning back in his chair, said, 'There is a poem that has been a great favorite with me for years, to which my attention was first called when a young man, by a friend, and which I afterward saw and cut from a newspaper, and carried in my pocket, till by frequent reading I had it by heart. I would give a great deal,' he added, 'to know who wrote it, but I never could ascertain.' Then, half closing his eyes, he repeated the poem, 'Oh! why should the spirit of mortal be proud?'"[3] Carpenter's reaction was typical of Lincoln's listeners: he was surprised and delighted, and he asked for a copy of the text.

Unlike its special meaning for Abraham Lincoln, "Mortality"'s meanings are not at all obscure. Its theme—that life is fleeting and death inevitable—is modulated in each of its fourteen quatrains and accented by the framing question of the first and last lines:

O why should the spirit of mortal be proud!
Like a swift flying meteor—a fast flying cloud—
A flash of the lightning—a break of the wave,
He passeth from life to his rest in the grave.

The leaves of the Oak, and the Willow shall fade,
Be scattered around, and together be laid.
And the young and the old, and the low and the high,
Shall moulder to dust, and together shall lie.

The infant a mother attended and loved—
The mother that infant's affection who proved
The husband that mother and infant who blest,
Each—all are away to their dwellings of rest.

The maid on whose brow, on whose cheek, in whose eye
Shone beauty and pleasure—her triumphs are by;
And alike from the memory of the living erased
And the memory of mortals, who loved her and praised—

The hand of the King, that the scepter hath borne,
The brow of the priest that the mitre hath worn,
The eye of the Sage, and the heart of the Brave,
Are hidden, and lost in the depth of the grave—

The saint who enjoyed the communion of Heaven,
The sinner who dared to remain unforgiven;
The wise and the foolish, the gentle and just,
Have quietly mingled their bones in the dust—

The peasant whose lot was to sow and to reap.
The herdsman who climbed with his goats up the steep,
The beggar who wandered in search of his bread,
Have faded away like the grass that we tread.

So the multitude goes like the flower or weed,
That withers away to let other succeed,
So the multitude comes, even those we behold,
To repeat every tale that has often been told.

For we are the same our fathers have been,
We see the same sights our fathers have seen,
We drink the same stream, and view the same sun,
And run the same course our fathers have run—

The thoughts we are thinking our fathers would think,
From the death we are shrinking our fathers would shrink;
To the life we are clinging they also would cling,
But it speeds from us all like a bird on the wing—

They loved, but the story we can not unfold,
They scorned, but the heart of the haughty is cold,
They grieved, but no wail from their slumber will come,
They joyed, but the tongue of their gladness is dumb—

They died! Aye, they died. We things that are now—
That walk on the turf that lies over their brow,
And make in their dwellings a transient abode,
Meet the things that they met on their pilgrimage road.

Yea, hope and despondency, pleasure and pain,
Are mingled together in sun shine and rain—
And the smile, and the tear, and the song, and the dirge,
Still follow each other like surge upon surge—

Tis the wink of an eye, tis the draught of a breath
From the blossom of health to the paleness of death—
From the gilded saloon to the bier and the shroud—
O why should the spirit of mortal be proud?[4]

Intended by the poet as a recapitulation of the third chapter of Job and
the first chapter of Ecclesiastes, its Old Testament fatalism is unremitting and notably unrelieved by any suggestion of an afterlife. The fate
of man—low or high, young or old—is that of the leaves: both "shall
moulder to dust." Man's joys and his grief, his love and his scorn, are
all mere repetitions of those of his forebears and come to nothing. The
predominant fact of life is death. Pride in so transient a thing as mortality is obviously misplaced.

↬

There can be little doubt that there was a connection between Lincoln's affinity for "Mortality" and his recurrent melancholy. One of the most conspicuous features of Lincoln's personal demeanor was his frequent lapses into moods of profound depression. He seems to have been subject to these spells from an early date, although he probably attempted to disguise them at first. He told a fellow legislator in his New Salem days "that although he appeared to enjoy life rapturusly[,] Still he was the victim of terrible melancholly. He sought Company and indulged in fun and hilarity without restraint, or Stint as to time[.] Still when by himself, he told me that he was so overcome with mental depression, that he never dare carry a knife in his pocket."[5]

Albert J. Beveridge noted that those who rode the circuit with Lincoln all referred to these moods. "Everybody observed his abysmal sadness. His gloom was not periodical and succeeded by weeks of brightness, but was made manifest every day, yet interwoven with hours of abnormal gayety—black despondency and boisterous humor following one another like cloud and sunshine in a day of doubtful storm."[6] Jesse W. Weik thought these reports must be exaggerated and so made a point of questioning those who knew Lincoln best: John T. Stuart, James H. Matheny, Judge Samuel Treat, Judge David Davis, Leonard Swett, Henry C. Whitney, and others. Their responses convinced him "that men who never saw him could scarcely realize this tendency to melancholy."[7]

Whether Lincoln was seriously suicidal when he told Robert Wilson that he dared not carry a pocket knife is not certain, but the association of his despondent moods with the contemplation of death would eventually become evident. His closest friends were concerned for his safety as well as his sanity when he lapsed into despondency after the death of Ann Rutledge. And the agony of his emotional crisis over his engagement to Mary Todd caused him to contemplate death and possibly even suicide as a remedy. But his darkest moods were more than tinged with morbidity; as Beveridge has pointed out, they were "strongly colored by apprehension of personal disaster. 'Billy, I fear that I shall meet with some terrible end,' he said to his partner upon coming out of one of these fits of dejection."[8]

What is notable here is that these moods or spells were often associated with a recurrence to poetry. Although his stories were known for their humor, his favorite poems were most often sad. His attraction for Oliver Wendell Holmes's "The Last Leaf" was such that some regarded it as his favorite, particularly the fourth stanza:

The mossy marbles rest
   On lips that he has pressed
      In their bloom;

And the names he loved to hear
Have been carved for many a year
    On the tomb.

Lincoln told Carpenter, "For pure pathos, in my judgment, there is
nothing finer than those six lines in the English language!"[9] He also
evinced a partiality for Edgar Allan Poe's "The Raven," which he often
recited. "The music of Lincoln's thought," wrote John G. Nicolay, "was
always in a minor key."[10]

But the poem most closely associated with Lincoln's melancholy by
those who knew him was Knox's "Mortality," a title so little recognized
that the poem is almost always referred to by its first line, "O why
should the spirit of mortal be proud?" Harriet Chapman, who lived with
the Lincolns in Springfield for a time in the mid-1840s, told Herndon,
"When he would be or appeard to be in a deep Study — Commence and
repeat aloud Some piece that he had taken a fancy to and Commited to
Memory Such as the one you *have already* in print ["Mortality"]."[11]
Judge Lawrence Weldon, who as a young man traveled with Lincoln on
the circuit, described Lincoln's habit of rising early before the other
lawyers and seating himself before the fire. There the others would find
him, "his mind apparently concentrated on some subject, and with the
saddest expression I have ever seen in a human being's eyes."[12] Weldon
remembered that on one of these occasions Lincoln "quoted aloud and
at length from the poem called 'Immortality.'"[13] During his presidency, Lincoln recited and praised the poem so often that it was sometimes
reprinted and attributed to him. By then it had taken on a special importance for Lincoln, for he is reported to have told a group of friends
that the poem was his "constant companion; indeed, I may say it is
continually present with me, as it crosses my mind whenever I have
relief from anxiety."[14]

↬

Lincoln's law partner and biographer, William H. Herndon, thought he
had discovered the special meaning that "Mortality" held for Lincoln.
In gathering information on the early years in New Salem, Herndon
unexpectedly came across the story of Lincoln's tragic love affair with
Ann Rutledge, something he had previously known nothing about. From
two dozen informants he gathered overwhelming testimony that Lincoln not only courted and became engaged to Ann Rutledge but also that
he became temporarily deranged with grief after her death in 1835.[15]
When he further discovered that Jason Duncan, who, Lincoln told Carpenter, had first showed him the poem as a young man, was an acquaintance in New Salem, Herndon conceived a bold hypothesis. "I've found

out the history of the poem called 'Immortality,'" he informed a friend. "The facts which I shall reveal, for the first time in the world, throw a footlight on Mr. Lincoln's sad life."[16]

The footlight came in a lecture Herndon delivered in Springfield on November 16, 1866, which he had printed up for distribution in advance and entitled "Abraham Lincoln. Miss Ann Rutledge. New Salem. Pioneering, and THE POEM." In a "pre-Raphaelite" mode of address as eccentric as his title, Herndon speculated that Lincoln's famous melancholy was precipitated by the death of Ann Rutledge and that "O why should the spirit of mortal be proud?" was shown to him at the time, became fixed in his mind, and was thereafter recited in memory of Ann, the only woman he ever loved. This and other aspects of the lecture offended the Lincoln family and much of his nineteenth-century audience and consequently earned Herndon a name for irresponsible speculation that continues to this day.

In his biography, published twenty-three years later, Herndon put forward a more moderate version of his theory: "It was shortly after this [Lincoln's derangement at the death of Ann Rutledge] that Dr. Jason Duncan placed in Lincoln's hands a poem called 'Immortality.' . . . He committed these lines to memory, and any reference to or mention of Miss Rutledge would suggest them, as if 'to celebrate a grief which lay with continual heaviness on his heart.' There is no question that from this time forward Mr. Lincoln's spells of melancholy became more intense than ever."[17] Herndon had thus satisfied himself that the significance of Lincoln's favorite poem and his peculiar affinity for it lay deep in his great partner's psyche, that it bore a direct relationship to the traumatic death of his first love, Ann Rutledge, and that the poem's hold on Lincoln was therefore datable from shortly after Ann's death. This is an intriguing conjecture, and Herndon had collected reliable testimony that lent it credence. The most telling was Isaac Cogdal's reported conversation with Lincoln in 1860 or 1861 in which the president-elect admitted not only that he had loved Ann dearly but also that he still thought of her often.[18] As David C. Mearns allowed, if we can accept the reality of Lincoln's romance with Ann Rutledge, Lincoln's attachment to the poem is thus "perfectly explained."[19]

But even though scholarship has demonstrated that the basic elements of the Ann Rutledge romance can be confidently accepted, other factual difficulties make Herndon's theory altogether unlikely.[20] His biographer David Donald thought Herndon had no reason to think that Lincoln had known "Mortality" at New Salem, but he was mistaken.[21] The key to Herndon's theory is the role of Jason Duncan.[22] Herndon had no idea who Duncan was or how or when he was acquainted with Lincoln, but by a

persistence that was characteristic of his investigations he tracked Duncan down late in 1866 and subsequently corresponded with him.[23] Only
one letter from Duncan survives in the Herndon-Weik Collection, a rather
full reminiscence of his years in New Salem as a close personal friend of
Lincoln's. No mention is made, however, of the thing Herndon was most
interested in: the Knox poem. Moreover, although Duncan volunteered
that he "knew [Lincoln] had great partialities for Miss Ann Rutledge," he
reported that he left New Salem in the autumn of 1834 and said nothing
about the love affair or Ann's death, which occurred a year later.[24]

In his 1866 lecture Herndon said Lincoln had been shown the poem
in September 1833 and that he then took it up two years later at the
time of Ann's death. What evidence Herndon had for this is not apparent, but in his biography he changed the time of Lincoln's first acquaintance with the poem to after Ann's death in 1835.[25] None of the surviving documentation supports either conclusion. Nor does there seem
to be any testimony to support Herndon's contention in his lecture that
Lincoln began reciting the poem to his friends at this time. Often abused
for taking positions that subsequently proved to be fully warranted,
Herndon's strong intuition about Lincoln's attachment to "THE POEM"
seems here to have caused him to overreach his evidence.

⤿

A series of letters that Herndon may never have seen puts "Mortality,"
and Lincoln's attraction for it, in a different light.[26] In 1846 and 1847
Lincoln sent four letters to a lawyer and political associate, Andrew
Johnston of Quincy, enclosing some poetry in each of them. In the first
letter, dated February 24, 1846, he included the text of "Mortality,"
which Johnston had previously requested. But Lincoln seems to have
had a further motive for writing. "By the way," he asks Johnston, "how
would you like to see a piece of poetry of my own making?"[27] Johnston
must have expressed interest, for each of the next three letters contained
what Lincoln described as a separate division or canto of a longer poem
that he had written.[28]

Lincoln had been something of a poet much of his life. As a young
man in Indiana, he not only wrote verses but also gained something of
a reputation by doing so. He even recited some of his Indiana verses to
his friends in New Salem in the 1830s.[29] Herndon discovered that there
were old friends in Indiana who could still remember and recite some
of his verses thirty-five years after he had moved away.[30] In the provocative essay "Lincoln and the Riddle of Death," Robert V. Bruce has
called attention to some verses Lincoln wrote in his commonplace book
of 1824 through 1826:

Time what an emty vaper tis and days how swift they are
swift as an indian arrow fly on like a shooting star
the present moment Just is here then slides away in haste
that we can never say they're ours but only say they're past[31]

Lincoln did not compose these lines, which constitute the opening of
a hymn by Isaac Watts.[32] The fact that he wrote them down, however,
as Bruce notes, "ought to have interested his biographers."[33] Certainly
what Bruce calls Lincoln's "adolescent keynote" sounds what would
become, with the mature Lincoln, a very familiar theme.

Although little of Lincoln's verse survives, Gibson Harris testified
that when he was a clerk in Lincoln's law office from 1845 to 1847, he
found in a drawer a substantial manuscript of what appeared to be original poetry in Lincoln's hand. As he remembered, these "stanzaed
effusions . . . were all, or nearly all, iambics and pensive in tone." Lincoln would not discuss them, but Herndon told Harris "Yes, he has
sometimes scribbled verses, I believe, but he seems unwilling to have
it known."[34] Lincoln's letters to Johnston of this same period seem to
represent a cautious venturing in another direction.

In the second letter to Johnston, dated April 18, 1846, Lincoln combined an explanation of what he knew about "Mortality" with an account of the circumstances under which he was led to compose the
original canto he was sending to Johnston. After denying authorship of
"Mortality," he told Johnston, "I met it in a straggling form in a newspaper last summer, and I remember to have seen it once before, about
fifteen years ago, and this is all I know about it."[35] This would put his
first acquaintance with the poem at about the time he first arrived in
New Salem in 1831, at approximately the same time Jason Duncan told
Herndon he arrived. The letter then turns immediately to the poem
Lincoln included: "The piece of poetry of my own which I alluded to, I
was led to write under the following circumstances. In the fall of 1844,
thinking I might aid some to carry the State of Indiana for Mr. Clay, I
went into the neighborhood in that State in which I was raised, where
my mother and only sister were buried, and from which I had been
absent about fifteen years. That part of the country is, within itself, as
unpoetical as any spot of earth; but still, seeing it and its objects and
inhabitants aroused feelings in me which were certainly poetry; though
whether my expression of those feelings is poetry is quite another question."[36] The original verses thus described constitute a forty-line poem
beginning, "My childhood's home I see again."[37]

The association of "Mortality" with his own poem about his return
to southwestern Indiana can hardly have been accidental. Lincoln's

poem begins with the pleasures of memory and moves toward a dramatic recognition of death as the principal force in the passage of time. Memory, the poem says, purifies and transforms the past:

> And, freed from all that's earthly vile,
>   Seem hallowed, pure, and bright,
> Like scenes in some enchanted isle
>   All bathed in liquid light.[38]

But to come to terms with the reality of the present, the poet is forced to acknowledge the overwhelming presence of death.

> The friends I left that parting day,
>   How changed, as time has sped!
> Young childhood grown, strong manhood gray,
>   And half of all are dead.

> I hear the loved survivors tell
>   How nought from death could save,
> Till every sound appears a knell,
>   And every spot a grave.

The swiftness of time and the all-conquering grave are, of course, precisely the motifs of "Mortality," the poem that Lincoln said he had first seen some fifteen years previously.[39] Although his characterization of the poem as appearing in "a straggling form" may mean that he remembered its proper form from his previous acquaintance with it, the implication of what Lincoln told Johnston seems to be that he had taken little cognizance of the poem in the fifteen intervening years. Herndon convinced himself that Lincoln recited it frequently from the time of Ann Rutledge's death, although Lincoln's closest friend of the ensuing years, Joshua F. Speed, may not even have recognized it.[40] But the second time around, in the summer of 1845, there is no question that "Mortality" made a profound impression on Lincoln. We know that this was the case, for Gibson Harris remembered that in his two years at Lincoln's law office, which began in September 1845, it was Lincoln's "favorite of favorites." "Many a time at the office did he recite this poem, in whole or in part; for a while I actually thought he had written it, so nearly did it resemble, in tone and meter, one of several compositions of his own that I had found in the office desk."[41]

The electioneering trip to his unpoetical childhood neighborhood in Indiana in October 1844 is an obscure event in Lincoln biography, and the year 1845 is barely noticed by most biographers. But something important seems to have come out of the Indiana experience, and the rediscovery of "Mortality" the following summer may have crystalized it in Lincoln's mind and given it expression. He had come very far in the world since leaving Indiana in 1830. From his hardscrabble beginnings with nothing to encourage education, he had risen to surprising heights. He had become educated, he had gained a profession, and he had achieved, by his political efforts, a measure of recognition. As Benjamin Thomas observes, "He had been disciplined by marriage and family responsibilities and by four years of association with Stephen T. Logan. He had regained his mental balance after the fiasco of 'the fatal first of January.' Home life and political disappointments had taught him patience and self-control. He had come to the front in politics against strong and determined rivals."[42] Of the man who became his law partner about the time of this trip, Herndon says, "Mr. Lincoln had unbounded and unlimited confidence in his own mental powers, he was himself and wholly self-reliant, asking no man anything."[43] What this confident and self-reliant man encountered in his boyhood neighborhood in Indiana was probably as unexpected as it was unforgettable— the humbling fact of human mortality.

This is not, of course, to say that Lincoln had never confronted the fact or the prospect of death before 1844. He had endured devastating losses through the deaths of his mother, his only sister, and his fiancée Ann Rutledge and had contemplated self-destruction as a means of escaping his torturous mental depression. But having survived these traumatic events and surmounted the formidable obstacles of poverty, ignorance, and obscurity, his experience in Indiana seems to have presented him with the reality of his own mortality in a new perspective.

The profound emotional effect that Lincoln felt on his visit to Indiana calls to mind the plight of one of Lincoln's idols, Thomas Jefferson, when stationed in Paris. Replying to a correspondent who had reported much local news, including the deaths of some of his acquaintances, Jefferson conjured up a fate for himself that is almost exactly that of Lincoln's: "Fancy to yourself," he told his correspondent, "a being who is withdrawn from his connections of blood, of marriage, or friendship, of acquaintance in all their gradations, who for years should hear nothing of what has passed among them, who returns again to see them and finds the one half dead. This strikes him like a pestilence sweeping off the half of mankind. Events which had they come to him one by one and in detail he would have weathered as other people do, when presented to his mind all at once are overwhelming."[44]

If Lincoln's beguilement with "Mortality" in the summer of 1845 was prompted by what had happened to him on his trip to Indiana the previous fall, his poem "My childhood's home I see again" may be regarded as an autobiographical record of that incident. As such, it appears to be an enactment of why the "spirit of mortal" should not be proud. The poem's most forceful passages are of the boyhood friends he expected to see and the startling changes time had interposed:

> Young childhood grown, strong manhood gray,
>   And half of all are dead.

The poem tells how listening to the "survivors" speak of those who have died magnifies the sense of mortality and produces the sensation that every sound is a death knell "and every spot a grave." To visit old friends and familiar places is hardly to bask in the honors of the present or even relive the pleasures of the past, for the poem ends:

> I range the fields with pensive tread,
>   And pace the hollow rooms,
> And feel (companion of the dead)
>   I'm living in the tombs.

The former friends and neighbors by whom the moderately triumphant Lincoln had expected to be greeted were greatly changed—and half of all were dead.

⌐

Lincoln became a very different man over the course of the next twenty years and yet his attachment to "Mortality" remained. If anything, it deepened. One of the things that makes it difficult for us to fathom this connection is the difference in sensibility between Lincoln's time and our own. Lincoln's taste was very much a product of the nineteenth century, with its notorious appetite for sorrow and sentimentality artfully laid on. As a result, the poem that to a twentieth-century reader may seem a "jingle" and a "tedious dirge" was to Lincoln a very different thing.[45] The anapestic meter that we may regard as artificial and inappropriate to its subject, he seems to have found soothing. Sentiments that may seem to us lugubrious or depressing actually consoled him in times of anxiety and grief. Far from sounding trite or bathetic, the poem, Lincoln told a friend, "sounded as much like true poetry as anything he had ever heard."[46]

What Lincoln got from the poem is not easy to specify, although it was undoubtedly related to his chronic melancholy and his well-established preoccupation with death. Robert V. Bruce, whose discussion of Lincoln and the "riddle of death" is especially penetrating, says, "The hold this poem had on Lincoln's mind was extraordinary. It obviously spoke to his soul."[47] By Lincoln's own testimony, the poem crossed his mind whenever he experienced "relief from anxiety."[48] His eulogy on

Zachary Taylor in 1850, which he concluded by quoting six stanzas of "Mortality," yields further clues.[49] Immediately before quoting the lines, Lincoln observed, "The death of the late President may not be without its use, in reminding us, that *we*, too, must die. Death, abstractly considered, is the same with the high as with the low; but practically, we are not so much aroused to the contemplation of our own mortal natures, by the fall of *many* undistinguished, as that of *one* great, and well known, name. By the latter, we are forced to muse, and ponder, sadly: 'Oh, why should the spirit of mortal be proud.'"[50]

At the time of his trip to Indiana in 1844, and perhaps in succeeding years as well, the one great name that filled the mind of the inordinately ambitious and self-confident Abraham Lincoln was his own. That half of all the people he had known as a boy should have been claimed by death was a shock for which, as his autobiographical poem suggests, he was wholly unprepared. As he confessed to his friend Johnston, seeing those things had aroused strong feelings. The experience forced him to see himself not as the returning prodigal but as a "companion of the dead." For a man who had once professed the "doctrine of necessity" and was inclined toward fatalism, this unexpected confrontation with mortality may have resulted in something like a revelation. Death was inevitable. It was not, as his previous experience had led him to think, an unlucky misfortune for the victim or an undeserved affliction for the bereft; rather, it was an irreducible fact—the crowning fact of all human striving no matter how vaunted or satisfying or successful. Such a discovery was not without its consolations, and these would prove even more useful later on. But the prodigal's pride had been misplaced, and his mood was caught by a poem he realized he had been shown fifteen years earlier, soon after leaving his childhood home in Indiana, but whose meaning he had been unprepared by experience to appreciate.

Seeing the inception of Lincoln's affinity for "Mortality" in this context holds out the possibility of enhancing our understanding of his development, for it helps to explain how and under what circumstances a touchstone expression became firmly established in his consciousness. From 1845 onward, "Mortality" served as an emotional tonic for a man subject to recurrent and virtually disabling melancholy. He recited it frequently for his friends and invoked it as a means of relief from anxiety in times of despondency and grief. Its appeal, to be sure, was partly esthetic, but it must also have been substantive. It seems to have appealed to the same susceptibility that made Watts's lines about time as an empty vapor of interest in the 1820s. The appeal of "Mortality" must also have been grounded in an identification with the basic imagery of the poem—fathers and sons, time, birth and death, and the earth—imagery, as James Hurt has argued, that is thematically continuous in Lincoln's writings from the Lyceum speech of 1838 to the Gettysburg Address.[51]

Finally, the poem was undoubtedly related to what Robert V. Bruce has aptly characterized as the "haunting sense of human transience and ultimate helplessness—a sense in which all men are indeed equal—[that] deepened [Lincoln's] compassion, forbearance, and ability to comprehend both the extent and the bounds of what was possible in the brevity of life."[52] For Abraham Lincoln, Knox's "Mortality" seemed to lay out the fatalistic facts of life and death in a way that assuaged his anguish, which, as his life unfolded toward greatness, was an anguish that embraced an ever-widening circle of mortality.

NOTES

1. Abraham Lincoln to Andrew Johnston, April 18, 1846, in *The Collected Works of Abraham Lincoln*, ed. Roy P. Basler, asst. eds. Marion D. Pratt and Lloyd A. Dunlap (New Brunswick: Rutgers University Press, 1953), 1:378 (hereafter cited as *Collected Works*).

2. David C. Mearns, "'The Great Invention of the World': Mr. Lincoln and the Books He Read," in *Three Presidents and Their Books: The Reading of Jefferson, Lincoln, and Franklin D. Roosevelt* (Urbana: University of Illinois Press, 1955), 83.

3. Francis B. Carpenter, *Six Months at the White House with Abraham Lincoln* (New York: Hurd and Houghton, 1867), 58.

4. The text cited is that written out by Lincoln in 1849 for Lois E. Newhall, transcribed from the photographic reproduction in Maurice Boyd, *William Knox and Abraham Lincoln: The Story of a Poetic Legacy* (Denver: Sage Books, 1966), xlv-vii. This differs slightly from the authoritative text of the poem in the extremely rare collected edition of Knox's poetry (1847), which is reproduced in Boyd. Another version in Lincoln's hand, written out for Mrs. Edwin Stanton during his presidency and reproduced by Boyd, is lacking one stanza (seven); the version dictated to Francis B. Carpenter lacked two (four and seven). The earliest known Lincoln version, dictated to his law clerk Gibson Harris between 1845 and 1847, is in the Illinois State Historical Library.

5. Robert L. Wilson to William H. Herndon, Feb. 10, 1866, Herndon-Weik Collection, Manuscript Division, Library of Congress (hereafter cited as H-W).

6. Albert J. Beveridge, *Abraham Lincoln, 1809–1858* (Boston: Houghton Mifflin, 1928), 1:521.

7. Jesse W. Weik, *The Real Lincoln* (Boston: Houghton Mifflin, 1922), 112.

8. Beveridge, *Abraham Lincoln,* 1:524. Herndon referred to Lincoln's predisposition to melancholy as a "morbid condition." Weik, *The Real Lincoln,* 113.

9. Carpenter, *Six Months at the White House,* 59. Several people mention

Lincoln's fondness for this poem, but Henry Clay Whitney singles it out as Lincoln's "all the year round" favorite. See *Life on the Circuit with Lincoln*, ed. Paul M. Angle (Caldwell, Idaho: Caxton Printers, 1940), 425.

10. John G. Nicolay quoted in Helen Nicolay, *Personal Traits of Abraham Lincoln* (New York: Century, 1912), 367.

11. Mrs. Harriet Chapman to William H. Herndon, Nov. 21, 1866, H-W. Harriet's memory had been prompted by just having read Herndon's lecture on Ann Rutledge, in which "Mortality" is prominently featured.

12. Judge Lawrence Weldon quoted in Beveridge, *Abraham Lincoln*, 1:523.

13. Weldon quoted in William H. Herndon and Jesse W. Weik, *Herndon's Life of Lincoln*, ed. Paul M. Angle (Cleveland: World Publishing, 1949), 257. Strangely, Herndon and other contemporaries believed the title of the poem was "Immortality."

14. Reported by William D. Kelley in *Reminiscences of Abraham Lincoln by Distinguished Men of His Time*, ed. Allen Thorndyke Rice (New York: North American Review Publishing, 1886), 268. See Boyd, *William Knox and Abraham Lincoln*, xv-xviii, for references to Lincoln's recitations of the poem during his presidential years and much other useful information on the poem. Boyd's citations are not always accurate, however.

15. See "Abraham Lincoln, Ann Rutledge, and the Evidence of Herndon's Informants" in this volume.

16. William H. Herndon to Charles H. Hart, Nov. 1, 1866, in *The Hidden Lincoln: From the Letters and Papers of William H. Herndon*, ed. Emanuel Hertz (New York: Viking Press, 1938), 35.

17. Herndon and Weik, *Herndon's Life of Lincoln*, 114. Herndon also believed that Lincoln's melancholy was also "part of his nature." See Weik, *The Real Lincoln*, 113.

18. Undated interview with Isaac Cogdal, H-W.

19. Mearns, "'The Great Invention of the World,'" 85.

20. For a critical reexamination of the Ann Rutledge affair in Lincoln scholarship, see John Y. Simon, "Abraham Lincoln and Ann Rutledge," *Journal of the Abraham Lincoln Association* 11 (1990): 13–33; for a discussion of Herndon's evidence in this regard, see "Abraham Lincoln, Ann Rutledge, and the Evidence of Herndon's Informants" in this volume. See also John Evangelist Walsh, *The Shadows Rise: Abraham Lincoln and the Ann Rutledge Legend* (Urbana: University of Illinois Press, 1993).

21. David Donald, *Lincoln's Herndon: A Biography* (1948, repr. New York: Da Capo, 1989), 229.

22. For the reference to Jason Duncan as the one who first showed Lincoln this poem, see Carpenter, *Six Months in the White House*, 59.

23. For the search for Duncan and the many false leads Herndon turned up before locating his man see the letters of William G. Greene, R. B. Rutledge, John M. Rutledge, A. Y. Ellis, David Turnham, and the statements of J. Gains Green, W. G. Greene, and Royal Clary to William H. Herndon for the period from September to November 1866, H-W.

24. Jason Duncan, undated statement, H-W. Duncan says that he came to

New Salem at the same time Lincoln did and lodged with him for some time. For confirmation of the friendship of Duncan and Lincoln see the interview with J. Gaines Green, Oct. 5, 1866, H-W.

25. In a manuscript that may have been prepared for the use of his collaborator Jesse W. Weik, Herndon first wrote, "Some years before this Doct Jason Duncan placed in his hands a poem" but subsequently changed this to "some year after." See Herndon, "Miss Rutledge amd Lincoln," undated manuscript, H-W.

26. These four letters to Andrew Johnston were all first published after Herndon's death. See *Collected Works*, 1:366–67, 377–78, 384–85, 392.

27. Abraham Lincoln to Andrew Johnston, Feb. 24, 1846, *Collected Works*, 1:367.

28. In addition to the first canto discussed in this essay, Beveridge notes something else about Lincoln's poetry: "More than once after a successful political contest he indulged in the making of verses. Lincoln did this when Hardin withdrew from the fight for the congressional nomination, and again when he had beaten Cartwright at the polls." Beveridge, *Abraham Lincoln*, 383. One might add to this the light-hearted quatrain he got off after Lee's defeat at Gettysburg. See "Verses on Lee's Invasion of the North," in *The Collected Works of Abraham Lincoln: Supplement 1832–1865*, ed. Roy P. Basler (Westport: Greenwood Press, 1974), 194.

29. See W. G. Greene to William H. Herndon, Jan. 23, 1866, H-W: "I am not positive as to the year he wrote potery in relation to Mrs Noah *Gordon* & her Geese[.]   my impression is that it was 1825[.]   I have seen the poetry it was charmingly good[.]   I thought he was well pleased with his effort himself." Presumably, this refers to Lincoln's Indiana period, judging from the date Greene gives it, but there was a Noah Gordon in the New Salem neighborhood when Lincoln lived there. If the reference is to comic verse from the New Salem period, it is one of the only ones on record.

30. For example, see the verses remembered by Elizabeth Crawford in an interview with William H. Herndon, Sept. 16, 1865, and her letter of May 3, 1866, in *The Hidden Lincoln*, ed. Hertz, 367, 294–95.

31. Robert V. Bruce, *Lincoln and the Riddle of Death* (Fort Wayne: Louis A. Warren Lincoln Library and Museum, 1981), 1. The arrangement of the lines is by Bruce. I am indebted to this stimulating essay for a number of references and insights.

32. See Isaac Watts, *Hymns and Spiritual Songs 1707–1748*, ed. Selma L. Bishop (London: Faith Press, 1962), book 2, no. 58, 220–21.

33. Bruce, *Lincoln and the Riddle of Death*, 1.

34. Gibson William Harris, "My Recollections of Abraham Lincoln," *Farm and Fireside*, Jan. 15, 1905, 24. I am grateful to Roger D. Bridges for bringing this material and Harris's dictated copy of "Mortality" to my attention.

35. Abraham Lincoln to Andrew Johnston, April 18, 1846, *Collected Works*, 1:378.

36. Ibid.

37. Ibid., 1:378–39. Lincoln subsequently sent two more cantos: one was a

description of the madness and pitiable condition of an Indiana contemporary, Matthew Gentry, and the other a description of a frontier bear hunt. Although separate and sufficiently distinct from "My childhood's home I see again," both pieces were apparently conceived as parts of a retrospective poem about Indiana, which may never have been completed.

38. Ibid., 1:378. The text exists in two slightly different versions. The one given was that printed in the Quincy *Whig* on May 5, 1847, and is presumed by the editors of the *Collected Works* to represent a revision of the manuscript version in Lincoln's hand in the Library of Congress.

39. Although only an approximation, this estimate of fifteen years clearly places the date well before the death of Ann Rutledge, which would have been only ten years before Lincoln's rediscovery of the poem in the summer of 1845.

40. Herndon seems to have raised the question of where Lincoln learned "Mortality" with Speed when he was looking for Duncan and bearing down on the Ann Rutledge affair. See J. F. Speed to William H. Herndon, Sept. 13, 1866, H-W: "I know nothing of where he learned the Poem alluded to."

41. Harris, "Recollections of Abraham Lincoln," 24.

42. Benjamin Thomas, *Abraham Lincoln: A Biography* (New York: Modern Library, 1968), 110.

43. William H. Herndon to Jesse W. Weik, Oct. 8, 1881, in *The Hidden Lincoln,* ed. Hertz, 84.

44. Thomas Jefferson to Dr. James Currie, Paris, Sept. 27, 1785, in *The Papers of Thomas Jefferson,* ed. Julian P. Boyd et al. (Princeton: Princeton University Press, 1950–), 8:558.

45. Donald, *Lincoln's Herndon,* 229.

46. Herndon and Weik, *Herndon's Life of Lincoln,* 257–58.

47. Bruce, *Lincoln and the Riddle of Death,* 10.

48. Rice, ed., *Reminiscenses of Abraham Lincoln,* 268.

49. *Collected Works,* 290; the stanzas quoted are eight through nine and eleven through fourteen.

50. Ibid. I have edited the punctuation of the newspaper text slightly to make the line "Oh, why should the spirit of mortal be proud" appear the object of "ponder," as I believe was Lincoln's intention, rather than as a title for the poem, as the newspaper rendered it.

51. James Hurt, "All the Living and the Dead: Lincoln's Imagery," *American Literature* 52 (Nov. 1980): 351–80.

52. Bruce, *Lincoln and the Riddle of Death,* 23.

PART FOUR

Lincoln and Jefferson

—— 8 ——

The Lincoln-Douglas Debates:
An Unfinished Text

When Abraham Lincoln concluded his series of debates with Stephen A. Douglas in the fall of 1858, he lost no time in acquiring copies of the newspapers that had carried verbatim reports of the principal speeches and compiling a scrapbook of the campaign. For the texts of the debates at his seven joint appearances with Douglas, he used clippings from the leading Republican newspaper, the *Chicago Press and Tribune*, for his own remarks and the Democratic *Chicago Times* for those of his opponent. His unstated assumption was that these zealously partisan papers presented the most reliable accounts of the remarks of the respective speakers. Arranging the speeches in chronological order and providing a few sentences of handwritten continuity as needed, he made some marginal corrections in his own speeches but left Douglas's alone.

At one point, he substituted a clipping from an unnamed newspaper, duly noting in the margin: "This extract from Mr. Lincoln's Peoria Speech of 1854, was read by him in the Ottawa debate but was not reported fully or accurately in either the Times or Press & Tribune. It is inserted now as necessary to a complete report of the debate."[1] As is clear from the tone and form of address he adopted in this note, Lincoln had in mind for his scrapbook something more than a personal memento. A few inquiries by prospective publishers came to nothing, but when the Republican party of Ohio proposed to reprint the texts of the debates a year later Lincoln was prepared and promptly sent his scrapbook by courier to Columbus to provide copy for the printer. The text set from Lincoln's scrapbook became, in the spring of 1860, a prime document in the presidential campaign that sent Lincoln to the White

House. Subsequently, of course, the widely reprinted debates became one of the most celebrated documents in American history, and until the mid-twentieth century the 1860 text was the only one available.

The scrapbook itself was largely forgotten and little regarded, even by those who knew of its role. John G. Nicolay, Lincoln's personal secretary and biographer, although he had been the courier who carried it to Columbus, thought so little of its importance that he advised his partner, John Hay, that he did not think it was worth $50.[2] Twentieth-century Lincoln scholars subsequently rediscovered it, and the editors of *The Collected Works of Abraham Lincoln* (1953) used it as the copy-text for their rendering of the Lincoln-Douglas debates. It thus occurs that Lincoln's scrapbook has been the primary document behind every text of the famous debates that has been published since 1858. Although a number of editors along the way have duly consulted the original newspaper texts to check on the accuracy of the 1860 edition and the completeness of the scrapbook clippings, Lincoln has largely succeeded in being the principal editor of his own debates with Douglas.

⤷

The entirely new edition of the debates offered in 1993 was edited by Harold Holzer and based not on Lincoln's scrapbook but on an distinctly different set of texts and a novel theory of authenticity.[3] Holzer employs the texts from the same two Chicago newspapers Lincoln used, but instead of using the *Press and Tribune* for Lincoln's speeches and the *Times* for Douglas's, he reverses the procedure, printing Lincoln's speeches as they appeared in the Democratic *Times* and Douglas's from the Republican *Press and Tribune*. In making these opposition texts available, Holzer has performed a rare feat in Lincoln studies: bringing to light for the first time documents of great interest and importance that shed real light on the Lincoln-Douglas debates.

It has long been assumed that the editors of both papers took pains to present the remarks of their candidate in the best possible light, smoothing over the rough spots and providing clarity and continuity as needed while giving the text of the opposing candidate short shrift. Holzer's theory is simply that the opposition texts, in not having been polished and improved by the friendly editors, are closer to what the speakers actually said. The differences between the two sets of texts are considerable, and Holzer goes so far as to say that the Lincoln-Douglas debates "have largely been lost to us" because of the partisan press.

In an effort to showcase the debaters to the best advantage, the raw power and unexpurgated spontaneity of the speakers were permanent-

ly sanitized by partisan stenographers, transcribers, and editors. Together they reproduced the speeches and rebuttals as they perceived
their equally partisan readers wanted them preserved. Inevitably, their
approved (and improved) versions of the debates became the basis of
the permanent historical archive. It would be hyperbolic to suggest
that the original record was suppressed, but inaccurate to deny that
it was enhanced.[4]

Holzer insists that the debate texts as published and reprinted from
the scrapbook were "sanitized," as undoubtedly they were. What he
does not investigate is the question of the extent to which they were
sanitized and whether the resulting text produced by the friendly paper was more of a distortion than that offered by the opposition. His
offering the opposition texts as more authentic than their counterparts
is partly based on certain assumptions about the editorial process that
prevailed in 1858. "On the Democratic side, supportive editors apparently gave a careful critical reading to Douglas transcripts, deleting
ungrammatical sentences, improving stylistic transgressions, plugging
up run-on sentences, and extending fragmentary thoughts . . . and in the
interest of time, left Lincoln's portion alone." The *Press and Tribune*
is accused of "performing comparable cosmetic surgery" on Lincoln's
speeches and "printing the Douglas texts verbatim." This leads logically
to an arresting conclusion: "that only Democrats got to read the unexpurgated Lincoln, and only Republicans the unedited Douglas."[5]

This is an intriguing theory that, given the wide differences between
the two versions, would, if accepted, make for a very different picture
of these important debates. "*Tribune* 'verbatim' accounts of the debates," Holzer believes, "magically transformed Lincoln's occasionally
bumpy impromptu prose into seamless, cogent writing while presenting Douglas's words as informal and coarse. *Times* reports, in turn,
abbreviated Douglas's windier phrases and also diluted some of his ven-
om, frequently deleting the inflammatory adjective from one of his favorite attack phrases, 'Black Republican,' or changing his use of 'nig-
ger' to 'negro.'"[6]

But interesting and instructive as these texts undoubtedly are, there
is serious a problem with Holzer's theory. How does he know that Lincoln's prose was magically transformed or that Douglas's attack phrases were changed? Only by assuming that the opposition texts are accurate and that the friendly paper's deviations are all embellishments. If
this is intended as proof, it is a glaringly circular argument. Assuming
what is to be proved takes us nowhere, and these same assumptions put
us in the awkward position of trusting extremely partisan newspapers
without strong and compelling reasons for doing so.

To inquire only about Lincoln's side of the debate, what makes Holzer think that the openly hostile Chicago *Times* printed a reasonably authentic record of what Lincoln actually said in the debates, particularly given the unflattering and inarticulate character of the result? The germ of this idea seems to be Holzer's doubt that Lincoln was a good extemporaneous speaker. As Holzer puts it: "as an impromptu speaker, he could be dreadful. Notwithstanding his reputation as an engaging storyteller and spellbinding courtroom lawyer, an unprepared Lincoln could be a surprisingly hapless spouter of hollow banality."[7] Holzer asks the question: "Given his lackluster record in unrehearsed oratory, how did he summon the skill to make cogent, hour-long speeches, along with ninety-minute rebuttals, and thirty-minute rejoinders, in his debates with Stephen A. Douglas?"[8] The answer, he believes, is to be found in the originally published accounts of the debates taken down by opposition reporters as "so-called 'exact' transcriptions."[9]

Holzer is surely flying in the face of overwhelming evidence about Lincoln's skill as a stump speaker or debater. Lincoln first distinguished himself and earned recognition as a standout stump speaker. His eventual prominence and leadership in his political party was squarely based on his abilities not only to speak extemporaneously on the stump but also to put down live opponents in debate on the floor of the legislature and elsewhere. For more than twenty years before the debates with Douglas, he matched words with the best orators of his time and place— W. L. D. Ewing, George Forquer, Usher F. Linder, John Calhoun, and Douglas himself—and was acknowledged by contemporaries on all sides as a superior speaker. One of those who knew him longest and best, Joseph Gillespie, wrote: "As early [as] 1834, 5, he was put forward as the spokesman of the whig party, and he never disappointed them or fell below their expectation."[10]

Holzer's examples of Lincoln's awkwardness or ineffectiveness as an impromptu speaker seem to be taken mainly from occasions when Lincoln, as president, was deliberately holding himself back and trying to avoid impromptu remarks as possible pitfalls of misunderstanding. Although it is true, as Holzer asserts, that Lincoln tried to improve his Springfield Farewell Address when writing it out for the press, the speech as given was far from a lame performance and was regarded by those who heard it as very eloquent and affecting. And why, if Lincoln was ineffective on the platform, did Douglas tell a friend in the middle of the debates: "I have known Lincoln for many years, and I have continually met him in debate. I regard him as the most difficult and dangerous opponent that I have ever met and I have serious misgivings as to what may be the result of this debate."[11] The evidence from all quarters indicates that the Lincoln who was put up against Douglas was a formidable speaker, a feared debater, and a master performer on the platform.

Virtually the only contemporary observers who portray Lincoln's speaking performance as inept are the reporters and editors of the highly partisan opposition newspapers of the time. It is notorious, as Holzer acknowledges, that in the heat of a campaign these papers made little pretense to objectivity and published strictly for political effect—to disparage their opponents and glorify their own. But in spite of this, Holzer's theory requires him to argue that when one reads Lincoln's speeches in the hostile *Times* accounts and finds that he is often halting and incoherent, that he uses strange locutions and awkward phraseology, that his arguments contain lapses in logic and non-sequiturs, and that he occasionally makes no sense at all, this is all to be regarded as convincing evidence of Lincoln's ineptitude as a public speaker.

Holzer admits that the best text would be a comparative one with the *Press and Tribune* and *Times* texts in adjacent columns, but he offers instead what he frankly describes as a "compromise system" that is somehow "better suited to the effort to exhume these old texts and present them to new readers."[12] What is the compromise system? The basic text is that of the opposing newspaper—Lincoln from the *Times* and Douglas from the *Press and Tribune*—except where there are "huge discrepancies" in the reports. In such cases, Holzer says, "we chose to present *both* versions, with the 'friendly' alternative in the form of a bracketed insert."[13] But while sampling shows that discrepancies are present in profusion and that many of these are interesting and possibly significant, only a small minority are actually noted.

The theory of having it both ways is attractive, but in practice it is more than a little problematical. Having frequently to interrupt the flow of the text with bracketed alternative readings is one thing for those already familiar with the debates, but it must surely be maddening for the "new readers" Holzer hopes to entice. The resulting "compromise system" seems less than satisfactory for both. To be able to gauge the differences effectively, scholars and serious students of the debates need much fuller reporting on discrepancies than Holzer offers, whereas new readers, who are grappling with the arguments and issues for the first time, would seem to need far less.

Valuable and interesting as these opposition texts are, they frankly do not seem to me a very suitable place for new readers to engage the debates. Indeed, it is difficult to see what advantage there could be for a novice to begin here, which is why the subtitle, *The First Complete, Unexpurgated Text*, appears misleading. In what sense may this be considered either "unexpurgated" or the first "complete" edition? Others have been more complete, if only in the sense of including texts of other speeches from the campaign. And that a "compromise" text should be at the same time "unexpurgated" suggests a complicated, if not conflict-ed, definition of terms.

↩

Dubious and unpromising as Holzer's theory may be, the proof, final-ly, is in the pudding. What do comparisons of the texts really show? As expected, Lincoln's witching use of words in the Republican paper is often muted or even mutilated in the Democratic. One need go no fur-ther than Lincoln's first speech in the first debate at Ottawa to see that the opposition paper's account shows untoward qualities in abundance, but is the clumsy and ineffective performance recorded there evidence of Lincoln's ineptitude or of an unfaithful report?

Although Holzer does not go into it, strong evidence suggests that there was a marked difference in the integrity with which the opposi-tion texts were reported. Robert Hitt, the reporter who took down the speeches of both Lincoln and Douglas for the *Press and Tribune,* was said to have received "the hightest praise from Mr. Lincoln for the ac-curacy of his work."[14] Hitt claimed that Douglas also complimented him on his accuracy, and a sampling of his reporting of Douglas for the *Press and Tribune* compared with the text printed by the *Times* indi-cates no great disparity where Douglas's speeches were concerned. The furor in the press at the time seems to have been mostly about wheth-er or not the *Times* was doing justice to Lincoln. The reputable report-er who took down Douglas's remarks for the *Times* was James Sheri-dan, a Philadelphia phonographer, but Sheridan was not responsible for Lincoln's speeches. These were reported by one Henry Binsmore, whose performance, according to Hitt, was regarded by his fellow newspaper-men as deliberately slovenly in his reporting of Lincoln. Thus the boast of the *Times*'s editor that "Lincoln's speech was printed verbatim, just as it came from the reporter" had a different meaning for the press corps from the one assumed by the reading public.[15]

To make a conclusive case about the relative authority of the texts one way or the other would require extensive comparison, but for an example of the general differences between the *Times* and the *Press and Tribune* accounts consider a brief passage from Lincoln's speech in the Ottawa debate. The first version is from the friendly paper, the *Press and Tribune:* "Now gentlemen, I hate to waste my time on such things, but in regard to that general abolition tilt that Judge Douglas makes,

when he says that I was engaged at that time in selling out and aboli-
tionizing the old Whig party—I hope you will permit me to read a part
of a printed speech that I made then at Peoria, which will show altogether a different view of the position I took in that contest of 1854."

The opposition paper, the *Times*, rendered the same passage: "Now,
I hate to waste my time on some things. But on the abolition tilt, that
the Judge thinks that I was engaged in, I hope you will permit me to
read a part of a speech that I made at Peoria, which will show altogether a different state of case."

The *Times* account here, as throughout the debates when reporting
Lincoln, is significantly shorter than that of the *Press and Tribune*. In
this fairly neutral passage, where nothing very controversial is being
offered, one can see why. Consider the resulting text when the words
and phrases not found in the *Times* are eliminated from the *Press and
Tribune* account:

> Now ~~gentlemen,~~ I hate to waste my time on such things, but ~~in re-
> gard to~~ that ~~general~~ abolition tilt that Judge Douglas ~~makes, when he
> says that~~ I was engaged ~~at that time~~ in ~~selling out and abolitionizing
> the old Whig party—~~ I hope you will permit me to read a part of a
> ~~printed~~ speech that I made ~~then~~ at Peoria, which will show altogeth-
> er a different ~~view~~ of the ~~position I took in that contest of 1854.~~

Such an exercise is revealing for it yields a text that matches that of
the *Times* almost word for word. If Holzer's theory applies, Lincoln
expressed himself throughout the debates in stripped-down, telegraphic language that the *Times* reported accurately but the *Press and Tribune* had constantly to refurbish and augment. Is this a credible explanation, or is it more likely that the *Times* account is pared down and
skeletal, either through the fecklessness of the stenographer or because
of an editor's ruthless pencil?

If this passage is at all typical, it suggests that the tendency of the
Times was to reduce Lincoln's statements to essentials. The inevitable
result is a text that is deliberately deaf to the nuances of Lincoln's
meaning, to say nothing of his artfulness with words and expressions.
Not surprisingly, this seems to be true even when the *Times* report more
closely parallels that of the *Press and Tribune*. Consider, for example,
a passage from the Galesburg debate. The *Times* account is fairly close
to the *Press and Tribune*'s, but a notable exception is its failure to do
justice to Lincoln's deft application of a quotation from Henry Clay
alluding to the Declaration of Independence he had just read to the
crowd. The *Press and Tribune* version:

And I do think—I repeat, though I said it on a former occasion—that Judge Douglas, and whoever like him teaches that the negro has no share, humble though it may be, in the Declaration of Independence, is going back to the era of our liberty and independence, and, so far as in him lies, muzzling the cannon that thunders its annual joyous return; that he is blotting out the moral lights around us, when he contends that whoever wants slaves has a right to hold them; that he is penetrating, so far as lies in his power, the human soul, and eradicating the light of reason and the love of liberty, when he is in every possible way preparing the public mind, by his vast influence, for making the institution of slavery perpetual and national.

The *Times:*

I do think, and must repeat, because I think it—I do think that Judge Douglas and whoever teaches that the negro has no humble share in the Declaration of Independence, is going back to the hour of our own liberty and independence, and so far as in him lies, is muzzling the cannon that thunders its annual joyous return; that he is blowing out the moral lights around us, and perverting the human soul and eradicating from the human soul the love of liberty, and in every possible way, preparing the public mind with his vast influence for making that institution of slavery perpetual and national.

The *Press and Tribune* against *Times* version:

~~And~~ I do think—I repeat, ~~though I said it on a former occasion~~—that Judge Douglas, and whoever like him teaches that the negro has no share, humble ~~though it may be,~~ in the Declaration of Independence, is going back to the era of our liberty and independence, and, so far as in him lies, muzzling the cannon that thunders its annual joyous return; that he is blowing out the moral lights around us, ~~when he contends that whoever wants slaves has a right to hold them;~~ that he is penetrating, ~~so far as lies in his power,~~ the human soul, and eradicating ~~the light of reason and~~ the love of liberty, ~~when he is~~ in every possible way preparing the public mind, by his vast influence, for making the institution of slavery perpetual and national.

As in the case of the passage from Lincoln's speech at Ottawa, the *Times* text appears to be a stripped-down version of the text printed by the *Press and Tribune,* but one of the casualties is language critical to Lincoln's meaning—the passage bearing on the immorality of slaveholding. When he used the same Clay quotation at Ottawa even the *Times* version incorporated his meaning: "When he is saying, as he often does, that if any people want slavery they have a right to have it, he is blowing out the moral lights around us." But at Galesburg, Lincoln seemed to have found a more felicitous and memorable way of expressing himself, which may explain why no trace of it survives in the *Times* account. This prompted a Galesburg newspaper to complain that the *Times*, not content with making Lincoln "talk like a booby, a half-witted numbskull," could not even permit Clay's "beautiful apostrophe" to go "unmutilated."[16]

꒰꒱

Roy P. Basler and his fellow editors were reportedly under a great deal of pressure to complete their edition of the *Collected Works*, which may explain their willingness to settle for the text of the famous scrapbook, and if they calculated that no one would complain or find fault with that decision they were right. It would, in fact, be idle to claim that a more sophisticated editorial treatment of the debates would greatly alter our understanding of them or their place in history, which is undoubtedly the reason that practicing historians have had little interest in pursuing an improvement in the text.

But that the text can be improved upon is beyond dispute. All parties responsible for generating the text of the debates as they were presented to the public, from the speakers themselves to the stenographers and editors who rendered them into print, have testified about the less-than-favorable conditions that prevailed for producing an accurate account of what was said.[17] The speakers were often interrupted by hecklers or other voices from the crowd as well as by the noise of general crowd reactions. These crowd reactions had to be characterized by the reporters at the same time they were attempting to determine what the speakers and the crowd said. The wind occasionally made it hard for the reporters to hear, and it sometimes disturbed the paper on which they were writing. There were times when the noise and disruption were such that the reporters stated frankly that they could not hear what was said.

Stenographers' shorthand notes had to be transcribed, and not always by the same person who made the notations. The reporter who took down Lincoln's speeches for the Chicago *Times* was said to have produced notes that were virtually unintelligible to other stenographers, which probably meant that he had to make his own transcriptions. The transcriptions themselves had to be done at white heat, for time was of the essence in this enterprise and deadlines had to be met at all costs. Once the transcriptions reached the editors' desks, they had to be edited for such things as spelling, punctuation, continuity, and coherence. And then the edited transcriptions had to be set into type.

All of these steps and conditions presented manifold opportunities for error if by "error" we mean all the differences between what the speakers said and what eventually appeared in print. Because the result of all that effort would be not one text but two—that of the *Times* and the *Press and Tribune*—all such contingencies must be multiplied by two. That Lincoln believed that the texts of his speeches printed by the *Press and Tribune* were more accurate and representative of what he actually said than those of the *Times* is important evidence that it would be foolish to ignore. But it is hardly reason for writing off the opposition accounts as worthless and disregarding them altogether. This is why and how Holzer's publication of the texts constitutes a welcome contribution to an unfinished agenda in Lincoln scholarship—a critical text of the Lincoln-Douglas debates.

The samples from the Galesburg debate offer a glimpse of an important use of the opposing texts. Much of Holzer's criticism of previous editions of the debate texts is well taken, for historians and editors have made no significant advancement beyond Lincoln's own editing of the text. Such lassitude is, in one sense, defensible, for Lincoln's text is the one that was printed and read during the campaign of 1860, much to Douglas's chagrin, and it thereby assumed an authority and historical importance of its own. But Holzer is surely on the right track in inquiring about an essentially different matter, namely, what the contestants actually uttered on those seven occasions. These are the lost texts that he seeks to recover.

The assumptions that he makes in embracing the opposition texts wholeheartedly are, I believe, unwarranted by the available evidence and do not stand up under scrutiny. But questionable and imperfect as they may be, these are nonetheless very valuable texts, and Holzer has done Lincoln scholarship a great service in bringing them forth. For one thing, Lincoln's editorial tinkering with the text has not gone unnoticed, and he has been criticized accordingly. The editors of the *Collected Works* assumed, for example, that Lincoln was responsible for the suppression of crowd responses and references to byplay on the platform in the 1860 edition of the debates. These editors made a point of restoring them to the text of the debates even though much of this material is not reporting but calculated editorializing. Holzer follows their example and frequently implies in his annotation that Lincoln's "suppression" of the crowd responses was deliberately self-serving.

But Lincoln was not responsible for these omissions in the 1860 edition. The pencil strikeouts in the scrapbook do not appear, upon inspection, to be his, a fact confirmed by the publishers' reply to Douglas, who had written to protest unfair treatment: "The speeches of Mr. Lincoln were never 'revised, corrected or improved' in the sense you use those words. Remarks by the crowd, which were not responded to, and the reporter's insertions of 'cheers,' 'great applause,' and so forth, which received no answer or comment from the speaker, were, by our direction omitted, as well from Mr. Lincoln's speeches as yours, as we thought their perpetuation in book form would be in bad taste, and were in no manner pertinent to or a part of the speech."[18]

It is true that an examination of the opposition texts would not be sufficient to clear Lincoln of this charge, but they do shed light on another: that in making marginal changes he took unwarranted liberties with the text of his own words. Lincoln said of his scrapbook editing that his changes were "verbal only, and very few in number."[19] He has often been accused of having understated the extent of his editorial changes, and it is true that the number of changes (I count at least thirty-three) does add up to more than anyone's definition of "a few." Under such circumstances one can legitimately question whether the basis of his decision to alter the printed text was to correct errors or second-guess himself and improve his text.

Consider, as a test case, the five changes he made in his remarks at Freeport. Near the beginning of his opening speech, the *Press and Tribune* reported him saying: "I then distinctly intimated to him that I would answer the rest of his interrogatories." In his scrapbook, Lincoln added to this sentence "on condition only that he should agree to answer as many of mine." This has the look of Lincoln's not only second-guessing his own reporter but also fixing up the record to suit himself. A little further along he was reported by the *Press and Tribune* as saying in answer to one of Douglas's questions: "I would not oppose such acquisition, accordingly as I might think such acquisition would or would not agitate the slavery question among ourselves," but in the scrapbook Lincoln changed "agitate" to "agravate." The distinction is subtle, but with the connotations of "agitate" being associated with the disruptive and unpopular activities of the abolitionists, it seems clear that Lincoln's political interests were being served by the change, and readers have a right to question whether the basis of this change is accuracy or expediency. The next change Lincoln made, "offensive" substituted for "affirmed," seems merely to correct an aural error on the part of the reporter not caught by the editors, and the same might be said for the next change, where "decide" is substituted for "decree."

What is notable, and what Holzer's text enables us to determine, is that all of Lincoln's changes, with a single exception, are taken from the *Times* account. And even the change not confirmed by the *Times* text is unconfirmable as part of a construction that is simply not present in the *Times*. What is more, comparison of all thirty-three of Lincoln's changes shows that twenty-six are taken directly from the *Times*; three of the remaining seven are unconfirmable because the construction is not present in the *Times*, two are mere clarifications, and only two out of the thirty-three could qualify as out-and-out changes in the text. This suggests at least two things worth knowing: that even though he did not paste them into his scrapbook, Lincoln consulted the opposition texts in his possession before making any changes in the *Press and Tribune* text, and, more important, he can not be accused of taking unwarranted liberties with the text or with the truth. The changes he made were, as he insisted, "verbal only, and very few in number."

In consulting the opposition texts to augment or correct his own paper's reporting, Lincoln provides a small but telling example of the kind of critical editing of the debate texts that has never been attempted. Shakespearian editors discovered as early as the eighteenth century that the text of the great poet's plays published by his theatrical colleagues in 1623, the First Folio, was not the definitive be-all and end-all text that it appeared. Although most of the earlier editions of the plays represented imperfect and inferior versions of the text, they could often be sources of words, lines, and even whole scenes that were lacking in the First Folio. By closely comparing all versions, and by ingeniously untangling errors of transcription and the press, editors of Shakespeare from that time on have steadily improved the accuracy and authenticity of his text.

By comparison, the editorial procedures employed thus far by scholars in rendering the Lincoln-Douglas debates appear crude indeed. It is evident that if we edited the Lincoln-Douglas debates as rigorously and as resourcefully as Shakespeare's plays, we would long ago have discovered the utility of the neglected texts that Holzer has so usefully resurrected. The lesson to be learned is the value of comparison. This means making a critical comparison of all known versions of the text that emanated from on-the-spot reporters. It is, of course, a reasonable assumption that the friendly press produced the most reliable text, but it seems to have occurred to no one but Holzer to take a serious look at the opposition texts. Although he has embraced them almost as uncritically as his predecessors have accepted their counterparts, his volume makes possible a new and illuminating look at the textual problem of the debates and provides us with a working text of one of the principal ingredients that has been heretofore been missing. Both are important contributions to the future editorial work of improving the texts of the debates.

↬

A modest example of how such improvement would work is apparent in the differing texts that have been cited from the Galesburg debate. Lincoln was reported by his paper, the *Press and Tribune*, as saying, "He is blotting out the moral lights around us," whereas the *Times* printed not "blotting" but "blowing." There is every reason to believe that the *Times* here printed what Lincoln actually said and that his own paper got it wrong. He was quoting Henry Clay, who wrote "blowing," a marginal correction Lincoln duly made in his scrapbook. Unless there were compelling evidence that Lincoln misspoke and said "blotting," a critical edition of the debates would render the word "blowing" and note the circumstances. The evidence in this simple example may be uncharacteristically abundant, but the example clearly illustrates the basic principle involved in emending a primary text, the key being a close critical comparison of all differences.

Holzer only offers one extended comparison, and although its value in demonstrating his thesis is doubtful, it is instructive nonetheless. Holzer compares the reports of a justly famous passage from the Alton debate, where Lincoln universalized his contention with Douglas by insisting that the "real issue" being debated was the "eternal struggle" of right and wrong. The *Press and Tribune* version was:

> That is the real issue. That is the issue that will continue in this country when these poor tongues of Judge Douglas and myself shall be silent. It is the eternal struggle between these two principles—right and wrong—throughout the world. They are the two principles that have stood face to face from beginning of time; and will ever continue to struggle. The one is the common right of humanity and the other the divine right of kings. It is the same principle in whatever shape it develops itself. It is the same spirit that says, 'You work and toil and earn bread, and I'll eat it.' No matter what shape it comes, whether from the mouth of a king who seeks to bestride the people of his own nation and live by the fruit of their labor, or from one race of men as an apology for enslaving another race, it is the same tyrannical principle.

And the *Times* reported the passage as:

> That is the real issue! An issue that will continue in this country when these poor tongues of Douglas and myself shall be silent. These are the two principles that are made the eternal struggle between right and wrong. They are the two principles that have stood face to face, one of them asserting the divine right of kings, the same principle that says you work, you toil, you earn bread, and I will eat it. It is the same old serpent, whether it come from the mouth of a king who seeks to bestride the people of his nation, and to live upon the fat of his neighbor, or whether it comes from one race of men as an apology for the enslaving of another race of men.

Holzer contends that "while the Democratic version lacks polish, it echoes with an impromptu-sounding immediacy lacking in the version published by Lincoln's allies." This is the extent of his argument that the *Times* text is preferable on the basis of accuracy, except to add that "these newly unearthed rival transcripts may be no more perfectly dependable than the texts produced last century by the candidates' backers, but they may well be no more flawed, either."[20]

Although it is not favorable to Holzer's thesis, there is, nevertheless, something further that can be said about the comparison. It seems clear, for example, that in this part of his speech Lincoln must have named both of his principles, whereas the *Times* account has him naming only one, "the divine right of kings." The *Press and Tribune* account supplies the opposing principle, "the common right of humanity," which seems far more likely to have come from the speaker than from an editor. In fact, the *Times* account, when compared with its opposition here and elsewhere, shows signs of the stenographer either not quite keeping up or not taking sufficient pains to capture the speech in its entirety. Lincoln might have referred to a king who sought to "live upon the fat of his neighbor," but it seems far more likely and more in keeping with his sentiment that he spoke of a king who sought to bestride his people and "live by the fruit of their labor."

But a king bestriding his people was not a novel trope in Lincoln's oratory; he had used it a few months earlier in his speech at Chicago, in precisely the same context, and had spoken of "the same old serpent," a phrase that occurs in the lackluster *Times* account but not in the *Press and Tribune*. Is it more likely that the Democratic reporter or editor inserted so distinctive a phrase on his own or that the *Press and Tribune*, for whatever reason, left it out? I have no hesitation in opting for the latter, and this is evidence of precisely the kind of thing for which Holzer is looking, namely, something actually uttered by Lincoln in the debates but either not heard, not understood, or edited out of the account in the *Press and Tribune*.

The opposition texts of the Lincoln-Douglas debates are of undoubted interest to serious students of the debates, and Holzer has performed a valuable and noteworthy service in getting them finally into print. Not only do they add flavor and dimension to the dramatic occasions that were the Lincoln-Douglas debates but they also provide the essential raw material for serious textual emendation. That Holzer's theory about the significance of these opposition texts may be disputed is of far less importance to students of Lincoln and the debates than the fact that he has made the texts themselves readily accessible. And at least one of his claims for these texts deserves to be endorsed heartily: "In the light of its long-delayed exposure, it can clearly be argued that the opposition version of all the transcripts deserve to be included on history's bookshelf, at the very least alongside the editions once approved by Lincoln, Douglas, and their supporters."[21]

NOTES

1. David C. Mearns, ed., *The Illinois Political Campaign of 1858: A Facsimile of the Printer's Copy of His Debates with Stephen A. Douglas as Edited and Prepared for the Press by Abraham Lincoln* (Washington: Library of Congress, n.d.), 97.

2. Mearns, ed., *The Illinois Political Campaign of 1858,* 19.

3. Harold Holzer, ed., *The Lincoln-Douglas Debates: The First Complete, Unexpurgated Text* (New York: HarperCollins, 1993).

4. Holzer, ed., *The Lincoln-Douglas Debates,* 4–5.

5. Ibid., 9.

6. Ibid., 11.

7. Ibid., xii.

8. Ibid., xiii.

9. Ibid., xiv.

10. Joseph Gillespie to M. D. Hardin, April 22, 1880, Hardin Papers, Chicago Historical Society.

11. Stephen A. Douglas quoted in Francis Lynde Stetson to Horace White, Dec. 7, 1908, in Horace White, *The Life of Lyman Trumbull* (Boston: Houghton Mifflin, 1913), 40.

12. Holzer, ed., *The Lincoln-Douglas Debates,* 35.

13. Ibid., 35.

14. Edwin Erle Sparks, ed., *The Lincoln-Douglas Debates of 1858* (Springfield: Illinois State Historical Library, 1908), 78.

15. See the account in Walter B. Stevens, *A Reporter's Lincoln* (St. Louis: Missouri Historical Society, 1916), [3–4], 52ff. For a revealing account of the reporting of the debates, see Michael Burlingame, "How Shorthand Reporters Covered the Lincoln-Douglas Debates of 1858," *Lincoln Herald* 96 (Spring 1994): 18–23.

16. Sparks, ed., *The Lincoln-Douglas Debates of 1858,* 83–84.

17. Ibid., 75–84.

18. Mearns, ed., *The Illinois Political Campaign of 1858,* 18.

19. Ibid., 9.

20. Holzer, ed., *The Lincoln-Douglas Debates,* 36.

21. Ibid., 36.

—— 9 ——

Lincoln's Declaration

Abraham Lincoln had a special affinity for the Declaration of Independence. It became, in the phrase of John G. Nicolay, "his political chart and inspiration."[1] Lincoln seems to have come to a belief that the Declaration occupied a place in American politics superior to the Constitution itself, because it not only preceded it in time but also stated grandly and forthrightly the principles that the Constitution sought to implement in practical form. In an undated manuscript he characterized the basic principle of the Declaration as "Liberty to all" and drew an analogy to the Book of Proverbs, in which this great principle was the "apple of gold," the word "fitly spoken," whereas the *"Union,* and the *Constitution,* are the *picture* of *silver,* subsequently framed around it. The picture was made," Lincoln insisted, "not to *conceal,* or *destroy* the apple; but to *adorn,* and *preserve* it. The *picture* was made for the apple — *not* the apple for the picture."[2]

The literature dealing with Lincoln's views of the Constitution with respect to the Declaration is voluminous and diverse, but the discussion that follows has a narrower focus.[3] It represents an attempt to trace the development of Lincoln's thinking on the Declaration of Independence as reflected in his speeches and writings, culminating in his most famous pronouncement on this theme, the Gettysburg Address. The perspective offered by such an approach puts a much-examined subject in an unaccustomed light. It indicates that, contrary to the way it is most often represented, Lincoln's thinking about the Declaration and its application to the political issues of his day was not static but rather that it developed and matured. It indicates further that this process of maturation did not belong to Lincoln's early political development but was something that emerged later as the political disputes of the 1850s progressed.[4] The shaping of Lincoln's view of this subject is not merely an academic matter. Thomas Jefferson's Declaration of Independence is still a vital document, its prologue being as close as Americans have ever come to a common creed. But as Garry Wills has affirmed in *Lincoln at Gettysburg,* Lincoln's views have had much to do with determining the way Americans now read and understand Jefferson's Declaration.[5]

⤶

The first occurrence of the Declaration of Independence in Lincoln's published writings is a passing reference in the Young Man's Lyceum Address of 1838, "The Perpetuations of Our Political Institutions." Valuable as it is in many ways, the Lyceum Address is nonetheless an early set-piece on a conventional theme that perhaps tells us less about Lincoln's mature political thought than about the state of his development, at the age of twenty-eight, as a formal platform speaker.[6] That his surviving writings contain no reference to the Declaration during the subsequent period of his political ascendency, which culminated in his election to Congress, is partly explained by the next reference, which occurred some fourteen years after the Lyceum speech in his eulogy of Henry Clay.

Speaking in Springfield in 1852, he used the occasion to take note of "an increasing number of men, who, for the sake of perpetuating slavery, are beginning to assail and to ridicule the white-man's charter of freedom—the declaration that 'all men are created free and equal.'"[7] By way of reply, Lincoln quoted at length from Clay's 1827 speech before the American Colonization Society, when he argued that critics and opponents who would suppress the work of the Colonization Society must logically do more: "They must go back to the era of our liberty and independence, and muzzle the cannon which thunders its annual joyous return. . . . They must blow out the moral lights around us, and extinguish that greatest torch of all which America presents to a benighted world—pointing the way to their rights, their liberties, and their happiness."[8]

Lincoln took up the Declaration in 1852 principally because it had come under attack. Quoting a specimen of anti-Declaration opinion, he allowed that this "sounds strangely in republican America."[9] Heretofore, defending the Declaration had been largely unnecessary and hardly worth a politician's time except as an exercise in commonplace and cliché. But with Jefferson's words and ideas under attack, a new order of things presented itself, and the eulogy to Henry Clay registers Lincoln's earliest recorded reaction. Referring to it as "the white-man's charter of freedom" and misquoting the equality clause, Lincoln seemed to be at an early stage of thinking about the Declaration and its meaning, especially as it related to his own time. It is noteworthy, however, that he had already seized upon the power and strategic relevance of Clay's colonization speech, which he would use in the 1858 debates, first at Ottawa and later at Galesburg.

᭝

Lincoln's great speech at Peoria in 1854—for the light that it sheds on his thinking about slavery and for its eloquent exposition of the issue of extension—must rank as one of his most important. By the time he came to give this speech two years after the Clay eulogy he had evidently given serious thought to the Declaration as it related to contemporary political issues, particularly its relevance to the crisis created by the passage of the Kansas-Nebraska bill. He may at first have been attracted largely by the broad popular appeal of the Declaration, which was the emotional centerpiece of the most widely celebrated national holiday, where it was solemnly read aloud as a sacred text in every hamlet of America. But the frequent use he subsequently made of the Declaration in his political writings is anything but perfunctory and reveals a deepening absorption with its meaning.

In the Peoria speech he attacked Douglas for his role in opening the new territories to slavery, which the senator claimed had been done purely on the basis of self-government. Lincoln argued: "When the white man governs himself that is self-government, but when he governs himself, and also governs *another* man, that is *more* than self-government — that is despotism. If the negro is a *man*, why then my ancient faith teaches me that 'all men are created equal;' and that there can be no moral right in connection with one man's making a slave of another."[10] Having hoisted the banner of the Declaration in the cause of the humanity of blacks and the immorality of slavery, Lincoln zeroed in on the issue of despotism by arguing "that no man is good enough to govern another man, *without that other's consent*. I say this is the leading principle—the sheet anchor of American republicanism." Slavery, he insisted, is "a total violation of this principle."[11]

A year later, in 1855, Lincoln's preoccupation with the Declaration as the basic gauge of political principles was again evident in a well-known letter to his friend Joshua F. Speed in which he voiced his concern about the nativist turn that politics was taking: "Our progress in degeneracy appears to me to be pretty rapid. As a nation, we began by declaring that *'all men are created equal.'* We now practically read it 'all men are created equal, *except negroes.'* When the Know-Nothings get control, it will read 'all man are created equal, except negroes, *and foreigners, and catholics.'* When it comes to this I should prefer emigrating to some country where they make no pretence of loving liberty — to Russia, for instance, where despotism can be taken pure, and without the base alloy of hypocracy."[12] Here the threat of despotism, the keynote at Peoria, is closely associated with a concern for the unraveling of the Declaration's commitment to equality. This suggests that in Lincoln's thinking there was something fundamental about the connection between America's nationhood and the Declaration's affirmation of equality. It further suggests that he was already troubled by the way in which admitting exceptions to Jefferson's great maxim effectively undermined its meaning.

Reports of his electioneering for the newly formed Republican party the following year, 1856, show Lincoln raising the issue of the Declaration in varying ways for political effect. In Princeton, before an audience sympathetic to abolitionism, he invoked the equality clause. In Petersburg, where the audience was heavily Democratic, he pointed out that Democratic politicians were shamefully calling the Declaration a "self-evident lie." In Belleville, before an audience containing a number of German immigrants, he presented himself as the defender of the Declaration against the attacks of Douglas.[13]

By the close of the campaign he seems not only to have thought further about the Declaration but also to have come to a determination about its meaning for the public at large and its potential relation to the politics of the day. Perhaps prompted by a famous remark of Jefferson's, Lincoln told his fellow Republicans in a post-election speech at Chicago:

> Our government rests in public opinion. Whoever can change public opinion can change the government, practically just so much. Public opinion, on any subject, always has a *"central idea,"* from which all its minor thoughts radiate. That "central idea" in our political public opinion, at the beginning was, and until recently has continued to be, "the equality of men." And although it was always submitted patiently to whatever of inequality there seemed to be as a matter of actual necessity, its constant working has been a steady progress towards the practical equality of all men.[14]

Much as it may now seem to readers that Lincoln was merely employing commonplaces and preaching to the choir, it is important to realize that both for himself and his audience he was actually beginning to break new ground. What he was acknowledging, in effect, was that although "consent of the governed" may arguably be the "leading principle" of the Declaration, as he had said in his Peoria speech two years earlier, the idea that is most deeply rooted in the hearts of Americans is something else. "Liberty to all" might epitomize the *sense* of the Declaration, but the words that resonate most memorably with the public are "all men are created equal." He was urging his political colleagues, in short, to recognize and make use of this phenomenon, to seize the high ground of the Declaration and hold it.

By any meaningful standard he was asking a great deal. Of the familiar precepts in the prologue of the Declaration that might have been employed in the fight against slavery and its extension, "liberty" would seem the most directly applicable, although "consent of the governed" and "the pursuit of happiness" would have served very well. Lincoln had fixed upon what was undoubtedly, in the heated political climate of the time, the most controversial and problematical—the equality of all human beings. There were many aspects of slavery and its extension into the territories that concerned the citizens of Illinois—and the rest of the country for that matter—but affirming the equality of blacks was definitely not one of them. For an Illinois politician seeking statewide office, to appear to be espousing or even suggesting anything like Negro equality was to risk political suicide. How was it possible, his Republican colleagues at Chicago might have demanded, to exploit the deep attachment of white voters to the Declaration's affirmation of equality without handing one's opponents a lethal political weapon?

In the Peoria speech, Lincoln had granted that blacks could not, at that time and at that place, be made the political and social equals of whites because, as he said, "a universal feeling, whether well or ill-founded, can not be safely disregarded," a watchword of practical politics that he never forgot.[15] But the speech to his fellow Republicans suggests that he may have come to see this rule of conduct, at least where slavery was concerned, as a two-edged sword. If deep-seated attachment to the idea that "all men are created equal" were indeed a "universal feeling," why should they disregard it? Why could this not be somehow captured and made use of in the struggle against Douglas and extension, where the most egregious form of inequality was at issue?

Lincoln's ideas may not have been fully developed on how this difficult matter could be made politically practicable in December of 1856, but they were soon to be put to the test. The Dred Scott decision was announced by the Supreme Court just three months later in March 1857, ruling that blacks were chattel property and could not be citizens. Lincoln promptly undertook to contest the opinion of Justice Taney. The result was a carefully elaborated interpretation of the Declaration's equality clause that would become an important part of Lincoln's subsequent opposition to slavery and extension. In a speech at Springfield on June 26, Lincoln insisted that contrary to what Justice Taney and Senator Douglas had claimed, the authors of the Declaration, in declaring "all men are created equal," "intended to include *all* men, but they did not intend to declare all men equal *in all respects.* They did not mean to say all were equal in color, size, intellect, moral developments, or social capacity. They defined with tolerable distinctness, in what respects they did consider all men created equal—equal in 'certain inalienable rights, among which are life, liberty, and the pursuit of happiness.'" They did not mean "that all men were then actually enjoying that equality," which would, Lincoln allowed, have been an "untruth." The intention of the authors of Declaration was something different. "They meant to set up a standard maxim for free society, which should be familiar to all, and revered by all; constantly looked to, constantly labored for, and even though never perfectly attained, constantly approximated, and thereby constantly spreading and deepening its influence." They meant it, in short, to be a "stumbling block" to future lapses into despotism so that would-be tyrants in years to come would find in it "at least one hard nut to crack."[16]

In the same speech, Lincoln showed how what might be regarded as a weakness in his position could be turned into a strength. If "all men are created equal" did not include blacks, who did it include? Douglas, perhaps unguardedly, had offered a narrowly historical interpretation, which Lincoln tellingly characterized as "We hold these truths to be self-evident that all British subjects who were on this continent eighty-one years ago, were created equal to all British subjects born and *then* residing in Great Britain."[17] Try reading that on the Fourth of July, he suggested. Lincoln, the consummate logician, had effectively driven Douglas into a corner in which, as Harry V. Jaffa puts it, the "only logical reconciliation of Douglas's statement with the language of the Declaration would be by means of the proposition that all true men are by nature British!" a proposition that "might find its place in some undiscovered operetta by Gilbert and Sullivan."[18] Douglas's interpretation, Lincoln told his audience, made a "wreck," "a mangled ruin . . . of our once glorious Declaration" because it denied its continuing relevance to present and future generations and left the Declaration "without the *germ* or even the *suggestion* of the individual rights of man in it."[19]

In the Dred Scott speech at Springfield, Lincoln took what, for a Illinois politician seeking statewide support in 1857, must be regarded as a bold stand on the Declaration. "The white-man's charter of freedom," which he had spoken of five years earlier in his eulogy to Henry Clay, had been not only discarded but also repudiated in favor of a universal application. Equality was now to be understood as the key, and the Declaration meant what it says: All human beings are equal as regards their inalienable rights to life, liberty, and the pursuit of happiness. But perhaps the most notable new element in the equation was the emphasis on the equality clause as a transcendent ideal—not a statement of objective fact but a proposition by which future actions and decisions may be guided and judged.[20] The value of such a reading is that it provides a way to view the Declaration as a living document rather than a merely historical one and affords a way of reconciling its special or abstract "truth" as an ideal with its all-too-evident "untruth" in the world at hand.

To Douglas and the Democrats, as to many Republicans, it must have seemed that Lincoln had placed himself in a hopelessly vulnerable position. Could it not be readily shown, through his own words, that he was in favor of Negro equality and as such was but an abolitionist in Whig's clothing? Lincoln was, of course, not an abolitionist, and he did not intend to advocate social and political equality for blacks, as he tried over and over to make clear. But he was a politician, and he saw that there was political advantage to be gained in preempting the most revered clause of the most revered statement of national purpose. Just how calculating and shrewdly pragmatic his decision to take this position was is difficult to judge, for he was secretive on such matters and kept his own counsel. And, as he would demonstrate in the "House Divided" speech, he sometimes liked long odds. But there can be no doubt that Lincoln recognized the Declaration as a moral document, one that distinguished between right and wrong, and that he meant to depict slavery as a moral issue. He also perceived that making exceptions to the Declaration's inclusiveness was a slippery slope and that there was political utility in its universality, particularly in a nation that, with a growing proportion of immigrants, was becoming less and less homogeneous. The question to be answered was, Could the political benefits be made to outweigh the risks?

~

In 1858 Lincoln's evolving interpretation of the Declaration and its essential meaning was tested in the fire of the senatorial campaign with Stephen A. Douglas. Although the subject is absent from the "House Divided" speech at the time of his nomination in June, Lincoln put his view of the Declaration prominently on record early in the campaign in an important speech the following month at Chicago. Devoting a long section at the end of the speech to the Declaration, he made a special appeal to immigrants, whose ancestors had no part in the Revolution and who, by Douglas's logic, had no connection to the Declaration. But, said Lincoln, when these new citizens—Germans, Irish, French, and Scandinavians—"look through that old Declaration of Independence they find that those old men say that 'We hold these truths to be self-evident, that all men are created equal,' and then they feel that that moral sentiment taught in that day evidences their relation to those men, that it is the father of all moral principle in them, and that they have a right to claim it as though they were blood of the blood, and flesh of the flesh of the men who wrote that Declaration, and so they are."[21]

This passage is a perfect demonstration of how Lincoln proposed to use the universal application and the essential morality of the Declaration to political advantage. Far from being the narrowly historical and exclusively national document that Douglas held it to be, the Declaration, according to Lincoln, appeals to something deeper and more fundamental than race or nationality: "the father of all moral principle." "It is," he went on to say in a memorable phrase, "the electric cord in that Declaration that links the hearts of patriotic and liberty-loving men together."[22]

To illustrate his somewhat more abstruse position regarding the transcendental nature of the Declaration's equality clause, Lincoln concluded the speech at Chicago by resorting to a familiar rhetorical strategy—a biblical parallel. In the scriptural admonition "as your Father in Heaven is perfect, be ye also perfect," Lincoln said, Jesus meant not to insist upon human perfection, which is impossible, but to "set up a standard" such that "he who did most towards reaching that standard, attained the highest degree of moral perfection." This suggests a parallel with the Declaration's equality clause: "So I say in relation to the principle that all men are created equal, let it be as nearly reached as we can. If we cannot give freedom to every creature, let us do nothing that will impose slavery upon any other creature."[23] Thus Lincoln demonstrated how the Declaration, with an assist from the Bible, could be roundly invoked against the extension of slavery.

The forthright position that Lincoln had taken on the Declaration at Chicago made his task against Douglas doubly difficult. In arguing that slavery violated the most sacred principle of the nation's creed, he was treading on a political land mine, for whatever his inclination, Lincoln did not have the luxury of arguing, with Frederick Douglass and the abolitionists, that the Declaration should be read as a mandate for total political equality, regardless of color. He was clearly counting on the countervailing influence of a deep popular feeling, morally grounded, that the Declaration invoked. Horace White remembered that after the debates with Douglas were arranged Lincoln punctuated his first scheduled speech, at Beardstown, with a passionate apostrophe on the Declaration that, in White's reconstructed version, was widely circulated. It concluded:

> Think nothing of me—take no thought for the political fate of any man whomsoever—but come back to the truths that are in the Declaration of Independence. You may do anything with me you choose, if you will but heed these sacred principles. You may not only defeat me for the Senate, but you may take me and put me to death. While pretending no indifference to earthly honors, I *do claim* to be actuated in this contest by something higher than an anxiety for office. . . . I am nothing; Judge Douglas is nothing. *But do not destroy that immortal emblem of Humanity—the Declaration of American Independence.*[24]

Predictably, Douglas bore down on the implications of equality as a universal principle and attempted to make Lincoln pay the political price of seeming to advocate social and political equality for blacks. Hewing to the interpretation of the Declaration he had developed in previous pronouncements, especially the Dred Scott speech, Lincoln sought to steer a tight middle course between two looming alternatives: the moral acceptance of slavery on the one hand and total equality for the Negro on the other.

Lincoln's failure to embrace the second of these alternatives has, in recent years, overshadowed his advanced and principled position on the first. Quoting his famous disclaimer at Charleston (which repeated what he had already said in the first debate at Ottawa) has become an all-too-familiar way of demonstrating that Lincoln was not really a friend of civil rights:

> I will say then that I am not, nor ever have been in favor of bringing about in any way the social and political equality of the white and black races,—that I am not nor ever have been in favor of making voters or jurors of negroes, nor of qualifying them to hold office, nor to intermarry with white people; and I will say in addition to this that there is a physical difference between the white and black races which I believe will for ever forbid the two races living together on terms of social and political equality. And inasmuch as they cannot so live, while they do remain together, there must be the position of superior and inferior; and I, as much as any other man, am in favor of having the superior position assigned to the white race.[25]

"But for that pledge," Garry Wills has pointed out, "Lincoln had no hope of winning office."[26] But by contrast with the effect these words have on late-twentieth-century readers, Lincoln seems to have had trouble convincing his contemporaries that this was where he actually stood. Even his friends apparently found it hard to understand and defend Lincoln's position, which is why he prepared a scrapbook of his statements on this issue late in the campaign for his friend and fellow candidate James N. Brown. Including clippings from his 1854 Peoria speech, the Dred Scott speech of 1857, the Chicago speech of July 1858, and the Ottawa and Charleston debates, he tried to show Brown—an old line Whig, Kentuckian, and former slaveholder—that he was maintaining the principle of human equality found in the Declaration but disavowing advocacy of social and political equality for Negroes. "I have expressly disclaimed all intention to bring about social and political equality between the white and black races," he wrote. "I have made it equally plain that I think the negro is included in the word 'men' used in the Declaration of Independence — I believe the declaration that 'all men are created equal' is the great fundamental principle upon which our free institutions rest; that negro slavery is violative of that principle; but that, by our frame of government, that principle has not been made one of legal obligation."[27]

The distinction may have been hard to put across effectively, but the issues Lincoln was attempting to place in the foreground were, for him, logically prior to, and thus more immediately important than, civil rights for free blacks: the moral wrong of slavery and the threat to freedom everywhere posed by what he represented as the deadly combination of extension and the Dred Scott decision. The most elegant and effective instrument for advancing and defending these positions was the Declaration of Independence. As a moral document incompatible with slavery, and as an authoritative statement of basic human equality, the Declaration could be made directly relevant to his leading arguments. His strategy, quite simply, was to make Douglas attack the Declaration and the principles it affirmed.

~

For this he did not have long to wait. Douglas attacked Lincoln's position on the Declaration in his first speech at the very first debate at Ottawa, ridiculing the notion that the Declaration's statement of equality applied to blacks, as Lincoln and "Abolitionist orators" maintained. Lincoln answered briefly and defensively although he managed to end on a strongly positive note: "I agree with Judge Douglas he [the Negro] is not my equal in many respects—certainly not in color, perhaps not in moral or intellectual endowment. But in the right to eat the bread, without leave of anybody else, which his own hand earns, *he is my equal and the equal of Judge Douglas, and the equal of every living man.*"[28]

But the matter really came to a head in the fifth debate at Galesburg. Douglas opened by ridiculing the notion that the author of the Declaration, Thomas Jefferson, could have intended "that his negro slaves, which he held and treated as property, were created his equals by Divine law, and that he was violating the law of God every day of his life by holding them as slaves."[29] With a strong contingent of sympathetic listeners in the audience, Lincoln vigorously counterattacked. He defied Douglas to point to a single affirmation, before the agitation over the Kansas-Nebraska bill, "that the negro was not included in the Declaration of Independence." With a boldness calculated to produce a dramatic effect, Lincoln directly challenged his opponent: "I think I may defy Judge Douglas to show that he ever said so, that Washington ever said so, that any President ever said so, that any member of Congress ever said so, or that any living man upon the whole earth ever said so, until the necessities of the present policy of the Democratic party, in regard to slavery, had to invent that affirmation."[30] Douglas, in fact, produced no satisfactory reply.

The Declaration was useful to Lincoln in other ways. To Douglas's charge that he was appealing to antislavery sentiment in the North while disguising his views in southern Illinois, Lincoln could respond that his stand on the equality of the races was drawn directly from the Declaration of Independence and had been consistently presented. To reinforce his identification with the revered politician Henry Clay, Lincoln quoted again from Clay's defense of the Colonization Society, which alludes metaphorically to the Declaration. Douglas, Lincoln said at Galesburg, "and whoever like him teaches that the negro has no share, humble though it may be, in the Declaration of Independence, is going back to the era of our liberty and independence, and, so far as in him lies, muzzling the cannon that thunders its annual joyous return; that he is blowing out the moral lights around us when he contends that whoever wants slaves has a right to hold them."[31]

Lincoln's friends at Springfield's *Illinois State Journal*, who certainly recognized Lincoln's strategy, lent support by focussing attention on the issue on October 11, 1858: "The principal stock in trade of Douglas and his satellites consists now-a-days in denunciations of the glorious old Declaration of Independence. . . . their chief card against Mr. Lincoln is that he is a believer in that ancient and venerable instrument."[32] Although unable to frame an effective reply to Lincoln's challenge at

Galesburg, Douglas repeated his charge at the remaining two debates that Lincoln's position on the Declaration followed the abolitionists' notion of "the negro being on an equality with the white man."[33] Instead of denials, Lincoln responded positively by reading from Henry Clay at Quincy and from his own Dred Scott speech at Alton. The authors of the Declaration, he had said, "did not mean to assert the obvious untruth, that all were then actually enjoying that equality, nor yet, that they were about to confer it immediately upon them. . . . They meant simply to declare the *right* so that the *enforcement* of it might follow as fast as circumstance should permit."[34]

↩

Douglas won the senatorial battle of 1858 only to lose the presidential war in 1860. The intervening year of 1859 is notable for two developments with regard to Lincoln and Jefferson's Declaration. The first, Lincoln's public lecture on "Discoveries and Inventions," may appear incidental or unrelated. His close friend Joseph Gillespie recalled that on this occasion Lincoln, in endeavoring "to trace out the source and development of language," told him that he "was surprised to find his investigations in that direction so interesting and instructive to himself."[35] In the lecture he developed the idea that "writing—the art of communicating thoughts to the mind, through the eye—is the great invention of the world." It deserves this distinction because it enables us "to converse with the dead, the absent, and the unborn, at all distances of time and space."[36] Because we are able to write down our ideas and so preserve them for posterity,

> the observation of a single individual might lead to an important invention, years, and even centuries after he was dead. It is very probable—almost certain—that the great mass of men, at that time [when printing was invented], were utterly unconscious, that their *conditions*, or their *minds* were capable of improvement. They not only looked upon the educated few as superior beings; but they supposed themselves to be naturally incapable of rising to equality. To immancipate the mind from this false and under estimate of itself, is the great task which printing came into the world to perform.[37]

Lincoln realized that he had risen to the heights he had, in the legal profession as well as politics, by his mastery of language, so it not surprising that he should find this line of inquiry so "instructive." What Lincoln had rediscovered in practical terms was a version of the age-old boast of poets—that words are deathless and that language transcends the limitations of time and mortality.

The second notable development in 1859 was a letter written a few months later in which Lincoln found a propitious occasion for employing his newly articulated theory. Replying to an invitation to attend a festival in Boston honoring Jefferson, Lincoln saluted him as a man who had written something that looked toward the emancipation of the mind from its "false under estimate of itself" and that the future could not ignore. "All honor to Jefferson," Lincoln wrote, "to the man who, in the concrete pressure of a struggle for national independence by a single people, had the coolness, forecast, and capacity to introduce into a merely revolutionary document, an abstract truth, applicable to all men and all times, and so to embalm it there, that to-day, and in all coming days, it shall be a rebuke and a stumbling-block to the very harbingers of re-appearing tyranny and oppression."[38] Lincoln had been steadily working his way toward this view of Jefferson's Declaration since 1854. The final piece in the puzzle was the recognition or insight that putting an idea down in writing gives it a ceaseless potential and that its utility is thereafter virtually inextinguishable.

Before taking the oath of office as president, Lincoln made a point of raising a flag at Independence Hall in Philadelphia, where the Declaration had come into being, and saying, "I have never had a feeling politically that did not spring from the sentiments embodied in the Declaration of Independence."[39] As president, he continued to appeal to the Declaration and the equality clause as a gauge of what was transpiring and what was at stake. In its third year he characterized the Civil War as, at bottom, "an effort to overthrow the principle that all men were created equal," and, underlining this, he pointed out how fitting it was that on the triumphant Fourth of July 1863 "the cohorts of those who opposed the declaration that all men are created equal, 'turned tail' and run."[40] At Gettysburg, he took the final step and in a miracle of succinctness proclaimed that the meaning of the war and of the national purpose itself was embodied in the Declaration's equality clause.

> Four score and seven years ago our fathers brought forth on this continent, a new nation, conceived in Liberty, and dedicated to the proposition that all men are created equal.
> Now we are engaged in a great civil war, testing whether that nation, or any nation so conceived and so dedicated, can long endure.[41]

In the most stunning act of statesmanship in our history, he invested Jefferson's eighteenth-century idea of equality with an essentially new meaning and projected it onto the future of the nation, where, in the words of the Dred Scott speech, it has remained "familiar to all, and revered by all; constantly looked to, constantly labored for, and even though never perfectly attained, constantly approximated, and thereby constantly spreading and deepening its influence."[42] He had taken a leaf from the book of his earliest idol Thomas Jefferson and had left the future adversaries of equality "at least one [more] hard nut to crack."

NOTES

1. Nicolay quoted in Ida M. Tarbell, *The Early Life of Abraham Lincoln* (New York: S. S. McClure, 1896), 166.

2. Roy P. Basler, ed., Marion D. Pratt and Lloyd A. Dunlap, asst. eds., *The Collected Works of Abraham Lincoln* (New Brunswick: Rutgers University Press, 1953), 4:169 (hereafter cited as *Collected Works*). Emphasis here and in the quotations that follow is in the original. The editors suggest that this fragment may have been written in 1861 after Lincoln was elected president but also allow that it "may have been written earlier." The contextual evidence presented here about Lincoln's changing views on the Declaration points to a much earlier date than 1861.

3. The classic treatment of Lincoln and the Declaration is Harry V. Jaffa, *Crisis in the House Divided: An Interpretation of the Issues in the Lincoln-Douglas Debates* (Garden City: Doubleday, 1959). Among the countless subsequent discussions see Glen E. Thurow, "The Gettysburg Address and the Declaration of Independence," in *Abraham Lincoln, the Gettysburg Address, and American Constitutionalism*, ed. Leo Paul S. de Alvarez (Dallas: University of Dallas Press, 1976), 55–75; Richard N. Current, "Lincoln, the Civil War, and the American Mission," in *The Public and the Private Lincoln*, ed. Cullom Davis et al. (Carbondale: Southern Illinois University Press, 1979), 137–46; Merrill D. Peterson, *"This Grand Pertinacity": Abraham Lincoln and the Declaration of Independence* (Fort Wayne: Louis A. Warren Lincoln Library and Museum, 1991); and Ronald D. Rietveld, "Lincoln's View of the Founding Fathers," in *Abraham Lincoln: Sources and Style of Leadership*, ed. Frank J. Williams, William D. Pederson, and Vincent J. Marsala (Westport: Greenwood Press, 1994), 17–44. A notable recent reatement of this theme is Phillip Shaw Paludan, *The Presidency of Abraham Lincoln* (Lawrence: University Press of Kansas, 1994).

4. For a contrasting perspective on this point, see the discussion by Allen C. Guelzo, "'That All Men Are Created Equal': Lincoln's Declaration of Independence," *Lincoln Herald* 96 (Winter 1995): 119–26.

5. Garry Wills, *Lincoln at Gettysburg: The Words That Remade America* (New York: Simon and Schuster, 1992), 147.

6. *Collected Works*, 1:112.

7. Ibid., 2:130.

8. Ibid., 2:131.

9. Ibid.

10. Speech at Peoria, Ill., Oct. 16, 1854, *Collected Works*, 2:266.

11. Ibid.

12. Abraham Lincoln to J. F. Speed, Aug. 24, 1855, *Collected Works*, 2:323.

13. See the *Collected Works* for speeches at Princeton on July 4 (2:346), Petersburg on September 6 (2:368), and Belleville on October 18 (2:380).

14. Speech at Chicago, Dec. 10, 1856, *Collected Works*, 2:385. Jefferson's famous remark was in a letter to Edward Carrington of January 16, 1787: "The basis of our governments being the opinion of the people, the very first object should be to keep that right; and were it left to me to decide whether we should have a government without newspapers or newspapers without government, I should not hesitate a moment to prefer the latter. But I should mean that every man should receive those papers & be capable of reading them." *Writings*, ed. Merrill D. Peterson (New York: Library of America, 1984), 880.

15. *Collected Works*, 2:256.

16. Speech at Springfield, Ill., June 26, 1857, *Collected Works*, 2:405–6. This is substantially the passage Lincoln read to his audience in the final debate at Alton.

17. *Collected Works*, 2:407.

18. Harry V. Jaffa, *Crisis in the House Divided: An Interpretation of the Issues in the Lincoln-Douglas Debates* (Garden City: Doubleday, 1959), 317.

19. *Collected Works*, 2:406, 407.

20. Jaffa points out that Lincoln "treats the proposition that 'all men are created equal' as a transcendental goal and not as the immanent and effective basis of actual political right." See *Crisis in the House Divided*, 318. Garry Wills has given this subject and its context in the romantic era a rich treatment in "The Transcendental Declaration" in *Lincoln at Gettysburg*, 90–120.

21. *Collected Works*, 2:499–500.

22. Ibid., 2:500.

23. Ibid., 2:501.

24. Ibid., 2:547. White's account of this incident is in William H. Herndon and Jesse W. Weik, *Herndon's Life of Lincoln*, ed. Paul M. Angle (Cleveland: World Publishing, 1949), 340–41; see also Basler's editorial note in *Collected Works*.

25. Abraham Lincoln, *Speeches and Writings*, vol. 1: *1832–1858*, ed. Don E. Fehrenbacher (New York: Library of America, 1989), 636.

26. Garry Wills, *Certain Trumpets: The Call of Leaders* (New York: Simon and Schuster, 1994), 14.

27. Lincoln, *Speeches and Writings*, 1:822. The scrapbook has been published in facsimile as *Abraham Lincoln, His Book: A Facsimile Reproduction of the Original*, ed. J. McCan Davis (New York: McClure, Phillips, 1903).

28. Lincoln, *Speeches and Writings*, 1:512.

29. Ibid., 1:697.

30. Ibid., 1:702.

31. Ibid., 1:717–18.

32. Quoted in David Zarefsky, *Lincoln, Douglas, and Slavery: In the Crucible of Public Debate* (Chicago: University of Chicago Press, 1990), 151.

33. Lincoln, *Speeches and Writings*, 1:775.

34. Ibid., 1:794.

35. Joseph Gillespie to William H. Herndon, Dec. 8, 1866, Herndon-Weik Collection, Library of Congress.

36. *Collected Works*, 3:360.
37. Ibid., 3:362–63.
38. Ibid., 3:376.
39. Lincoln, *Speeches and Writings*, 2:213.
40. *Collected Works*, 6:320.
41. Ibid., 7:23.
42. *Collected Works*, 2:406.

INDEX

AL: Abraham Lincoln; L-D: Lincoln-Douglas

Abell, Elizabeth H., 82; on AL's reaction to death of Ann Rutledge, 82
Abolitionists, 172, 173, 175
Abraham Lincoln Association, 16n
The Abraham Lincoln Encyclopedia (Mark E. Neely, Jr.), 26
Adams, John, 9, 12, 17n
Aesop's Fables, 7
Alton debate: texts compared, 163–64; AL quotes Dred Scott speech, 177
American Colonization Society, 167; Clay's defense of, 167–68, 176
Angle, Paul M. 22, 29, 81, 118, 131n; disputes the Ann Rutledge story, 22–23, 24, 75, 78, 80, 88; on Isaac Cogdal, 31, 86; misconceptions about Herndon, 34n; on the "disastrous effect" legend, 89; on Al's broken engagement, 100, 120; and evidence AL was jilted, 116–17
Arenz, Francis: editor of *Beardstown Chronicle,* 55, 56, 63, 70; sketch of, 59; and canal company, 59
Armstrong, Duff, 9
Armstrong, Hannah (Mrs. Jack), 9, 79
Armstrong, Jack, 9, 72n, 81, 92, 93
Arnold, Isaac N., 41, 42, 43, 45, 48

Baker, Edward D.: as political rival of AL, 107
Baker, Jean H.: on Herndon, 26
Bale, Hardin: as Ann Rutledge informant, 79, 82
Bale, Mrs. Hardin: as Ann Rutledge informant, 82; 97n

Barret, Richard F., 128n
Barret, Sarah Rickard, 120, 128n, 131n; as object of AL's affections, 109, 124; mentioned in Speed's letters to AL, 123–24; as sister of Elizabeth Butler, 124; and possible romantic connection to Speed, 125, 132n
Basler, Roy P., 22, 159
Baxter, John, 11
Beardstown Chronicle and Illinois Military Bounty Land Advertiser, 55, 56, 60, 67, 70
Bell, Ann, 110
Bell, James, 110, 129n
Bell, Jane D., 129n; on AL's involvement with Mary Todd and Matilda Edwards, 110, 114, 118
Bell, Lizzie Herndon: as Ann Rutledge informant, 81, 82, 96n; on AL's engagement, 83; Herndon's opinion of, 97n
Bennett, William, 81, 82
Berry, William, 57
Beveridge, Albert J., 96n; use of Herndon's materials, 75; on Herndon's search for the truth, 79; on effect of AL's wrestling match, 92; and Herndon's story of the defaulting bridegroom, 126n; on AL's melancholy, 136; on AL's penchant for celebratory verse, 147n
The Bible, 6, 8
Binsmore, Henry: reporting of AL speeches for *Chicago Times,* 156; on reporting of debates, 156
Black, Chauncey F.: as Lamon's ghostwriter, 48, 128n; and Matilda Edwards story, 108

Black Hawk War, 81
Bogue's Mill, 33
Booton, Joseph, 35n
Bray, Robert, 57, 68, 72n
Bridges, Roger D., 94n, 147n
Broadwell, Judge, 127n
Brown, James N.: and AL scrapbook, 175
Brown, John L., 116
Browning, O. H., 48, 114, 129n; on AL's involvement with Mary Todd and Matilda Edwards, 109, 115; on AL's derangement, 119–20
Bruce, Robert V.: on verses in AL commonplace book, 139–40; on AL's attachment to "Mortality," 143, 145
Burlingame, Michael, 35n, 71n, 128n
Burns, Robert, 8, 13, 16n, 81, 133
Butler, Elizabeth (Mrs. William), 105; inquiry about AL's condition, 120, 124
Butler, William, 124, 131n; on encounter of AL and Cartwright, 58
Byron, Lord, 133

Calhoun, John, 154
Carman, Caleb, 96n; on AL's newspaper article on Peter Cartwright, 55, 56, 57, 66, 67; as Ann Rutledge informant, 82
Carpenter, Francis B., 43; on AL's recitation of "Mortality," 133–34; and version of "Mortality" dictated by AL, 145n
Cartwright, Peter, 147n; rivalry with AL, 55–73; AL attack on in *Beardstown Chronicle*, 55–56; and Samuel Hill, 56, 57, 59; career in Illinois, 57–58; letter to *Christian Advocate*, 60; letter to *Sangamo Journal*, 61–63
Cass, Lewis, 69
Chapman, Harriet: on AL quoting "Mortality," 137
Charleston debate, 174, 175
Chicago Press and Tribune, 151–64; and reporter for L-D debates, 156
Chicago speech, 164, 173–74, 175; appeal to immigrants, 173
Chicago Times, 151–64; and coverage of AL, 156; reports of L-D debates, 156

Child, Francis James, 37
Chrisco, Mrs. R. H., 130n
Christian Advocate and Journal, 60, 63, 64
Cicero, 6
Clark, Henry: as witness to AL's wrestling match, 92
Clark, John B., 129n
Clary, Louisa: on AL and New Salem, 32–33
Clay, Henry: quoted by AL in Galesburg debate, 157–59, 163, 176; AL's eulogy of, 167–68, 172; quoted by AL in Quincy debate, 177
Cogdal, Isaac: and AL as source of Ann Rutledge story, 31, 86–88, 138; as friend and law pupil of AL, 31; as Ann Rutledge informant, 82; and McGrady Rutledge, 96n; and AL as "Abe," 97n
Conkling, James C., 116, 118, 119; description of AL in 1841, 117; on Mary Todd and Matilda Edwards, 117, 119
Crawford, Elizabeth, 72n

Dall, Caroline, 51n
Darnton, Robert, 13
Davis, Judge David, 136; as AL's executor, 43
Declaration of Independence, 8, 179n; in L-D debates, 157–59; and AL, 166–81; "white-man's charter of freedom," 168; AL's use of in Peoria speech, 168; as gauge of political principles, 168; and "central idea" of equality of all men, 169–70; interpreted in Dred Scott speech, 171–72; equality clause, 171, 172, 173; as living, moral document, 172, 173, 175; as the "father of all moral principle," 173; AL's apostrophe on, 174; Douglas vs. AL on, 176; AL and identification of political feelings with, 178; AL and transformation of meaning of, 178–79
Dickinson, Emily, 13–14
Dilworth's Spelling-Book, 7
"Discoveries and Inventions": AL lecture on, 177

Donald, David Herbert, 29, 39, 41, 81, 95n; *Lincoln's Herndon*, 24–25, 28–29; on Herndon's truthfulness, 25; on Herndon's foibles, 27; on Herndon's alcoholism, 28; treatment of Herndon's informants, 31, 77; on AL's and Matilda Edwards, 128n; on AL and "Mortality," 138

Douglas, Jeffrey, 129n

Douglas, Stephen A., 69, 169, 170; and Matilda Edwards, 105, 109, 116; as possible suitor of Mary Todd, 112; L-D debates, 151–65, 172–77; and AL, 154, 175; opinion of AL as debater, 154; comments on reporting of Robert Hitt, 156; and 1860 text of debates, 160; Peoria speech and, 168; on equality clause of Declaration, 171; 1858 campaign against AL, 172–77

Douglass, Frederick, 173

Drake, Dr. Daniel, 119

Dred Scott decision, 170, 175

Dred Scott speech, 174, 175; AL's interpretation of Declaration's equality clause in, 171–72

Dubois, Jesse K. ("Uncle"), 128n

Duff, John J.: as critic of Herndon, 25, 35n

Duncan, Jason: AL and "Mortality" and, 137, 138–39, 140; friendship with AL confirmed, 147n

Edwards, Albert S., 100, 109, 126n

Edwards, Mrs. Benjamin S., 129n; on AL and Matilda Edwards, 109

Edwards, Cyrus, 104; on Matilda Edwards and trip to Jacksonville, 116

Edwards, Elizabeth Todd (Mrs. Ninian W.), 28, 30, 107, 108, 113, 118, 127n, 129n; account of AL's courtship, 100, 105–6, 126n; and AL's broken engagement, 105–6; story of defaulting bridegroom, 106; on Speed's courtship of Matilda Edwards, 111; on Matilda Edwards as factor in AL's broken engagement, 129n

Edwards, Matilda, 104, 113, 114, 118, 125, 127n, 128n; AL's feelings for, 102, 103, 106; role in AL's broken engagement, 104, 106, 107, 108–10;

marriage to Newton Strong, 104; refusal of Speed and Douglas, 105, 116; AL's and Speed's pursuit of, 111, 115; as center of attention, 117

Edwards, Nelson, 116, 127n

Edwards, Ninian W., 109, 110 112, 113, 116, 128n, 129n; on AL's broken engagement, 104–5; governor of Illinois, 104; on AL's and Mary Todd's marriage, 105, 106, 108; on Speed and Matilda Edwards, 111; and Matilda Edwards attending ball, 115–16; on defaulting bridegroom story, 127n

Ellis, A. Y., 95n; on Mary Todd-AL engagement, 131n

Euclid, 8

Ewing, W. L. D., 154

Fauquier, Francis, 5

Fehrenbacher, Don E., 10

Fell, Jesse W., 15n, 98n

Ferguson, John, 72n

Forquer, George, 68, 154

Fortune, William, 15n

Francis, Simeon, 68; refusal to publish AL article in *Sangamo Journal*, 55, 56, 67, 70

Freeport debate: AL's editorial changes in text of, 161–62

Galesburg debate, 73n, 177; comparison of newspaper texts, 157–59, 160, 162; Clay's colonization speech quoted in, 168; Douglas and AL on Negro equality, 176

Garrison, William Lloyd, 25

Gettysburg Address, 145, 166, 167, 178–79

Gillespie, Joseph, 116, 177; on AL's ability as speaker, 154

Gilreath, James, 96n

Gordon, Mrs. Noah, 147n

Gordon, Noah, 147

Goudy, Jane, 120; as author of verse romances, 130n

Graham, Mentor, 12; and claim to have taught AL, 80; as Ann Rutledge informant, 82; and source of Ann Rutledge, 86

Grant, Ulysses S., 28

Green, Bowling: care of AL, 86
Green, Mrs. Nancy: as Ann Rutledge informant, 82; testimony about AL, 86, 88, 97n
Greene, William G., 68, 98n; on Mentor Graham and AL, 80
Grigsby, Nathaniel, 16n, 72n

Hanks, Dennis: interviewed by Herndon, 78
Hanks, John: interviewed by Herndon, 78
Hanks, Nancy (AL's mother): reputation of in Kentucky, 40, 49, 50; AL's belief in illegitimacy, 40
Hardin, John J., 114; and 1840 excursion to Jacksonville, 120; family reaction to AL's mental condition, 120
Hardin, Martinette. *See* McKee, Martinette Hardin
Hardin, Sarah, 120
Harris, Gibson: and AL's poetry, 140; on AL's "favorite of favorites," 141; version of "Mortality" dictated by AL, 145n, 147n
Hart, Charles H., 45, 48; as confidante of Herndon, 39–43
Hay, John, 10, 16n, 152
Hay, Milton, 16n
Helm, Emily, 49
Helm, Katherine, 100, 126n
Henning, Fanny, 115
Henry, Dr. Anson, 119, 131n
Henry, Patrick, 9–10
Herndon, J. Rowan: and information on AL, 78; as Ann Rutledge informant, 82, 98n
Herndon, William H., 37, 123; as AL's law partner, 8; on AL's reading habits, 8, 9, 16n; on AL's library, 12; scholarly reputation of, 21–27; and Ann Rutledge story, 21, 74–76, 77; on AL as defaulting bridegroom, 21, 29–30, 22–24, 106; truthfulness of, 25; "Lincoln Records," 25, 48, 126n; criticism for story of AL and syphilis, 26; drinking habits of, 27–28; civic activities of, 28; as a biographer, 28–29, 38, 45–46, 78; Mary Todd Lincoln and, 29–31; Lincoln informants and, 31–33, 77–78, 79,

80; problem of memory, 33; Robert T. Lincoln and, 37, 49; and AL biography, 38, 45–46; and facts about AL's early life, 38–40, 79; concerns about evidence, 40; lecture on Ann Rutledge story, 41–42, 43, 45, 80, 97n, 138, 139, 156n; doctrine of necessary truth, 42–43, 50; interviews with Kentucky informants, 46–47; inheritance of farm, 47; and sale of AL archive to Lamon, 48, 128n; and AL article on Cartwright, 55; misrepresentation of investigations, 79, 81; and McGrady Rutledge, 84; and Isaac Cogdal, 87; and story of AL in Coles County court, 93; on AL's broken engagement, 99, 101–4, 129n; interview with Ninian Edwards, 104–5; interview with Elizabeth Edwards, 105–6; and chronology of AL's courtship, 111; and AL-Speed exchange, 126n; on "Mortality" and AL, 137–39, 141; on AL as poet, 140; on AL's self-confidence, 142; on AL's melancholy, 145n
Herndon's Lincoln (William Henry Herndon), 74, 95n
Herndon-Weik Collection (Library of Congress), 23, 28, 29, 77, 97n, 127n, 139
The Hidden Lincoln (Emanuel Hertz), 29
Hill, John, 58, 81, 94n; on Herndon's drunkenness, 35n; as Ann Rutledge informant, 82
Hill, Parthena (Mrs. Samuel), 96n, 97n
Hill, Samuel: article against Cartwright, 56, 66, 70; "skinning" by Cartwright, 56, 66; sketch of, 58–59; and publication of letter, 66; authorship of Cartwright letter, 66–67, 68
History of England (Rapin), 6
Hitt, Robert: accuracy of reporting, 154
Hohimer, Henry: as Ann Rutledge informant, 82
Holland, Josiah G., 38
Holzer, Harold: edition of Lincoln-Douglas debates, 152–64; on the text of debates, 152–54, 155; on AL's speaking ability, 154; criticism of previous L-D texts, 160; contributions to

editorial work on L-D debates, 162; on Alton debate, 163
Homer, 10
Hood, Thomas, 10
Horace, 6, 11
"House Divided" speech, 172
Howard, James Quay, 98n
Howells, William Dean: on AL's wrestling match, 92, 98n
Hume, David, 11
Huntington Library, 23, 94n, 126n
Hurt, James: on imagery of AL's writings, 145

Illinois State Journal, 176
Independence Hall, 178
Irwin, B. F.: as Ann Rutledge informant, 81, 82

Jackson, Mary B. E. (Mrs. Henry), 129n
Jacksonville, Ill.: excursion to by AL and friends in 1840, 114, 116, 120
Jaffa, Harry V., 171, 180n
Jefferson, Isaac, 9
Jefferson, Peter, 6; library of, 15n
Jefferson, Thomas, 169, 179n; compared to AL, 4–14; legend of, 4; papers of, 4; sale of library to Congress, 4, 11, 14n; education of, 5–7; *Notes on the State of Virginia,* 9; as lawyer, 9–10; extracts from the Gospels, 11; and library collection, 11–12; retirement of, 12; Declaration as American creed, 167; invoked by Douglas, 176; AL's tribute to, 178; as AL's idol, 179
Johnston, Andrew, 139, 140, 141
Jones, John: as Ann Rutledge informant, 82; faulting of testimony, 90

Kansas-Nebraska bill, 168, 176
Kelso, Jack, 81
Kennedy, John F., 4
Kirkham's Grammar, 12
Know-Nothings, 169
Knox, William: as author of "Mortality," 133, 139

Lamon, Ward Hill, 50, 108–9; and copies of Herndon's documents, 23, 48, 128n; biography and Robert T. Lincoln, 49

"The Last Leaf" (Oliver Wendell Holmes), 136–37
Lee, Robert E., 89
Lessons in Elocution (William Scott), 10
Levering, Mrs. Lawrason, 117
Levering, Mercy, 111, 113, 116, 117, 118
Library of Congress, 3, 17n, 24, 75, 96n; AL's use of, 3,4; acquisition of Jefferson's library, 4, 11; purchase of Herndon-Weik Collection, 23
Lincoln, Abraham: as member of Congress, 3, 4; use of Library of Congress, 3, 4; Jefferson and, 4–14, 178; legend of, 4; education of, 5–7; and newspapers, 8; as anti-Jackson man, 8; and English poetry, 10; love affair with Ann Rutledge, 23–24, 31, 74–98, 137; alleged logrolling, 26; remembered by New Salem neighbors, 32–33; book on infidelity, 42; Peter Cartwright and, 55–73; life in New Salem, 57; as delegate to common schools convention, 60–61; challenge by Shields, 68; New Salem years, 75, 76, 80–81, 96n; early courtships, 79; touchstone questions about relationship to Ann Rutledge, 81; evidence on early life, 91–92; wrestling match with Jack Armstrong, 92; courtship of Mary Todd, 99–132; Speed on broken engagement, 101–4; Matilda Edwards and, 102, 111; depression and moods of, 91, 102, 104, 118, 119, 136; first "crazy spell" (1840), 104, 113, 118, 119; effect of unhappy love affairs, 110; leap from church window, 112; Christmas excursion to Jacksonville (1840), 116; "trials and embarrassments" of, 120; Mrs. William Butler as confidant, 120; meaning of "that fatal first of Jany. '41," 121–25; and Speed, 121–24; fondness for poetry, 133–48; "My childhood's home I see again," 140–42; return to Indiana neighborhood, 140, 141–43, 144; personal losses through death, 142; eulogies: for Zachary Taylor, 143–44, for Henry Clay, 167–68; scrap-

book of L-D debates, 151; as extemporaneous speaker, 154–55; on the accuracy of L-D texts, 160, 160–62; affinity for, defense of Declaration, 166, 167–69, 171–72, 172–77, 178–79; Peoria speech and Douglas, 168; on political and social equality of blacks, 170, 172, 174, 175; counterattacks in Galesburg debate, 176; public lecture on "Discoveries and Inventions," 177

Lincoln-Douglas debates, 9, 11, 69, 151–65; text of AL's scrapbook, 151–52; quality of reporting, 155–59; comparison of texts, 156–59, 162–64; conditions affecting reports, 159; quality of editing, 159–64: authority of 1860 text, 160; editorial procedures, 162

Lincoln at Gettysburg (Garry Wills), 167

Lincoln Legal Papers, 16n

Lincoln, Mary Todd, 26, 39, 77, 100, 136; courtship with AL, 21, 99–132; Herndon on, 21, 29–31; reputation in Springfield, 30; personality and effect on AL, 105, 110; letter to Mercy Levering (1840), 111, 113–14; Matilda Edwards and, 114

Lincoln, Robert, 8, 9, 12, 47, 48; and biography of AL, 37; dislike of Herndon, 38; objections to Herndon's Ann Rutledge lecture, 43–45; on biographies of father, 49

Lincoln, Sarah Bush Johnston, 15n, 16n

Lincoln scholarship, 21, 22, 160

Lincoln, Thomas, 48

Linder, Usher F., 154

Logan, Stephen T., 26, 142

Lyceum Address, 145, 167

Malone, Dumas, 4

Marsh, Mathew S.: letter on AL, 91

Mary Lincoln: Wife and Widow (Carl Sandburg), 100

Matheny, James H., 108, 110, 112, 129n, 136; account of AL's broken engagement, 107; on AL at marriage ceremony, 107; on story of AL's aborted wedding, 128n

Maury, Rev. James, 5

McHenry, Henry, 15n, 95n, 98n; as Ann Rutledge informant, 82; statement about AL, 90–91; on AL's wrestling match, 92

McKee, Alexander R., 130n

McKee, Martinette Hardin, 130n; and AL's mental condition, 120

McMurtry, R. Gerald, 129n

McNamar, John, 95n, 96n, 97n; on AL's article on Cartwright, 56, 57, 67; as Ann Rutledge's fiancé, 81, 83, 85, 88; testimony on marking Ann Rutledge's grave, 91

McNeely, T. W.: as Ann Rutledge informant, 81, 82

McPherson, James, 10

Mearns, David C.: quoted, 12, 49, 133

Menard County, Ill., 31, 32, 38, 40, 86

Miles, G. U., 86, 96n; Herndon and, 79

Miller's Ferry, 59

Monticello, 9

"Mortality" (William Knox), 137, 143, 156n; AL's recitation of, 133–34, 144; text, 134–35; theme, 135; and AL's melancholy, 136, 144; Herndon's theory of, 137–39; AL's own verses and, 140–41; motifs of, 141; versions dictated by AL, 145n, 147n

"My childhood's home I see again" (AL), 140–41, 142, 148n

Narrative (James Riley), 7

Negro equality, 172–73; and Illinois politicians, 170; effect of Dred Scott decision, 170–71; and AL, 172, 174; AL's middle course on, 174, 175

Newhall, Lois E., 145n

New Salem, Ill., 6, 12, 15n, 31, 32, 38, 55, 56, 57, 59, 67, 77, 78, 80, 81, 83, 87, 92, 136, 137, 138, 139, 140, 147n

New Testament, 11

Newton, Joseph Fort: study of Lincoln and Herndon, 27

Nicolay, John G., 26, 35n, 109, 115, 137; on value of AL's debates scrapbook, 152; on AL and Declaration, 166

Norton, Charles Eliot, 37

Offutt, Denton, 57

Old Salem League, 33

Onstot, T. G.: quoted, 58, 59
Orr, Oliver, 97n
Ossian, 10
Ottawa debate, 151, 158, 174, 175; comparison of press coverage, 156–57; quotation of Clay's colonization speech, 168; Douglas and on equality, 175–76
Ovid, 6
"O why should the spirit of mortal be proud?" *See* "Mortality" (William Knox)

Page, John, 6
Parks, Samuel, 98
Peck, John Mason, 59
Peoria speech (1854), 151, 157; AL's use of Declaration in, 168; and AL on equality of blacks, 170
Pilgrim's Progress (John Bunyan), 7
Pioneer and Western Baptist (Rock Spring, Ill.), 59
The Prairie Years (Carl Sandburg): treatment of Ann Rutledge story, 75, 76
Pratt, Harry, 22
Prewitt, Nancy Rutledge, 96n

Quigley, Alice Edwards: on AL and Matilda Edwards, 109
Quincy debate, 177

Ramsey, David, 7
Randall, James G., 22, 25, 28, 93, 97n, 129n; critiques the Ann Rutledge evidence, 23–24, 34n, 75–76, 92; on Herndon and his informants, 31–33, 77, 78, 81, 85, 88, 90, 92; papers of, 34n, 35n; on Robert B. Rutledge's testimony, 85–86; on McGrady Rutledge's testimony, 86; on Cogdal's testimony, 86, 87; on standards for historical evidence, 88, 89; use of hearsay and unconfirmed evidence, 90–91; *Lincoln the President*, 91; presuppositions about AL and Ann Rutledge, 98n; on Mary Todd's release of AL, 127n
Randall, Ruth Painter, 104, 125, 130n, 131n; as critic of Herndon, 25, 77, 88, 126n; on Herndon's representation of Mary Todd Lincoln, 29–30;

investigation of AL's courtship, 100, 126n; and gossip about AL and Matilda Edwards, 109–10; on Matilda Edwards story, 115; view of Ninian W. Edwards, 128n
Randolph, Edmund, 9
Rankin, Henry B., 15n
"The Raven" (Edgar Allan Poe), 137
The Readers Digest, 24, 35n
Reep, Thomas P., 33, 35n
Richardson, Joseph C., 72n
Rickard, Sarah. *See* Barret, Sarah Rickard
Roberts, Octavia, 109
Robinson Crusoe (Daniel Defoe), 7
Romine, John, 16n
Rutledge, Ann, 6, 12, 17n, 142; love affair with AL, 21, 31, 41, 51n, 74–98, 136; love affair disputed, 22–24, 74–93; as object of AL's despair, 42, 138–39; Ann Rutledge hoax, 75; family testimony about, 84–85; and AL's attachment to "Mortality," 137–39
Rutledge, David, 84
Rutledge family, 31, 84
Rutledge, James McGrady: as Ann Rutledge informant, 82; conversation with Ann Rutledge, 84; criticism of testimony, 86, 90
Rutledge, Jasper, 96n
Rutledge, John M.: as Ann Rutledge informant, 82
Rutledge, Robert B., 90, 96n; as Ann Rutledge informant, 82; on AL's engagement to Ann Rutledge, 83, 97n; on McGrady Rutledge and Herndon, 84; as representative of Rutledge family, 85; on his sister, 85; as witness to AL's wrestling match, 92
Rutledge, Mrs. William: as Ann Rutledge informant, 82, 98n; on Ann Rutledge and John McNamar, 83

Sanford, Nellie Crandall, 132n
Sangamo Journal, 55, 56, 57, 61, 68
Schwartz, Thomas F., 129n
Scripps, John L., 15n, 98n
Sellers, John R., 34n
Shakespeare, William, 8–9, 10, 11, 13, 16n, 133, 134; *King Lear*, 10; *Richard III*, 10; *Henry VIII*, 10; *Hamlet*,

10, 133; *Macbeth*, 10; AL's love of recitation, 81; editions of compared with L-D texts, 162
Sheridan, James, 156
Shields, James, 68
Short, James: as friend of AL, 31; on testimony, 80; as Ann Rutledge informant, 82; on AL and Ann Rutledge, 83, 88, 89, 91
Simon, John Y., 94n; on Ann Rutledge story, 24, 77, 82; on the Lincoln marriage, 31; on critics of the Ann Rutledge story, 88, 90, 93, 97n
Simon, Paul, 25–26
Skinner, Hubert M., 3, 7
Slavery, 170, 173; and Declaration, 168; as a moral issue, 172; and policy of Democratic Party, 176
Small, Dr. William, 5
Smith, Ashford, 59, 60; 62
Smith, Samuel H., 17n
Smoot, Coleman: on AL in New Salem, 32
Spears, George: on AL, 32, 78
The Spectator, 6
Speed, Joshua F., 68, 108, 110, 117, 118, 119, 127n, 129n, 131n, 141, 168; role in AL's courtship, 100; friendship with AL, 101, 124–25; on AL's broken engagement, 102–3; Matilda Edwards and, 105, 111, 113, 114, 116, 125; leaving Springfield, 118, 121; marriage to Fanny Henning, 121; unhappiness during engagement, 121; and "fatal first of Jany. '41," 122; as counselor of AL, 122, 123; and references to Sarah Rickard, 123
Spoon River Anthology (Edgar Lee Masters), 74–75
Springer, John G., 48; and Herndon's materials, 40, 94n, 126n
Springfield Farewell Address, 154
Stanton, Mrs. Edwin, 145n
Strong, Newton: marriage to Matilda Edwards, 104; attentions to Matilda Edwards, 115
Strozier, Charles B., 26; on AL's broken engagement, 100
Stuart, John T., 16n, 59, 98n, 119, 120, 136

Stuart, Mrs. John T., 127n
Supreme Court, 170
Swett, Leonard, 136; caution to Herndon, 49; on skeleton in AL's closet, 49–50

Taney, Justice Roger B., 171
Tanner, Terence A., 72n, 130n
Tarbell, Ida M., 109, 119, 127n; on credibility of defaulting bridegroom story, 99–100
Taylor, Richard S., 35n
Taylor, Zachary, 144
Thomas, Benjamin, 22; on AL's wrestling match, 92; on AL's rise, 142
Thomas, Jesse B., Jr., 68
Thornton, H. W., 119, 130n
Todd, Mary. *See* Lincoln, Mary Todd
Treat, Judge Samuel, 136
Trumbull, Lyman, 119

Virgil, 6, 10

Wallace, Mrs. Frances, 100, 126n
Warren, Louis A., 8; attack on Herndon, 24, 29; on Ann Rutledge story, 76–77
Washburne, Elihu B., 15n
Washington, George, 176; life of, 7
Watts, Isaac: verse in AL's commonplace book, 140, 144
Webb, Edwin B., 116, 130n; as suitor of Mary Todd, 112, 113, 114
Weems, Mason, 7
Weik, Jesse Weik, 26, 28, 30, 106; as collaborator on life of AL, 23, 50, 147n; use of Herndon's materials, 75; investigation of AL's melancholy, 136
Weldon, Judge Lawrence, 137
White, Horace, 174
Whitney, Henry C., 136, 146n
Williams, Gary L., 131n; characterization of AL-Speed relationship, 123
Wills, Garry, 179n; on AL's Charleston disclaimer, 175
Wilson, Robert: on AL's early melancholy, 136
Wythe, George, 5

DOUGLAS L. WILSON is coeditor, with Rodney O. Davis, of *Herndon's Informants: Letters, Interviews, and Statements about Abraham Lincoln.* He was formerly George A. Lawrence Professor of English at Knox College in Galesburg, Illinois, and is now Saunders Director of the International Center for Jefferson Studies at Monticello.

Riley